Invitation to Chinese Philosophy

SCANDINAVIAN UNIVERSITY BOOKS
Universitetsforlaget, Oslo, Bergen, Tromsö
Munksgaard, Copenhagen
AB Läromedelsförlagen, Stockholm, Göteborg, Lund

ARNE NAESS and ALASTAIR HANNAY (Eds.)

Invitation to
Chinese Philosophy

Eight Studies

Universitetsforlaget 1972
OSLO – BERGEN – TROMSÖ

Cover design by Bjørn Roggenbihl

ISBN 82 00 02264 1

Printed in Norway by
A.s John Griegs Boktrykkeri

Contents

AN APPEAL TO THE CRAMPED SCHOLAR
BY WAY OF FOREWORD

A collection of essays on Chinese philosophy needs no general justification. It is always illuminating to know what and how people with a different tradition think. And it is of course especially fitting at this time of tentative, and perhaps genuine, political *rapprochement* that the philosophers of East and West should also compare notes. But for philosophy such cross-cultural illumination has an added point, and this gives the present publication a special justification.

Most philosophers would claim to know what philosophy is. And if they do not always find it easy to *say* what it is, they can at least point to what they actually *do* as philosophers, and say 'That's what philosophy is'. Yet they often seem tempted to add: 'and that's all it is', implying that if someone calling himself a philosopher does something else then he is not really a philosopher, or, more diplomatically though just as dismissively, not a philosopher 'in the same sense'. Those prone to such bold dismissals may be well-advised to consider the Taoist philosopher Chuang Tzu's image of 'the cramped scholar'. The cramped scholar is a creature whose world, like that of the summer-insect and the well-frog, is very limited in relation to what *can* be known, to say nothing of what cannot. And the narrowness of his world is such as to make him 'unable in speech or thought' to deal with any topic that transcends its limitations (see Hansen's essay).

Cramped or not, philosophers — not least those reared in the Western tradition — tend to be disturbingly parochial at least about philosophy. They see their discipline as a very specific kind of activity, indeed as just one discipline, whether the old-style one of building metaphysical systems or the new-style ones that bring them down in ruins. Philosophy, accordingly, is looked upon as a task to be performed with special tools and methods, and the philosopher himself as a craftsman who is adept at a particular skill. Whatever value our philosopher sees in the products of another kind of activity, employing different aptitudes, tools, and skills, is not to be confused with the merits peculiar to a philosophical work properly so-called.

Examples are readily available. Protesting that it is precisely not for reasons of 'European parochialism' that he excludes any sources 'east of Suez' in his recent *Introduction to Western Philosophy*, Antony Flew justifies his retrenchment policy by saying that philosophy in his sense of the word is concerned 'first, last and all the time with arguments', while 'most of what is labelled *Eastern Philosophy* is not so concerned'.*

However, there is, we think, at least one principal parochialism at work here, namely a prejudice as to what alone may count as an argument in philosophy. In the Western tradition we have learned to interpret 'argument' somewhat narrowly; by an argument in philosophy we usually mean some statement or statements from which, in conjunction with other independently validated statements of fact or principle, it is possible to infer a conclusion. To interpret it any less narrowly, it is hinted, would be to fall into idle speculation, and therefore from professional grace, or else to renounce one's calling altogether by joining what Hume called 'the precipitate march of the multitude'. Care and precision in philosophy, it seems to be assumed, are to be safeguarded solely by obedience to the rule: 'Look to your inferences!'

Even a cursory acquaintance (as our own) with other traditions should suffice to dispel this latter illusion. Chinese philosophy itself provides a prime example, for despite a comparative dearth of inferential arguments in the writings of Chinese philosophers, their works are exemplary in care and precision, as well as in subtlety and sophistication. What we would like to advocate here, as a remedy for scholarly cramp, is the (local) heresy that inference, although obviously an important tool for philosophers, does not provide the only, or even the typical, form of philosophical argument. Indeed we would press the heresy further and suggest that the contrary belief gives a distorted picture of philosophy in general, that is, not only of Chinese philosophy among others, but also of the philosophical activity of those who hold the belief. In other words, the very philosophers who prize the tool of inference so highly fail to see how it actually functions in their own hands.

* Antony Flew, *An Introduction to Western Philosophy. Ideas and Argument from Plato to Sartre*, Thames & Hudson, London 1971, p. 36.

'Philosophising essentially incorporates argumentation', says Ryle. So far so good, but then note his explanation: it does so in such a way, he continues, that 'whereas a weak or faulty inference might by luck put Sherlock Holmes on the track of the murderer, a weak or faulty philosopher's argument is itself a blind alley', and adds: 'In this field there is no detachment of the conclusion from its premisses.'* It seems reasonable to assume that we can take the principle enunciated here to be 'No guesswork in philosophy!' That might seem not such a bad principle, if you accept that philosophy is not concerned, at least in the way that Sherlock Holmes is, with factual discovery; for if there is nothing analogous to Holmes's lucky identification of the murderer, that is, no possible cause to congratulate oneself or one's good fortune where the inference has been faulty or weak, then it seems that the guess will always remain just that, a speculation, but then surely a quite empty one. But all the same we think it a totally misconceived principle.

Consider how it would lead us to construe a simple, though typical philosophical exchange. Philosopher *A* claims that we do not perceive the physical world 'directly', but only via sense-impressions, and argues for this claim by appealing, say, to the 'argument from illusion'. Philosopher *B* thereupon proceeds to show that *A*'s claim does not *follow* from the premisses in which this argument is included. Now the principle would require him to reject *A*'s claim simply because it does not follow from these premisses. But whoever except a dyed-in-the-wool rationalist would say that it should? Indeed it seems to us much more plausible to say that the fact that a philosopher's conclusion does not follow from his premisses, far from being a reason for rejecting the conclusion, is a requirement of that conclusion's being at all philosophically interesting. Let us explain.

If what the argument from illusion points out is true, it serves merely to indicate a complexity to be accounted for in the analysis of perception. It points to a feature of *some* perceiving, a feature which makes that perceiving a kind of *mis*perceiving, the possibility of which must be accounted for in any acceptable account of *all* perceiving. It does not, as *A* perhaps hopes, force upon us the conclusion that all perception of the physical is indirect, let alone any of the other conclusions associated with the argument, e.g. that we only 'really perceive' our own subjective states. But then neither does the fact that no such conclusion follows from the argument show, as Ryle would apparently

* Gilbert Ryle, 'Autobiographical', in O. P. Wood and G. Pitcher (Eds.), *Ryle*, Macmillan, London 1970, p. 7.

have it, that any such conclusion is a philosophical dead-end. On the contrary, a conclusion is a live philosophical option so long as it is at least consistent with the facts it is introduced to explain. And it only ceases to be an option for the philosopher when it is shown, demonstrated, or proved, to be incoherent or not stateable without inconsistency. Perhaps there *are* conclusions that follow from the argument from illusion; some would claim that the impossibility of the view known as naïve realism was one such. Whether the example is a good one or not, this indicates at least one function of inferential argument in philosophy, that of eliminating a possible 'conclusion' on the grounds that it is demonstrably incoherent, or senseless. Another could be simply that of indicating the consequences of distinctions that a satisfactory solution must take account of. But then this does not even touch the question of how to argue positively in favour of a specific conclusion. Moreover, if we thought these two functions covered the uses of philosophical argument, we would have to conclude that there was no answer to this question. Rather than accept *this* implausible conclusion, we suggest we should ask ourselves what kind of arguments would be useful to the philosopher who wants to justify specifically *his* account, or *his* 'analysis', and not just demonstrate the impossibility of a rival account.

To answer this one must first realize that a philosopher's 'conclusion' is not really a conclusion at all, or rather it is not a product of valid inference from true premisses, but instead more like a statement of a fundamental doctrine which his particular analyses of experience, his 'premisses', are designed to support. If the latter do support it, they do so in the following way: the 'premisses' are in some sense derivable from the 'conclusion' — or, less misleadingly, the descriptions they contain are requirements of the doctrine, and the latter are then independently testable as plausible descriptions of the 'facts'. If this is the form of a philosophical argument, then the 'arguments' provided by the descriptions are by no means inferential, as Ryle suggests they should be. True, and as he specifies, there is no detachment here of conclusion from premisses, but that is because the 'premisses' are deliberately *derived* from the 'conclusion'. The value of the 'premisses' is simply as descriptions that *fit*, cohere with, or help to elaborate, the fundamental doctrine. And for that purpose the philosopher might just as persuasively include, as Sartre does, anecdotes and illustrations from life as the more traditional analyses of such general philosophical areas as, say, 'perception' and 'value'. Or equally he might, like Chinese philosophers, employ images and metaphors to transmit his fundamental doctrine.

One argument in favour of this inversion of the commonly assumed relation of premiss to conclusion in philosophical reasoning is that it at least renders intelligible such, not untypical, exchanges as the one outlined above between philosophers *A* and *B*. What *A* and *B* are really doing, according to this alternative picture, is defending incompatible 'conclusions'. *A* uses the argument from illusion, or some other argument, to support his 'conclusion', while *B* shows that because *A*'s arguments don't compel acceptance of *A*'s conclusion, then he is warranted in continuing to maintain his own conclusion (provided it can accommodate facts which *B* acknowledges the argument to have disclosed). *A* may be defending some form of idealism, and *B* some critical (scientifically informed) version of realism. And just as the argument from illusion is not conclusive for the former, so its lack of conclusiveness is not conclusive for the latter.

However, it was not the internal politics of Western philosophy that these observations were designed to throw light on, but its foreign policy, in particular Flew's decision on east of Suez. So let us begin by looking at his own example, the *Analects* of Confucius, since this probably provides his most favourable instance. Although 'such works of the classical Chinese Sages as the *Analects* of Confucius are in their own kind great', he says, 'that does not make them in the present sense philosophy'. Because the present sense requires that they be concerned, first, last and all the time, with arguments.

Now in an obvious way the *Analects* are not concerned with arguments. They are a collection of aphorisms and brief dialogues primarily to do with moral conduct. The reader of the *Analects* will not find that he is asked to accept certain premises and draw conclusions from these. He will look in vain for any definite or systematically defined *rules* of practical morality. And he will be similarly disappointed if he expects to find any justifying arguments for the specific moral conduct prescribed. Should he not, therefore, simply forget the *Analects* as philosophy? He might think so. Without arguments, after all, what is a rational man supposed to do with mere rules? Just accept them? Heaven forbid!

But suppose, as Professor Cua argues, the *Analects* do in fact incorporate a definite moral point of view. Suppose further that the point of view in question explicitly rejects the idea that to be moral is to act in a way that can be justified by appeal to rule. And indeed from

Cua's essay it appears that this is precisely the case. A main idea in the *Analects*, he shows, is that of a 'superior man' whose function is to be a 'paradigmatic standard for practical morality'; and it appears to be a special point of Confucian ethics that moral conduct should *not* conform with abstract principles or rules specifying what is 'correct' in any given situation. Rather, the ideal is to act as this exemplary moral agent does, out of a cultivated moral sense that allows him to see what is correct even in unusual, or 'exigent' situations for which no rules are available. But then if it is a requirement of Confucian ethics that moral prescriptions include no rules of 'relevance' or 'inference' to guide action, the absence of such rules can hardly be a deficiency on its part.

Furthermore, if there is something we can call a Confucian moral point of view, then it is presumably something that can be offered for acceptance, that is, argued for in a wide sense of 'argued for'. Now acceptance requires evaluation and evaluation clearly requires understanding, initially via the *Analects* themselves, but also by supplementary elaboration ('analysis') of the kind provided in large measure by Cua's essay. In the end we might come to regard the *Analects* as the expression of a highly sophisticated moral outlook, one which relates actions to specific situations but without tying them to these situations by rules. True, its focus on the specific 'requirements or qualities for a life of moral excellence' (p. 42), rather than on, say, what it means to say of some quality that it is morally excellent, strikes an unfashionable note to (some) Western ears. But the fact that what is presented is a moral philosophy and not a philosophy of morals should not incline us to dismiss it as philosophy.

We would go a step further. Although it is perfectly true that the *Analects* are far removed from what philosophers in the Western tradition would be inclined to *call* philosophy, and the same goes for Zen (or Ch'an) Buddhism, another powerful cultural influence represented in this collection, in neither case can a disinclination to apply the label be justified by appealing to an absence of argument in these traditions. In some cases, as with the *Analects*, the absence of argument can itself be part of an arguable point of view; while in others its absence is simply an illusion created by the myth that a philosophical argument must conform to a certain stereotype. To get rid of this myth it might be helpful to think of a philosophical argument as having the form of an invitation to accept a particular point of view by understanding it, though that of course also includes understanding all the conse-

quences of holding the point of view. If so, the criticism of a philosophical view will emerge from the judgment of its capacity to present a
coherent, self-consistent picture, and it would be quite misguided to
reject it because its fundamental theses cannot be derived as 'conclusions' from the observations comprising its 'premisses'.

Seen in this light Chinese philosophical thought becomes more
readily comparable to that of the West than Flew's policy-statement
allows. For now we can see Chinese philosophy as concentrating on an
aspect of philosophical thought in general which Western philosophers
have largely neglected, namely, the basic viewpoint which colours a
philosopher's aims and methods. True, in the case of the *Analects* this
aspect has to be reconstructed by supplementary analysis, but in others
it emerges more explicitly, as we see from Professor Tang Chun-i's
account of the development of neo-Confucian thought from the tenth
century A. D. until the death of Wang Yang-ming in the sixteenth.
What the neo-Confucianist philosophers provide, where the *Analects*
only leave it to our intuition, is an over-all account of human nature,
an account, as one might say, of the unity of experience. Professor
Tang sees the development of neo-Confucianism as a progress towards
an increasingly unified picture of what an Anglo-American philosopher
might call the 'conceptual ingredients' of the neo-Confucian moral
concept of self-perfectibility. Although the teachings of these philosophers appear as doctrines concerning the 'way' (*tao*) of self-perfection,
these doctrines themselves incorporate different and progressively more
unified philosophical views of 'mind, human nature, and the universe'
(p. 56).

It is really a matter of convention whether one calls such views
'speculations' or 'elaborations', rather than 'analyses'. If one thinks
of an analysis as a break-down of the constituents of some specific and
clearly identified phenomenon, then the word will not seem apt; and
similarly if one associates with analysis a certain procedure or set of
conceptual tools. But in fact any claim about the *nature* of some selected
phenomenon is part of an 'analysis' of the larger set of those phenomena
in respect of which the nature of the former is partly determined. And
a description of a part is a part of an analysis of the whole. As Professor
Tang's essay shows, the phenomenon selected in neo-Confucianist
philosophy is the wide one of self-cultivation. Being wide, its 'analysis'
requires a coherent account of the interrelationship of such large items
as, on the one hand, mind and human 'temperamental' nature, and
also, on the other, of these two and 'the investigation of things'. It is

the various attempts to give a satisfactory account of these interrelationships which comprise the 'development of neo-Confucianism'.

To begin with a specific conception of the unity of experience will strike many Western philosophers as putting the cart before the horse. What is needed first, they will say, is a clear statement of the method for stating and justifying such conceptions. Then it remains to be seen which, if any, *can* be stated and justified. The possibility we are venturing is that even such an apparent preliminary as stating a method can involve giving expression to a certain conception of the unity of experience. If so, then it is less a question of whether the cart or the horse comes first than it is of whether the one conceals the other, or of whether, when both stand in view, they can be seen to form a well-matched pair. Those who tend to see methodology as the horse and therefore consider that neo-Confucian philosophy provides only a cart will find in Professor Liu's essay on the contemporary development of neo-Confucian epistemology an attempt to complete the picture. Liu outlines two contemporary attempts to provide for the traditional moral and epistemological insights of neo-Confucianists the kind of methodological (and epistemological) bases the lack of which Western philosophers are most likely to identify as a failure to provide justifying argument. Whether the arguments thus provided give the kind of rational support the Western philosopher would ordinarily expect, the reader can himself decide. But whether the reader thinks it essential that they should do so depends on how much of a cramped scholar he still is, philosophically speaking. If he has begun to see other possibilities of rational persuasiveness than those that have stamped his style in one sense, but cramped it in another, so much the better. He will then be in a position to benefit from Professor Wu's advice to those taking their first step towards Chinese wisdom, by arming himself against such dangerous fallacies of interpretation as that of 'the misplaced hamburger'.

Two brief comments in conclusion. First, there are of course many gaps in this collection. None are deliberate, certainly not Chinese Marxism which is one we tried unsuccessfully to fill. But the gaps don't really matter, since the purpose of the collection is less to give a comprehensive survey of philosophy in China than to offer a prospect of a fruitful interchange of ideas and insights. As it happens, the topics included in these eight essays represent all four 'periods' of Chinese philosophy: the 'ancient' period up to 221 B. C., which includes Confucianism (Confucius 551–479 B. C.) (see Cua) and Taoism (Chuang

Tzu [b. *c.* 369 B. C.]) (see Hansen); the 'middle' period from 221 B. C. to A. D. 960 in which Confucianism (which became the State ideology in 136 B. C.) and then neo-Taoism and Buddhism (8th and 9th centuries A. D.) (see Wienpahl and Cheshier) flourished; the 'modern' period from 960 to 1900 which included the heyday as well as the decline of neo-Confucianism (see Tang); and the contemporary period with — prior to the advent of Marxism — the revival of neo-Confucianism (Hsiung Shih-li [b. 1883] and Mou Tsung-san [b. 1909]) (see Liu).* The remaining two essays (Wu and Cheng) provide surveys, one introductory and the other summative, though both also include valuable analyses of the tradition as a whole. **

Secondly, the reader may notice certain inconsistencies in the transcriptions of Chinese words. This is due to the fact that a number of different systems are currently in use. Most of the present authors have adopted the Wade-Giles system which has been in use since the 1850s, but Hansen has used the 'pinyin' system which is the official Chinese one. A further possible source of confusion lies in the fact that it is customary to refer to Chinese by their literary or honorary names as well as by their 'real' ones. Thus Cheng Ming-tao in Tang's essay is sometimes also referred to as Cheng (or Ch'eng) Hao. For help in this latter respect the reader may consult, e. g., Wing-tsit Chan's article on Chinese Philosophy in the *Encyclopedia of Philosophy* (see footnote below). We are grateful for advice on these matters to Professor Henry Henne of the East Asian Institute in the University of Oslo.

Oslo 1971   A. N.
                                                             A. H.

---

* See Wing-tsit Chan, 'Chinese Philosophy', in Paul Edwards (Ed.), *The Encyclopedia of Philosophy*, Collier-Macmillan, London 1967, Vol. 2.

** All of the essays except that of Lars Jul Hansen appeared in *Inquiry*, Vol. 14 (1971), Nos. 1–2.

JOSEPH S. WU

I. Western philosophy and the search for Chinese wisdom

This introductory essay begins by presenting the author's impression of contemporary Western philosophy as having become too professionalized to perform the functions of moral guidance and spiritual supervision. Herein lies a reason for the search for Oriental wisdom by some people in the West. The author then points out some fallacies often incurred in the pursuit of Chinese philosophy: the fallacy of 'craving for cash value', the fallacy of 'the Procrustean bed', and the fallacy of 'the misplaced hamburger'. In the second half of the paper the author attempts a characterization of Chinese philosophy as a whole. As he interprets it, Chinese philosophy as a distinct tradition possesses five characteristics: (1) human centrality, (2) unity of theory and practice, (3) pedagogic universality, (4) methodological simplicity, and (5) dynamic harmony.

Being introductory, this essay is intended to offer Western readers a threshold to Chinese philosophy rather than a detailed survey. First, from the viewpoint of a Chinese philosopher who is also a teacher of philosophy in a Western country, I will convey my impression of the contemporary situation of Western philosophy, particularly Western philosophy in the academic world of the American continent. Secondly, I will point out some methodological pitfalls that scholars should avoid in their pursuit of Chinese philosophy. And finally, I will attempt a general characterization of Chinese philosophy as a contrast with the main traditions of Western thought.

I

One of the most noticeable strains in recent European philosophy has been the Death of God. His death was pronounced as long ago as the nineteenth century.[1] To one brought up in a different culture, it is something of a puzzle that this should have been possible. In the Bible we learned that He is a perfect being, and loves all mankind; how then could He pass away and leave all His beloved children behind? How could a perfect being who is omniscient, omnipresent, and omnipotent suddenly give up His existence? Perhaps a more practical and urgent question is: Since the belief in God has formed the spiritual basis of Western culture, after His death who will be His successor as spiritual leader and moral supervisor of Western man? In contemporary theology and philosophy, a number of suggested solutions have been offered. In addition to the so-called 'Death of God Theology',[2] there are trends like secularization,[3] demythologization,[4] the symbolic approach to religious language,[5] humanistic existential theology,[6] and the kind of philosophy in which God is interpreted as becoming and creativity.[7] But from the viewpoint of a Chinese philosopher none of these suggestions can save the 'life' of God in the original Judaic-Christian tradition. All these attempts seem to be artificial compromises between traditional religious beliefs and the results of the development of science, which has so dominated contemporary Western life. Under such circumstances one would think that the best substitute for a belief in God is the moral teaching of a philosopher. But as soon as one turns to the contemporary scene in moral philosophy one is puzzled, mystified, and even frustrated. The paradoxical situation is that moral philosophers after G. E. Moore seem to be very hesitant to say something substantive.[8] Apparently they do not want to interfere with other people's lives by prescribing norms or setting up guidelines. They seem unwilling to assert any proposition which might be torn apart by a logician or analyst. In short, they want to be cautious, critical, and analytical. Consequently they have changed the direction of moral philosophy from the search for moral norms to the clarification of ethical usages. They try to make the unclear clear, the clear more clear; and they even find something unclear in what already seems clear. The spirit of such a search for clarity is admirable. But from the viewpoint of a Chinese philosopher it does not seem to get anywhere.[9]

Some have attempted to influence society by suggesting a way of life through their literary writings, but they have been ignored, degraded, and even excluded from the philosophical circle by scholars in philosophy.[10] The reason is that in contemporary Western society philosophers are no longer the easygoing, leisured wise men of antiquity, but members of a particular profession participating in the productive activities of modern industrial society. As a member of a profession one has to follow the professional code, or conventions, as set up, supported, and unconsciously enforced by the majority of the profession's members. No exception is made for the profession of philosophy. Western philosophy, in its highly professionalized state, has two basic characteristics: (1) a regard for philosophy as a serious discipline, following accepted scholarly patterns for research; and (2) a stress on the need of arguments and on the importance of methodology.

As a prospective member of the profession, a philosophy student in a graduate program is usually taught a kind of discipline which is formally no different from that taught to students in physics or chemistry. A doctoral student in philosophy, besides the foreign language tests, has to pass a qualifying examination which includes metaphysics, epistemology, logic, philosophy of science, philosophy of language, value theories, history of philosophy, and so on. While preparing for his dissertation he has to construct a thesis proposal, and compile a fairly extensive bibliography. When working on his thesis he has to observe the rules of style, at least those stated in the *MLA Style Sheet*. One wonders how the reincarnated Plato, were he to be enrolled in a philosophy department as a graduate student, would fare with the examiners. He might have difficulty even in passing a course on 'The Philosophy of Plato', without prior knowledge of the *MLA Style Sheet*, of the procedure for writing a term paper or thesis, or of Taylor's, Cornford's, or Brumbaugh's commentaries on his own philosophy.

I mentioned the stress in professional philosophy on the necessity of arguments, together with the emphasis on methodology. As a matter of fact, argumentation and methodology are intimately related to each other. An argument is a linguistic channel through which a philosophical method is embodied, while a philosophical method prescribes a procedure for constructing sound arguments. The use of arguments in philosophy has had a long tradition in the West. Zeno's paradoxes have occupied the interests of the professionals not because he made a great discovery, but because of his interesting arguments. Plato's dialectic method is a controlled argumentational process leading to more or less generalized first principles. The logical principles in the Aristotelian tradition have established a methodological model for the construction of sound arguments by later philosophers. From the non-theistic view of some professionals, medieval theology contributed rather little to later generations, yet they have to agree that the three arguments for the existence of God are of paramount importance. They are important not because the existence or non-existence of God is significant to us, but because the structure and the validity of the arguments constitute controversies in philosophical method. Perhaps it was due to his faith or religious enthusiasm that St. Anselm initiated the ontological argument. However, the rejection, acceptance, discussion, and revision of this argument have formed a glorious history of landmarks in philosophical method. After the downfall of the medieval period, when the existence of God had become less a matter of public concern, this particular argument was nevertheless reworked by Descartes, revised by Leibniz and Spinoza, criticized by Kant, rationalized by Hegel, supported by Collingwood, and reconstructed by such recent scholars as Charles Hartshorne and Norman Malcolm. When St. Anselm wrote *The Proslogion*, he could never have anticipated that in the twentieth century scholars would have compiled together this series of discussions of his argument into volumes and sold them to publishers for financial reward or out of some sort of academic vanity.[11]

From a non-professional or common-sense viewpoint, whether the ontological argument is valid or not is unimportant. Common-sense people are more interested in immediate answers and practical implications. For them, if God does exist, our prayers will be answered and our souls may be saved. But they can hardly see the value of the ontological argument. If the argument is valid, that is fine. But if it is invalid, it does not affect 'reality'. For ordinary people, philosophy consists of a set of enlightening ideas which provide guidance in life. No matter whether such ideas are expressed in the forms of a poem, a novel, a play, a speech, or a newspaper report, they do not care very much. From their viewpoint a poet or a novelist with enlightening ideas is a truer philosopher than a Carnap, a Quine, or a Strawson, because the novelist and the poet are more successful in communicating with them. It is an undeniable fact that, fettered by their concern with conceptual trivialities and with the infinite search for clarity, Western philosophers have today become far removed from the thinking and feeling of ordinary people, as well as of those highly educated in other fields. Thus ordinary people (or, better, people outside the circle of professional philosophers) are left with the choice of either condemning themselves for being incapable of talking philosophy or of blaming philosophy for being useless. Since so many people have been disappointed with contemporary Western philosophy in their search for moral leadership, spiritual supervision, and guidance in life, it is very natural that many of them, including scholars in philosophy, should turn to Oriental wisdom. But have they succeeded in their search? Have they gained anything from the Oriental sages? In the next section I will develop a critique of some methodological mistakes often incurred in studies of Oriental philosophy, particularly Chinese thought.

II

After World War II, particularly after the Chinese Communists took over the Chinese mainland, there have appeared a number of Asian Studies programs in the universities of the United States. Most of these programs have been devoted to the studies of *modern* Chinese history, government, economics, and society. Evidently such programs were established to 'honor' Mao Tze-tung rather than Confucius, in spite of the latter being the symbol of Chinese culture. Students searching for Chinese philosophy in these programs are usually encouraged to study the thoughts of Mao Tze-tung rather than explore Confucianism, Taoism, Buddhism, Ch'an, Chu Hsi, or Wang Yang-ming. In my view, this is a mistake in American higher education. I call it 'the fallacy of craving for cash value'. I hope my readers will not misinterpret me for holding the conservative view that the study of Chinese philosophy and culture should emphasize the classical period. My view is based on my understanding of Chinese culture as contrasted with modern Western culture. Chinese culture has been essentially a culture of the humanities, while modern Western culture has been predominantly occupied with the development of science. In scientific studies there is an emphasis upon recent developments. A dictum for the scientist is, 'the more up-to-date the more acceptable'. Newtonian physics is more acceptable than physics in Aristotle, and it in its turn has been superseded by Einstein's relativity and Planck's quantum mechanics. Because of the progressive nature of science, people in a scientific culture naturally put a higher value upon the modern, the recently discovered, and the up-to-date, than upon classical culture in antiquity. But in the humanities the corresponding dictum, 'the more recent the more acceptable', can no longer hold. It is absurd to say that Hemingway is more acceptable than Charles Dickens, or Robert Frost than Shakespeare. Moreover, a rule of thumb in science, particularly experimental science, is that one should follow prescribed rules. But in the humanities, and particularly in art and literature, what is important is not the following of rigid rules, but the imitation of great models in the past. It is therefore quite understandable that students of the humanities are less attracted to the moderns: they have to honor the ancients as well. Since Chinese culture is primarily a culture of the humanities, and these do not progress in the way a scientific culture does, any study of Chinese culture which conforms with the scientific dictum will lead only either to misunderstanding or to labor in vain. In Chinese culture the ancients and the moderns play an equally important role. In order to understand modern China a student in the Western tradition should study her whole history. For the ancient sages as well as the moderns are equally important in the shaping of modern China. Regarding this point, scholarship in Europe appears to be better than that in the American continent, probably because in American culture the spirit of 'knowledge for its own sake' has already been replaced by the craving for 'cash values'.

The second fallacy in the study of Chinese thought is, to use a Chinese idiom, *hsiao tsu shih chü*, meaning 'cutting one's toes to fit the shoes'. Or we may simply call it 'the fallacy of the Procrustean bed'. It is a result of the imposition of ready-made categories upon a subject-matter. This fallacy can be committed by Chinese scholars who have been trained in Western methodology as well as by Western scholars. As I have already pointed out, Western thinkers have a passion for clarity, but Chinese thinkers have not; they seem more aware of the uncategorizable nature of reality, particularly of the reality of the human world. Such a difference in modes of thought is revealed even at a more practical level. In a Western society we can generally identify a person by his religion: 'You are a Catholic, he is a Protestant, and I am a Jew.' But to classify Chinese people by calling them Buddhists, Taoists, or Confucians would be a serious mistake. In China, having faith in two or three religions at the same time is socially acceptable. This is because, according to the Chinese view, all religions lead to the same goal. In Chinese philosophy (not Chinese philosophy as prepared for Western readers by some scholars) we do not see the customary dichotomies such as form and matter, mind and body, idealism and materialism, *a priori* and *a posteriori*, analytic and synthetic, the empirical and the rationalistic, subjectivity and objectivity, and so on. In the Chinese language we do not find two distinct words correspondingly equivalent to 'heart' and 'mind' in the English language. The Chinese word *hsin* is used for both the emotional 'heart' and the more intellectually oriented 'mind'. From the beginning Chinese thinkers have not believed in the distinction between the rational and irrational parts of the soul; nor would they approve the distinction between the cognitive and the non-cognitive. Therefore, if we apply Western categories to Chinese philosophy without caution the result will only be what Whitehead called 'the fallacy of misplaced concreteness'.[12]

The third mistake is a very common one. It can best be explained by a metaphor describing what I have observed in ordinary experience. In the United States the hamburger is one of the most common kinds of food. As I am told by some of my friends who are owners of Chinese restaurants, many American customers come there to eat hamburgers, in spite of knowing very well that Chinese restaurants have many gourmet dishes to offer. Scholars in Chinese philosophy are often tempted to commit the same mistake. In Western philosophy there are important topics like 'causality', 'universals', 'the mind–body relation', and 'the analytic–synthetic distinction'. But it does not follow that Chinese philosophy, in order to be philosophy, must cover the same problems. If we are tempted to write a research paper on 'The Syllogistic Theory in Confucius' or 'Lao Tzu's Theory of Causality', this will be the same as asking for a hamburger in a Chinese restaurant. One may argue that ideas of syllogistic theory are to be found germinally in Confucius and embryonic notions of causality in Lao Tzu, and that it is the responsibility and interest of a scholar to bring them to light and systematic form. This argument differs little from saying that the kitchen of a Chinese restaurant has the materials for a hamburger. But the point is, why do we not, as a connoisseur of Chinese food, order something more typically Chinese, like Peking duck or steamed fish? It has been a fact that Chinese restaurants in the United States do try to sell hamburgers. It has also been a fact that some scholars in Chinese philosophy have tried to demonstrate that Chinese philosophers had theories about things that are considered important in Western philosophy. The reason in the case of the Chinese restaurateurs is very simple: they do not want to lose customers. But in the case of scholarship the reason may be more complex. Probably it is an attempt to promote the value of Chinese philosophy by demonstrating that what is found in Western philosophy is also to be found in the philosophy of China. It is also probable that scholars do this simply for the sake of intellectual gymnastics, or to fulfil the academic requirements under the 'publish or perish' policy.[13] But, in my view, the value of Chinese philosophy does not lie in its covering the topics of Western philosophy, no more than the value of Chinese gastronomy consists in having hamburgers on its menu. My thesis here is that in doing comparative philosophy we should have more *sense of importance*. When we search for Chinese wisdom we should search for what is significant, for what is typically Chinese. Now the important question is: How do we distinguish the typical from the non-typical? Or, how do we identify what is typical of Chinese philosophy? In answering this question we have to focus our attention on Chinese philosophy as a whole. In the next section I will attempt a characterization of the fundamental spirit of Chinese philosophy.

III

Any characterization of something complex is inclined to commit the fallacy of the blind men who attempted to describe the elephant on the basis of what they each felt with their hands. Although I will try to avoid bias or subjective feeling, selective emphasis is inevitable. Nevertheless my selective emphasis is based on my understanding of Chinese philosophy *as a whole*, rather than from the viewpoint of one single school of thought. As I observe it, Chinese philosophy as a distinctive tradition possesses the following five characteristics: (1) human centrality, (2) unity of theory and practice, (3) pedagogic universality, (4) methodological simplicity, and (5) dynamic harmony. To each of these characteristics I will give a brief explanation.

Human centrality: It has been an established belief that humanism is essential in the Chinese philosophical tradition. Many Chinese thinkers, particularly Confucius, have been often quoted to support this belief. I do not want to repeat what has been familiar to scholars in comparative philosophy. Here I am concerned with a very important question which may be raised by my Western readers. The question is: If Chinese philosophy is basically a form of humanism, how does it differ from the types of humanism that occur in the West, particularly Renaissance Humanism and twentieth-century Existentialist Humanism?

Strictly speaking, from a Chinese philosopher's viewpoint, Renaissance Humanism and Existentialist Humanism are not humanism in its full development. They are products of the outgrowth of non-humanistic thought. Renaissance Humanism signifies the previous dominance of religious supernaturalism more than it signifies humanism itself, for it is primarily a reaction against medieval thought. Throughout history Chinese Humanism has never been a reaction against any supernatural belief, probably because supernaturalism has played a very minor role in the development of Chinese philosophy. Even in popular Chinese thought, where there is a supernatural world it is a world full of humanistic spirit.[14] In the Judaic-Christian tradition God and man are sharply distinguished from each other. God is God, and man is man. But in China many of the gods were originally from the human world. They became gods primarily because of their possession of exceptional moral virtues and spiritual power. This means that in Chinese thought humanism has assimilated supernaturalism as an integral part of itself, since the supernatural world is basically an objectification of the humanistic spirit.

As to Existentialist Humanism, it is primarily a recent reaction against scientific naturalism. From the viewpoint of a Chinese thinker this form of humanism is not humanistic in the full sense. Scientific naturalism is not at all antagonistic to true humanism, since the development of science and technology can contribute to the well-being of mankind. It is antagonistic to the imperfect kind of humanism in which humanity is conceived only in a very narrow sense. If one follows the history of China, one may be surprised at the remarkable cooperation between Confucian Humanism and Taoist Naturalism. Professor W. T. Chan has rightly pointed out that 'Taoism and Confucianism run harmoniously parallel throughout Chinese history so that every Chinese is at once a Taoist and a Confucianist'.[15]

Therefore it seems quite justified to say that only Chinese Humanism deserves the term 'humanism' in its full sense, for it is not a reaction against any kind of thought which can ultimately contribute to the well-being of mankind. Being different from other types of humanism, Chinese Humanism is tolerant, accommodating (accommodating other types of thought as a part of itself), and even all-embracing. The dictum for Chinese Humanism is: *All that exists is for humanity, by humanity, and of humanity*.

Unity of theory and practice : Throughout the history of Chinese philosophy there has been a strong emphasis on the unity of theory and practice. Confucius is probably the first philosopher to have insisted on the necessary correspondence between words and actions.[16] Chu Hsi maintained that knowledge and action require each other.[17] Wang Yang-ming went a step further and advocated that knowledge and action are one.[18] The discussion of the unity of theory and practice, or knowledge and action, has been a central theme in Confucianism.

But a Western reader familiar with American philosophy may ask this question: In American Pragmatism the unity of theory and practice is also emphasized, how then does Chinese Confucianism differ from American Pragmatism in emphasizing such a unity? An answer to this question requires some understanding of the historical background of American thought as well as of the spirit of the Chinese philosophical tradition. American Pragmatism is a philosophy strongly influenced by Darwinism and the experimental sciences. Under the influence of Darwin, a pragmatist rejects 'knowledge for its own sake', and advocates that knowledge be the preparation for action, an instrument to solve problems, to satisfy our needs, including the need for survival in this precarious world. Under the influence of experimental science, a pragmatist holds that a theory or hypothesis performs the function of guiding our action in our inquiry. Regarding the logical structure (genetic and functional relations between theory and practice) of the unity of theory and practice, there is similarity between Confucianism and Pragmatism. But the basic stresses are qualitatively different. Generally speaking, the unity of theory and practice in pragmatism is more concerned with, in addition to human survival, scientific and epistemological problems. But Confucianism is deeply concerned with moral faith.[19] The term 'theory' as used in Confucianism is not to be understood in terms merely of conceptual framework or hypothesis. It should be conceived as *deep conviction* or even *ultimate concern*.[20] 'Practice' in Confucianism is not to be interpreted in terms merely of something to be exercised or performed in daily life, like 'diet', 'dance', or 'table-tennis'; it should be interpreted in terms of a deep moral sense; it is concerned with the *total moral performance of the individual*. From the Chinese viewpoint the total moral performance of the individual and the totality of his beliefs or theories should be in harmonious unity, without any gap or inconsistency.

When first exposed to logic in the Western tradition, I was very much surprised with the logic text which included '*Argumentum ad Hominem*' among the fallacies. Western logic has drawn a sharp distinction between one's personal character and one's theory, but no typical Chinese thinker (except one corrupted by Western logic) would approve of such a distinction. From the Chinese viewpoint a criticism of someone's theory through a criticism of his moral character commits no fallacy at all, since philosophy for a Chinese thinker is philosophy *lived* rather than philosophy constructed by the intellect, and one's personal character should be the exemplification of one's theory.

The traditional goal of moral life in Chinese culture is 'sageliness within and kingliness without'.[21] This ideal fully signifies the moral unity between theory and practice. Superficially this goal bears some resemblance to Plato's ideal of the philosopher king. But in fact the two are substantially different. For Plato, philosopher kings were those who were fully developed in intellect or the rational part of the soul. For the Chinese philosophers, sageliness is not to be achieved through the discipline of dialectics, but through the cultivation of a moral life. As an individual the ideal man is a sage; as a leader of society he is a king. But he does not lead his society by exercising power, nor does he lead it by exercising pure intellect. He leads his society through the total performance of his moral action, which is the exemplification of his convictions and ultimate concern.

Pedagogic universality: Unlike the Hindu caste system in which the teachings of the Vedas are possessed by only a few, and unlike contemporary Western society in which philosophy is possessed by only the professionals, Chinese society has never evinced aristocracy or professionalism in philosophy. On the contrary, in China philosophy is intended for every educated individual. Fung Yu-lan, in the opening chapter of his *A Short History of Chinese Philosophy*, gave the following description:

> In China, philosophy has been every educated person's concern. In the old days, if a man were educated at all, the first education he received was in philosophy. When children went to school, the *Four Books*, which consist of the *Confucian Analects*, the *Book of Mencius*, the *Great Learning*, and the *Doctrine of the Mean*, were the first ones they were taught to read. The *Four Books* were the most important texts of Neo-Confucianist philosophy. Sometimes when the children were just beginning to learn the characters, they were given a sort of textbook to read. This was known as the *Three Characters Classic*, and was so called because each sentence in the book consisted of three characters arranged so that when recited they produced a rhythmic effect, and thus helped the children to memorize them more easily. This book was in reality a primer, and the very first statement in it is that 'the nature of man is originally good'. This is one of the fundamental ideas of Mencius' philosophy.[22]

This is a very accurate and faithful description of the kind of elementary education thousands of Chinese intellectuals have undergone, including the present writer.[23] But the important question is: Why has philosophy in China occupied such a central place in children's education? To answer it we have to realize the fact that philosophy has taken the place of a formal religion in China. In the West the spiritual foundation was provided by the Judaic-Christian religious doctrines; religion has been pervasive and dominant in Western culture. In China, however, it is not religion but moral philosophy which has provided the spiritual basis for culture. Nevertheless, one may wonder how ethics without a religion can be the spiritual basis of a civilization. In answer I would like to cite the moral philosophy of Henri Bergson. According to Bergson, morality can be classified into two types corresponding to their sources. The first kind of morality lies in the necessity of social solidarity, while the second is the emotional appeal of great men. The first type is pragmatic, based on practical necessity, but the second type is mystical or religious. The morality which originates in practical necessity is closed and limited, but the morality that is generated by the appeal of great men is open, and without limitation.[24] It is Bergson's concept of open morality which throws light on the Chinese ethical tradition. Although formalized religion is not dominant in Chinese culture, Chinese ethics itself has a religious quality. It is religious because the influencing power of the sages has a universal appeal which is not too much different from the appeal of Jesus Christ and the Buddha.

Because philosophy, particularly moral philosophy, has been the spiritual basis of Chinese culture, philosophy in China has never been professionalized. At this point some of my Western readers, particularly professional philosophers, may doubt whether Chinese philosophy can be called 'philosophy' at all. To remove this doubt let me first point out that the absence of professional philosophy from Chinese culture does not imply that there is no philosophy in China, since the term 'philosophy' does not analytically imply that philosophy is professional. Professional philosophy is only a contingency, an historical fact in the modern West. Try to imagine a society in which there were no restaurants. Can we conclude that the members of this fictitious society had no art of cooking or eating at all? It might equally well be the case that each family could cook so well that no restaurants were needed. From the Chinese viewpoint the ultimate purpose of philosophy is not the acquiring of technical analytic skills or of historical knowledge about philosophers, but the cultivation of morals and self-realization. How can there be professional cultivators of morals or self-realizers? If we have to use the term 'professional', we may well say that in China the pedagogical goal is that every educated individual should become a professional philosopher. But this will be a self-contradiction. Once a profession is extended to include everyone, it is no longer a profession.

Methodological simplicity: Anyone familiar with Chinese culture may already have an impression of the simplicity that is a major characteristic of Chinese life. Since the unity of theory and practice has been so essential in that culture, simplicity in theory is a logical prerequisite. Unlike philosophers in the West, Chinese thinkers have never bothered to write long treatises comparable to Kant's *Critique of Pure Reason* or Whitehead's *Process and Reality*. In fact Chinese thinkers do not consider long treatises with elaborate arguments to be necessary, since the ultimate goal of philosophy is moral cultivation or self-realization, rather than the demonstration of the validity of one's own thesis. Artificial elaboration with linguistic symbols is, from a Chinese philosopher's viewpoint, a serious evil in that it hinders communication of thought. What is implied in the concept of simplicity is sincerity.[25] Long treatises with technical elaboration can easily promote an intellectual hypocrisy which can undermine this cardinal virtue.

Methodological simplicity in philosophical communication has been an underlying principle throughout the history of Chinese philosophy. The book which has had the greatest influence on Chinese thought is no doubt the *Confucian Analects*. It consists only of short aphorisms and brief dialogues. The *Tao Te Ching* is only a small pamphlet of no more than six thousand words, but it has initiated the whole Taoist philosophical tradition. Mencius, Motze, Chuang Tzu, and Han Fei expressed themselves in prose works of short or moderate length. Mahayana Buddhism, from India, has contained sophisticated epistemological and metaphysical systems which are, in form, not very different from the treatises of a Hume or a Hegel. But this is not the Chinese way, and Mahayana Buddhism was soon superseded by Ch'an Buddhism which holds fast to the principle of simplicity. It seems that all Chinese philosophers have had a built-in Occam's Razor which warns us: Do not complicate an issue with elaborate arguments which are not necessary.

My readers must not misinterpret me as saying that no Chinese philosophers ever used arguments. Many of them did. My point is that argument in Chinese philosophy is not sufficient as a method, nor is it necessary. Mencius is a philosopher who probably used arguments more than any other philosophers of his time, but he confessed that this was not his way.[26] However, if we look to the West, as I pointed out earlier, argumentation is a necessary method in philosophy. Why? And why is there such a substantial difference between Chinese philosophy and the philosophy of the West? To answer this question I will first relate it to the difference in linguistic background. Unlike European languages which encourage a linear or discursive way of thinking, the Chinese language does not proceed in a clear-cut linear way; so it leaves more room for grasping concrete diversified experiences simultaneously. Since I have already discussed the relation between Chinese language and Chinese thought in another paper,[27] I shall not go into details here.

It has been a general understanding that the major methodology in Chinese philosophy is *intuition*.[28] This term is a very unfortunate one, for it has so many meanings. If it has to be used, it must not be taken to denote the kind of intuition which is primitive, impulsive, instinctive, unreflective, and anti-scientific. Nor does it denote an occult vision which is possessed only by mystics. It is the kind of intuition which is the natural synthesis of the outcomes of moral maturation, intensive observation, direct experience, and persistent intellectual effort. This kind of methodology defies any ready-made categories in Western philosophy. If I have to give it a name, I would call it 'a natural synthetic intuitive grasp'. It is not antagonistic to logic or analysis. On the contrary, proper analysis and adequate logical thinking can contribute richly to such a synthesis. Since arriving at a conclusion here presupposes the complex processes of moral maturation, intensive observation, direct experience, and persistent intellectual effort, Chinese philosophers in communication usually present their conclusions without premises. This is simply because such premises are so complexly rooted in their moral, social, intellectual, and religious experiences that a complete presentation of them would require even a much longer treatise than any of the masterpieces of the Western world. So, I may conclude that the communicative method in Chinese philosophy is simple enough, but the processes behind the conclusions are far more complicated than any set of simplified premises in the treatises of Western philosophy.

Dynamic harmony: To my knowledge one of the most penetrating presentations in the English language of the spirit of Chinese philosophy remains Professor Thomè H. Fang's *The Chinese View of Life*.[29] It is more than what its title indicates. It has presented a system of metaphysics which is immanent in the whole history of Chinese philosophy. The title of its first chapter is 'Chinese Wisdom: A Vindication of Comprehensive Harmony'. The term 'harmony' very properly characterizes Chinese metaphysical thinking.

I am not going to repeat what Professor Fang has already presented in his work. Nor do I want to present an alternative view. My immediate concern is to answer a question which may be reasonably asked by my Western readers. The question is: If the concept of harmony is so essential in Chinese philosophy, how does it differ from the concept of harmony which dominated ancient Greece? To answer this question I would like to draw my readers' attention to the title of this section: 'dynamic harmony.' I used the term 'dynamic' expressly to distinguish the Chinese concept from that of ancient Greece. It has to be noted that Greek thinkers had a passion for mathematics. Plato was fond of geometry, and Pythagoras even tried to reduce music to numbers. The nature of mathematics is its transcendence of space and time. This is why the Platonic forms are 'located' in the world of eternity. The concept of harmony in Greek thought is based on the perfect forms and the aesthetic features of mathematics, particularly geometry. But when we shift our attention to China, we find that the concept of a separate realm of eternal forms is completely absent. The concept of *change* seems to have played a more dominant role. The book of *I Ching* is a classic built on the concepts of change and interaction. *Chung Yung* is an essay on the dynamic process of human nature. A central concept in this essay is called *chung ho*. *Chung* indicates the psychic state in which no feeling is aroused, and *ho* denotes the state of harmony attained through the balancing of all aroused feelings.[30] Now we may come to a general conclusion, namely that the Greek concept of harmony is modeled on the static form of *nature*, whereas the Chinese concept of harmony is modeled on the dynamic process of *life*. Although both Greek and Chinese culture are dominated by the concept of harmony, Chinese metaphysics is very different. Interestingly enough, Chinese metaphysics is similar to the process philosophy of Bergson and Whitehead, particularly the latter. This is probably why Joseph Needham has speculated that Whitehead might have been indirectly influenced by Chinese philosophers like Chuang Chou, Chou Tun-i, and Chu Hsi.[31] However, Needham was attracted to only one aspect of Chinese metaphysics, namely metaphysics of nature. While another aspect of Chinese metaphysics, metaphysics of morals, initiated by Mencius, richly implied in *Chung Yung* and *I Ching,* and developed by such neo-Confucianists as Lu Hsiang-shan and Wang Yang-ming, is very little known to the West. Had the Chinese concept of harmony not been modeled after *life,* the Chinese metaphysics of morals would probably not have been developed.

IV

To recapitulate, in this paper I have offered a critique of contemporary Western philosophy, a critique of methodological mistakes made in the pursuit of Chinese philosophy, and a characterization of Chinese philosophy as contrasted to the main traditions of Western thought. As a conclusion, I would like to take a final opportunity to make two points. First, I hope my Western readers do not get the impression that Chinese philosophy is so different from the philosophy of the West that it would be very difficult for a Westerner. With sufficient open-mindedness and intellectual effort I am sure that a Western scholar can achieve a certain degree of mastery of Chinese philosophy. Secondly, my article has been only a preliminary introduction. To catch a fish one needs a fishing pole (with its string, hook, and bait). But when you have caught the fish you no longer need the pole. My article is the pole; Chinese philosophy is the fish. I hope my readers will not take the fishing pole for the fish. This is the first step toward Chinese wisdom.

NOTES

1. I refer to the philosophy of Friedrich Nietzsche.
2. This theological movement is represented by Thomas J. J. Altizer and William Hamilton, *Radical Theology and the Death of God,* Bobbs-Merrill Co., Inc., Indianapolis 1966, and Thomas J. J. Altizer (Ed.), *Toward a New Christianity,* Harcourt, Brace & World, Inc., New York 1967.
3. This movement is represented by Harvey Cox, *The Secular City: Secularization and Urbanization in Theological Perspective,* rev. ed., Macmillan Co., New York 1966.
4. This movement is best represented by Rudolf Bultmann. For an introduction to his thought, see John B. Cobb, Jr., *Living Options in Protestant Theology,* Westminster Press, Philadelphia 1962, pp. 227–58.
5. This movement is represented by Paul Tillich. See his *Dynamics of Faith,* Harper & Brothers, New York 1957, and *Systematic Theology,* 3 Vols., University of Chicago Press, Chicago 1951–63.

6. This movement is represented by many theologians. See particularly John B. Cobb, Jr., op. cit.

7. The leading figure of this movement is Alfred North Whitehead. His concept of God is found in *Process and Reality*, Macmillan Co., New York 1929, Part V; *Religion in the Making*, Macmillan Co., New York 1926, Chs. III and IV; and *Science and the Modern World*, Macmillan Co., New York 1925, Ch. XI.
   My understanding of the contemporary scene of theology in the West is indebted to my reading of my friend Professor Shu-hsien Liu's unpublished paper 'The Religious Import of Confucian Philosophy: Its Traditional Outlook and Contemporary Significance'. Professor Liu, however, is not responsible for any inadequacies in my presentation.

8. John Dewey is probably the most important exception.

9. For a criticism of this kind of infinite search for clarity, see my 'Contemporary Western Philosophy from an Eastern Viewpoint', *International Philosophical Quarterly*, Vol. VIII (1968), No. 4, pp. 491–7.

10. A notable example is Ayn Rand; another is Will Durant. The works of these two writers are not taken seriously by professional scholars in philosophy in spite of the fact that both enjoy a celebrated reputation with the American public. Here I am describing a fact rather than pleading a defense.

11. A detailed bibliography is found in John Hick, 'Ontological Argument for the Existence of God', *The Encyclopedia of Philosophy*, 8 Vols., Macmillan Co., & Free Press, New York 1967, Vol. 5, pp. 538–42.

12. Whitehead, *Science and the Modern World*, op. cit., p. 85.

13. A criticism of this kind of scholarship is found in my article, 'Two Academic Dogmas in American Higher Education', *Educational Theory*, Vol. 20 (1970), No. 3, pp. 284–91.

14. Cf. my 'Some Humanistic Characteristics of Chinese Religious Thought', *Religious Studies*, Vol. V (1969), No. 1, pp. 269–75.

15. Wing-tsit Chan (Trans.), *The Way of Lao Tzu*, Bobbs-Merrill Co., Inc., Indianapolis 1963, p. 19.

16. See *Lun Yu* (*Confucian Analects*), Bk. V, Ch. 13.

17. Wing-tsit Chan (Ed.), *A Source Book in Chinese Philosophy*, Princeton University Press, Princeton 1963, p. 609.

18. Ibid., p. 656.

19. I have coined the term 'moral faith' to characterize the religious seriousness of the Confucians' concern with morality. The word 'faith' is not intended to denote any belief in the Divine.

20. I borrow this term ('ultimate concern') from Paul Tillich but use it in a stronger moral and humanistic sense.

21. Fung Yu-lan, *A Short History of Chinese Philosophy*, Macmillan Co., New York 1948, p. 8.

22. Ibid., p. 1.

23. Although the present writer is nearly forty years younger than Professor Fung he still had the same kind of moral and philosophical education as described in Professor Fung's work.

24. Henri Bergson, *The Two Sources of Morality and Religion*, Henry Holt, New York 1935, pp. 55–60.

25. The important point is not only that 'sincerity' is semantically implied in 'simplicity', but also that the concept of sincerity has become a very important concept in the metaphysics of morals in neo-Confucianism. Cf. Chan, *A Source Book*, op. cit., pp. 461, 465–7, 489, 507–8, 522, 552, and 560.
26. Chan, *A Source Book*, op. cit., p. 72.
27. Cf. my 'Chinese Language and Chinese Thought', *Philosophy East and West*, Vol. 19 (1969), No. 4, pp. 424–34.
28. This is a commonly held thesis which is probably a result of the influence of F. S. C. Northrop. Cf. his *The Meeting of East and West*, Macmillan Co., New York 1946, Ch. IX.
29. Thomè H. Fang, *The Chinese View of Life*, Union Press, Hong Kong 1957.
30. Chan, *A Source Book*, op. cit., p. 98.
31. Joseph Needham, *Science and Civilization in China*, Cambridge University Press, New York 1956, Vol. II, p. 505.

SHU HSIEN LIU

II. *The contemporary development of a neo-Confucian epistemology*

Until recently epistemology in the Western sense was never a central issue in Chinese philosophy. Contemporary Chinese neo-Confucian philosophers, however, realize that in order to reconstruct some of the important traditional philosophical insights and make them meaningful in the present time, certain methodological and epistemological considerations are indispensable. The present paper undertakes to examine some of these efforts. Since most neo-Confucian philosophers today have been influenced by Hsiung Shih-li, in one way or another, his epistemological theory is presented first. Then the further development of a neo-Confucian epistemological system in Mou Tsung-san's thought is discussed. Hsiung Shih-li has made an important distinction between what he calls the *hsing-chih* and the *liang-chih*. The former may be translated as the original wisdom and is what we rely upon to grasp ontological reality; the latter may be translated as the measuring wisdom and includes both our commonsensical and scientific ways of understanding which postulate a real, external world. A dialectical relation holds between the two. Mou Tsung-san further develops a comprehensive epistemological system which confirms the basic insights of Hsiung Shih-li. He has attempted a synthesis of the philosophical insights which he learns from Kant in the West and the Confucian tradition in China.

I. Introduction

Until recently epistemology in the Western sense was never a central issue in Chinese philosophy. All the three great traditions, Confucianism, Taoism, and Buddhism, maintain that ultimate truth can be reached. While it is true that intellectual sophistication, existential commitment, and diligent practice of the principle are needed in order to grasp the true meaning of either the Confucian *jên*, or the Taoist *wu*, or the Buddhist *k'ung* (*shunya*), theoretically there is nothing to prevent one from realizing truth if proper procedures are followed. Since scepticism had hardly achieved any distinction in the past,[1]

it is not difficult to understand why the epistemological issues that
have troubled the Western mind were largely ignored by traditional
Chinese thinkers.[2]

In the modern era, however, when traditional values are in doubt,
all sorts of Western philosophical points of view have flowed into
China. After more than half a century's struggle in ideas, three main
trends of thought are discernible, each with its specific epistemological
point of view. They are: Communism on the mainland; Pragmatism-
Logical Positivism,[3] and neo-Confucianism in so-called Free China.

I shall leave the discussion of the Communist ideology to experts
in that field. I shall not discuss Pragmatism-Logical Positivism, although this trend exerts an important influence on Chinese intellectuals today, because the basic ideas taught by this school are, for the
most part, merely a reiteration of views familiar to a Western audience.
The third trend may be more interesting in that it takes pains to seek
a synthesis of Chinese traditional values and Western values. Neo-
Confucian philosophers today are convinced that, although some
aspects of Chinese culture must be subject to drastic changes (for
example, China is in urgent need of Western science and democracy),
yet certain important philosophical insights developed in the past,
embodying the quintessence of the traditional Chinese culture, must
be kept intact. These insights must be revived and reconstructed in
such a way that the crisis of our times can be met. The neo-Confucian
philosophers realize that in order to justify their world-views and life-
views some sort of methodological and epistemological considerations
are indispensable. The present paper undertakes to examine some
of these efforts. Since most neo-Confucian philosophers today have
been influenced by Professor Hsiung Shih-li in one way or another, I
shall present his epistemological theory first.[4] Then I shall proceed to
examine the further development of a neo-Confucian epistemological
system in Professor Mou Tsung-san's thought.[5] Finally I shall make a
few remarks of my own in the concluding section of the paper.

II. HSIUNG SHIH-LI'S EPISTEMOLOGICAL THEORY

Hsiung Shih-li's way of reconciling Western science and traditional
Confucian metaphysical insight is to assign them to two distinct but
related universes of discourses. In epistemology he distinguishes sharply
between what he calls the *hsing-chih* and the *liang-chih*. The former may
be translated as the original wisdom or knowledge by nature, which

is what we rely upon to grasp ontological reality. The latter may be translated as the measuring wisdom or knowledge by measurement, which includes both our commonsensical and scientific ways of understanding which postulate a real, external world.

By *hsing-chih*, Hsiung understands that which correlates with the ontological principle within our being, or that which flows out of our depth of reason without obstruction. It is through the illuminating power of *hsing-chih* that we realize that the ontological principle within us is not different from the ontological principle of all beings. According to Hsiung, then, apart from such an illumination there can never be an authentic self. This illuminating self is without any want and without any conflicts. And such illumination does not exist apart from sense experience, although it is not bound by sense experience. In its normal condition this self is truly self-illuminating, self-enlightening; it is immaterial and contains all the principles within itself. In effect it is the only origin of all our knowledge.[6]

Liang-chih, the function of measurement which conducts inference, may be called the reason or the intellect. It is the principle which differentiates. It investigates the phenomenal world and makes judgments upon our experience. According to Hsiung, *liang-chih* in the final analysis is no other than the function or manifestation of *hsing-chih*, yet has the tendency to alienate itself from its origin and to falsely identify itself as having a separate existence of its own. Because *hsing-chih* has to depend upon the senses to manifest its function in the phenomenal world, it gives occasion for the senses to usurp its position just as slaves sometimes may usurp the position of a master. Once the senses alienate themselves from their origin and claim independence of their own, even though in fact they remain the function of *hsing-chih*, the latter is concealed and is twisted to serve the purpose of the senses as well as the intellect. The senses chase external things so as to form a deep-rooted habit, hence an external material world is artificially constructed. The habit, of course, has profound after-effects which continually accumulate and finally become inexhaustible. Thus knowledge by measurement is the kind of knowledge which we develop out of our experience of the phenomenal world, the basic characteristic of which is that it always directs its attention outward. And it is precisely because of its extrovert tendency that it always correlates itself with an external phenomenal universe. It is true that by means of *liang-chih* we are able to establish the order of the world and discover the principles of becoming in the phenomenal world. It can

certainly give us knowledge about the phenomenal world. But it is
unable to uncover the metaphysical truth, which we may realize
only through the cultivation of our inherent original wisdom. Hence
if we rely upon the information of *liang-chih* to construct arbitrary
metaphysical systems, it would be impossible for us to uncover the
true ontological principle of metaphysical reality within our own
being and the whole phenomenal universe.[7]

In the same spirit Hsiung also distinguishes between what he calls
the *pen-hsin* and the *hsi-hsin*. *Pen-hsin* is the original mind which is the
equivalent of *hsing-chih*, and *hsi-hsin* is the vulgar habitual mind which
is the equivalent of *liang-chih*. *Pen-hsin* is ontologically prior. It has
the following characteristics: In the first place it is both empty and
silent; silent because it transcends all confusion and anxieties of our
life and hence is regarded as subtle and divine; empty because its
creative power is always inexhaustible. In the second place, since it is
illuminating, it is the sole origin of all genuine knowledge. According
to Hsiung, the original mind is the ontological principle of our own being which is not different from the ontological principle of all beings.
Thus he traces this view back to Mencius's view that we realize our
mind in order to realize our nature as well as to realize Heaven.
Heaven, in this particular context, is the symbol for the metaphysical
origin of all things. Hence if we rely only on our habitual mind, which
makes all sorts of distinctions within the phenomenal world, which
distinguishes between what is internal and what is external, which
clings desperately to the small self and takes it as the only true self,
then it is certainly impossible for us to discover our true nature and
consequently the ontological principle of all beings. Moreover, the
original mind is not to be regarded as the opposite of matter. It is
the habitual mind which is the opposite of matter and, at the same
time, the correlate of matter. The original mind is nothing, if we take
a 'thing' to be a particular existent in time and space; time and space
themselves are products of the ontological principle. The original
mind is the creative power which operates within all things without
being limited by these things. It has to manifest its creative power
through matter and as matter, but it is not to be overwhelmed by
matter. In this sense it is the Absolute, but it is an Absolute which
has to manifest itself through what is relative. And it is only through
the realization of our original mind that we may hope to establish
any kind of genuine metaphysical knowledge at all.[8]

Once the distinction between the original mind and the habitual mind is granted, it is not difficult to see that human learning can be divided into two branches: sciences and metaphysics. The sciences appeal to the method of analysis used to investigate particular aspects of the phenomenal universe; metaphysics, on the other hand, relies on the method of inner illumination, which concerns itself with the universe as a whole.[9] The empirical sciences have their foundation in the habitual mind, whereas metaphysics has its foundation in the original mind. The sciences start from a pragmatic or operational point of view in which things are taken to have an independent objective existence of their own. As a consequence, the intellect always has to direct its attention outward. Metaphysics, on the other hand, from an ontological point of view takes the metaphysical principle to be immaterial, although it operates within all beings. It is only by appealing to the inner illumination springing forth out of the depth of our reason that we are able to realize the metaphysical principle inherent in us, just as a wave may truly reflect the whole ocean and is not apart from the whole ocean.[10]

According to Hsiung scientific truth in distinction from metaphysical truth has the following characteristics:

(1) It has to postulate the objective existence of the physical universe which is subject to empirical observation and which is not the product of our subjective imagination or mental construction.

(2) The discovery of scientific truths must be based upon sense experience, and they must also be verified by sense experience.

(3) The results of scientific investigations must be inter-subjectively verifiable, and once established they will be recognized by all men to some extent.

(4) These truths under the existing conditions must be relatively stable; they will hold invariably unless such conditions somehow change or disappear altogether. It does not matter whether these principles are exemplified by concrete facts so long as these conditions last.

(5) Although these truths are relatively stable, they are not absolutely unchangeable. Their objects are particular existents or states of affairs which are relative to one another. The sciences are instrumental in discovering the rules of correlation between phenomenal existents or events through experience. Hence scientific truths are always many, never one.

(6) The sciences rely heavily on the hypothetical method. They have to postulate a number of concepts which are subjective in origin, but which find their correspondence in an objective world.[11]

Metaphysical truth, on the other hand, has entirely different characteristics, which may be summarized in the following fashion:

(1) It is the ontological principle for all beings.

(2) It is absolute in itself, hence does not need further reasons to justify its existence. It cannot be reached by inference of the intellect, and it cannot be adequately expressed in terms of human language.

(3) Therefore, it can be realized only through inner illumination. Under such illumination the subject and the object are united. There is no longer the distinction between the internal and the external, the thing and the self, and so forth. The ontological truth transcends all relational concepts and therefore has nothing to do with all false conjectures of the mind based upon such concepts. In short, it is the most profound as well as the easiest and the simplest of all truths.[12]

Once the two different levels of truth are distinguished from each other, the next task for Hsiung is to relate the two together properly. According to him, negatively speaking, we may at least say that metaphysical truth cannot possibly contradict scientific truths, since the two belong to entirely different universes of discourse. They can both be valuable studies to be vigorously pursued on the human level of understanding. Moreover, positively speaking, we may say further that the two levels of truth are not only supplementary but complementary to each other. The sciences study the functional aspect of reality, whereas metaphysics studies the ontological aspect of the same reality. According to Hsiung no phenomenon or function can be so called without being the phenomenon or function of a certain ontological principle; also conversely, no ontological principle can be so called without manifesting itself in certain phenomena or embodying itself in certain functions. Hence we may conclude that scientific studies and metaphysical studies are interdependent in the sense that only by combining the two properly may we hope to apprehend both the phenomenal aspect and the ontological aspect of the same reality. Thus, according to Hsiung, philosophy has no conflict with the function of reason or intellect at all. It rejects reason only in so far as reason alienates itself from its own depth and attempts to do metaphysics itself. This is a state of confusion to be carefully avoided.[13]

Methodologically speaking we have to sweep away all phenomena in order to realize the ontological principle as it is. If we erroneously take what is merely phenomenal to be what is ontologically real, then it will be impossible for us to uncover metaphysical truth. However, we have to posit a phenomenal world as the functional aspect of the same principle, or else the world of our daily experience will be turned into nothing. If the objects of our empirical knowledge were not so grounded, then the validity of our scientific knowledge would be denied once and for all.[14]

Even though we accept the relative validity of scientific truths in the phenomenal realm, from a metaphysical point of view they cannot be put on a par with metaphysical truth. The scientific way of thinking has to posit an external physical world as having an independent existence of its own. From a pragmatic point of view this procedure is perfectly justifiable. But it has the danger of hypostatizing functions into ontological substances and hence committing a metaphysical fallacy. In order to guard against the natural tendency of man to fall into such a naïve attitude, philosophy has to adopt two important methodological procedures. In the first place, we have to appeal to a specific analytic method which purports to destroy all attempts to identify phenomenal functions with the ontological principle itself by finding out all the contradictions or absurdities involved in such untenable metaphysical conjectures. According to Hsiung this is exactly what the Buddhist philosophy has done in attempting to sweep away phenomena in order to realize the ontological depth of all beings. However, in adopting these negative procedures of the Buddhist philosophy one is tempted to emphasize only the silent aspect of the ontological principle and neglect its creative aspect. In the second place, therefore, we have to appeal to a specific method of inner illumination. It is only through such illumination that we are able to realize the infinite creative power of the ontological principle. It is here that Hsiung, who praises the great contributions of the Buddhist philosophy in all other respects, criticizes sharply that same philosophy for taking the ontological principle erroneously as no more than a silent ontological principle. The Buddhist philosophers have nothing to say about the creative aspect of the ontological reality, and hence fall victim to an unhealthy otherworldly sentiment which characterizes the whole Buddhist movement. They do not understand that precisely because the principle is silent and empty it is capable of releasing the infinite, creative power of being within it. In this respect we should follow the Confucian tradition in saying that paradoxically the principle does nothing and at the same time never neglects to accomplish everything. Since this creative philosophy is the very essence of Confucian teachings, Hsiung therefore claims that he has successfully synthesized the Buddhist philosophy with the Confucian philosophy.[15]

According to Hsiung, the Oriental philosophies such as Buddhism and Confucianism all take as their ultimate aim the realization of the ontological principle. Some may appeal to the way of sudden enlightenment, and this approach is for the wisest; some may follow a roundabout way, and this approach may need more time, but once it is successful it will produce essentially the same result. In any case, metaphysics has to depend upon *hsing-chih* for its establishment; this is a realm which cannot be penetrated by *liang-chih*, or the intellect. While *hsing-chih*, the original wisdom, is not different from *pen-hsin*, the original mind, the original mind is not different from the ontological principle of all beings. Hence in order to realize the profound metaphysical truth, we do not need any occult, mystical vision at all; in fact it is the original mind which is inherent in everyone of us that illumines for us the profound metaphysical truth. Once we understand that it is futile to appeal to *liang-chih* to establish any metaphysical truth from an epistemological point of view, then we will not seek 'far-away' by entrusting ourselves to inference of the intellect or the conjectures of the mind, but rather we will seek 'near-by' by realizing the selfsame ontological principle within our own being. When, under the illumination of the original mind, all our doubts have melted away, we may appreciate the philosophical message revealed in the following poem:

> Everywhere I look for him
> Over hundreds and thousands of times,
> . Suddenly I turn around
> And see that he is not far away
> Under the dim light yonder.[16]

In conclusion, according to Hsiung the way of the great learning starts with a discipline of the self and culminates with the realization of the profound metaphysical depth within us. One has to uncover the seeds of the great original wisdom within us, to cultivate them so as to enable us to reach a stage of mature understanding, to nourish them with great effort, and to prevent them from being choked by the weeds of evil habits and arbitrary opinions. If the original wisdom always illumines without obstruction, then one is able to penetrate into the root of creation, to remove the barriers between things and self, and to enjoy the highest metaphysical truth on all occasions. The great Ming dynasty philosopher, Wang Yang-ming has testified to the same point in a poem on original wisdom which may be freely rendered into English as follows:

When there is neither sound, nor smell
Only the true mind illumines;
The foundation of the whole universe is revealed.

Hsiung takes this poem as an excellent description of the ultimate ontological truth. Such illumination, of course, can never be reached by *liang-chih*. However, the principle has to manifest itself in functions. Once the phenomenal world is formed, we have to depend upon *liang-chih* in our daily experiences in order to investigate scientifically the phenomenal universe and to develop our inferring and inquiring powers. It is an indispensable tool for our practical life.

But if man confines himself to a practical life alone and follows his habit even to the degree of dehumanizing himself and others into merely phenomenal objects and completely loses sight of his inner divinity, this means the most miserable kind of life for man. We can save ourselves only by restoring *hsing-chih* and *liang-chih* to their proper functioning. Only if an ultimate concern is established in which *liang-chih* serves for *hsing-chih* without alienation will function and principle coalesce and find themselves in a perfect state of union. A dialectical relation holds between the two.

From the above discussion it is clear that for Hsiung philosophy is an existential concern, and his epistemology is not to be separated from his metaphysics, and from his philosophy of life.

Whether one agrees with Hsiung or not, I think his approach is typical of contemporary Confucian epistemological approaches. It is an empiricist approach insofar that he rejects all supernatural and mystical theories. The truth is the easiest and simplest which can be testified to by everybody so long as everyone can realize the metaphysical depth within himself. But Hsiung would certainly reject the Western type of empiricist approaches, because he rejects their sensationalistic psychology and their method of construction. From Hsiung's point of view these empiricists have not been able to realize the function of *hsing-chih* because they erroneously rely upon arbitrary methodological devices which will never bring them near to the truth.

III. Mou Tsung-san's Epistemological System

As a college student, Mou Tsung-san studied under Hsiung Shih-li and was greatly inspired by Hsiung's thought. It was from Hsiung that he first learned the essential metaphysical insights of the Confucian tradition. But the way he attempts to reconstruct the Confucian philosophy is very different from that of his teacher. While Hsiung takes the Buddhist philosophy as his point of departure and leaves Western philosophy on the periphery of his thought, Mou shows little interest in Buddhism and penetrates deeply into Western thought. Although some of Hsiung's writings bear the title of a treatise, he writes in traditional dialogue or essay form; Mou writes philosophical treatises in the Western fashion in which concepts are defined and expressed in a systematic way. Since it is impossible to give a detailed account of Mou's epistemological system here, the best that can be done is to give a description of the general direction of his thought.

In Mou's view traditional Chinese culture shows a penetrating understanding of the moral mind, but is woefully lacking in the development of the cognitive mind which serves as the foundation of logic and of the empirical sciences. On the conceptual level, Chinese philosophy has much to learn from Western philosophy; the limitations of traditional Chinese thought must be transcended, and traditional philosophical insights will then appear in their proper perspectives. Therefore Mou examines Western philosophies of the past, studies contemporary Western philosophers such as Russell, the early Wittgenstein, Dewey, and Whitehead. He is greatly indebted to these philosophers, but also realizes that none of them has given a satisfactory account of the cognitive mind. He finds that the spirit of Kant's philosophy is congenial to his own, but Kant's philosophical system is no longer acceptable. Therefore he undertakes to rewrite a critique of pure reason of his own which is entitled *A Critique of the Cognitive Mind*.[17] After laying bare the structure of the cognitive mind, he realizes that the cognitive mind cannot be the ultimate metaphysical principle. The function of the cognitive mind is to know; it is a formal principle, never an actualizing principle. Here, again, Mou finds himself in agreement with Kant in asserting the supremacy of practical reason over theoretical reason. But Mou is disappointed with the Kantian formulation of ideas. Instead of developing an autonomous moral metaphysics, Kant, limited by his Christian background, proceeds in a wrong direction and attempts to develop a moral theology in which the freedom of the will, the existence of God, and the immortality of the soul are regarded as postulates. It is here that Mou, after going in a full circle, returns to the traditional Confucian metaphysical insights. The next formidable task for Mou, then, is to determine the nature and function of the moral mind. This goal he has

few logical systems which can satisfy such a strict demand. In the sciences, we demand universal and necessary causal relations; in fact, we can never establish anything more than the merely probable. But the dilemma is only apparent, because the idea of certainty pertains only to the regulative principles of the cognitive mind. These principles are not established in terms of empirical generalization. It is through an intuitive illumination that the mind is capable of grasping these principles. Since ideals, as a rule, cannot be fully realized in the world, the validity of these ideals is not discredited simply by the fact that they have never been fully realized in the world. When the cognitive mind tries to objectify itself, it is limited by the schemata it has to impose on itself. If we reverse the process and trace the objectification of mind back to its origin, then we will find the inner illumination of the cognitive mind. It is through such illumination that we are capable of understanding those ideal principles which have never been fully realized in the world.[28]

In summary, the three stages of cognition are: immediate apprehension, discursive understanding, and intuitive illumination. After we have exhaustively analyzed the function and the structure of the cognitive mind, we find that we must go beyond the cognitive mind, because the cognitive mind is merely a knowing principle; it is not an actualizing principle, and it is unable to provide a metaphysical ground for the world.

Now we are in a position to examine the possibility of metaphysics. There have been many ways of doing metaphysics. In methodology Mou feels that, first of all, we must carefully avoid some of the erroneous ways of doing metaphysics. We must not try to establish metaphysical truth in terms of empirical generalization, because such generalization can establish only probable scientific truths. As Mou sees it, the way we do philosophy is essentially different from the way we do science. The main purpose of science is to accumulate knowledge about the phenomenal world, while the main purpose of philosophy is to uncover the transcendental ground underlying our empirical knowledge of the world, not to increase the bulk of our empirical knowledge. In the above, we have already seen how Mou proceeds to uncover the transcendental ground for empirical knowledge on all levels: the transcendental schema of space–time for immediate apprehension; the transcendental schemata of ground–consequence, whole–part, and affirmation–negation, for discursive understanding; and the intuitive illumination of the cognitive mind. Can we, then, establish metaphysical truth in terms of these transcendental principles? The answer is negative. Through the transcendental schema of space–time we find only changing phenomena, never the unchanging metaphysical principle; through the schemata of discursive understanding we find only a relational system of objects and events, never the self-sufficient metaphysical ultimate; through intuitive illumination of the cognitive mind we find only the regulative idea of perfection in the mind, never the pure actuality itself. This seems to be a rather hopeless situation. People may infer from the manifold of phenomenal existents a pluralistic metaphysical system, or people may stabilize the categories in such a way that they are elevated to something like Platonic ideas. But these are merely conjectures of the mind that cannot stand critical examination.[29]

Now the stage is set for Mou's transcendental dialectic. It is true that the cognitive mind cannot provide us with any genuine knowledge of the metaphysical ultimate, and it cannot produce any acceptable proof of the metaphysical principle. But the cognitive mind can help to reveal the logical structure of the metaphysical principle by projecting it as the exact opposite of the object of cognition. Thus, the metaphysical principle must be beyond all changes as against the changing phenomena encompassed by space and time; it must be self-sufficient in itself as against any object of understanding; and it must be an actual principle of infinite perfection as against the unfulfilled regulative ideas of the mind. But the cognitive mind can never guarantee the existence of such a metaphysical principle. It is here that we realize the intrinsic limitation of the cognitive mind.[30]

If the cognitive mind were the only thing that we could rely upon, then the ground of metaphysics would be completely cut off from us. We could never be sure that this universe had a rational structure, that it was going to forever perpetuate itself, and that it was driving toward infinite creative possibilities. Fortunately, this is not the case. It is here that Mou returns to the profound metaphysical insights of the Confucian tradition after his long journey to the rich kingdom of ideas developed in the West. The Confucian tradition never starts with a colorless cognitive mind which need have no existential commitment whatever. It is through the intuitive realization of the mind that we realize that there is an all-encompassing, creative, metaphysical principle that works incessantly in ourselves as well as in the universe. The mind here referred to must be not the cognitive mind, but the original mind, or the moral mind, which is the metaphysical origin of the cognitive mind. If we define a proposition to be either a formal statement in logic or a factual statement in empirical science, then metaphysical statements are not 'propositions', because they cannot either be traced back to the primitive terms and the axioms within a formal logical system or be possibly verified by our experience. Metaphysical statements do not belong to a universe of discourse in which we can use the literal mode of expression. But they are saturated with meaning for those who have realized the moral mind within themselves, and these statements are not equivocal statements without any definite meanings.[31]

When Kant goes beyond pure reason and discovers practical reason, Mou sees that Kant is heading in the right direction. But Kant establishes only a metaphysics of morals, he does not go all the way to establish a moral metaphysics. Instead he tries to establish a moral theology in which the freedom of the will, the existence of God, and the immortality of the soul, are taken to be the three indispensable postulates in his system. From Mou's point of view, however, the true metaphysical principle is always a presence, never just a postulate. Kant does not realize that intuitive realization can break through the confines of the cognitive mind and lay bare the ultimate creative metaphysical principle which works incessantly both in ourselves and in the whole universe. There are two ways of understanding the metaphysical principle. Westerners tend to see it as God, a purely transcendent principle, which cannot be penetrated by the human mind, while the Chinese tend to see it as the Great Ultimate, an immanent creative principle, which can be realized by the original mind. Mou rejects the first view, because God as an external super-object is the result of unwarranted metaphysical speculation that lacks intuitive certainty; furthermore the faith in God will eventually lead to moral heteronomy, which is contradictory to Kant's pursuit of moral autonomy. But Mou concedes that Kant is the only Western thinker who comes near to the heart of Confucian metaphysical insights.[32]

The Confucian creative metaphysical principle needs further elaboration. It does not create the universe out of nothing. The existence of matter is presupposed. Creation refers to the emergence of forms and order in the universe. The creative principle functions incessantly; the present universe is but the visible effect of the function of the principle. To say that creation has a beginning is absurd; the becoming process either exists or does not exist; it cannot appear from nowhere. And the becoming process will continue even if the present universe is destroyed. The all-encompassing creative principle is the guiding principle for becoming. Since it works incessantly to bring into existence new values and new forms, it is a 'moral principle' in the broad sense of the term. The created must be the limited. The creative spark within the created may be extinguished. But not so with the creative principle itself; its creative power is inexhaustible, and its creative activity is never thwarted, regardless of the actual condition of the empirical world. It alone is the true ontological principle.[33]

Of all animals man has the richest endowment. On the one hand, he lives according to the rules of the phenomenal world. On the other, he is capable of detecting the transcendental ground of empirical knowledge and of realizing the metaphysical principle within himself. He is a conscious being who can freely choose his life for himself. If he identifies himself with the small self with only empirical concerns, he will live a narrow, miserable life full of anxieties. If he realizes the metaphysical principle within himself and joins the creative process of the universe, he will transcend his limitations, and live a life full of meaning, free from anxieties.[34]

IV. CONCLUSION

A few remarks in conclusion:

(1) Mou Tsung-san, with his extensive background in Western philosophy, develops a philosophical system which confirms the basic insights of Hsiung Shih-li, who, in turn, inherits these insights from the Confucian tradition. These contemporary neo-Confucian philosophers believe that some of the essential insights of Confucianism are reconstructible,[35] and that they reveal to us important dimensions of life which ought not to be neglected by man. Continuity and novelty are the two important ingredients in the development of human thought.

(2) These contemporary neo-Confucian philosophers are opposed to all forms of reductionism, be it behavioristic, Freudian, or Marxist. In particular, they would be opposed to the late Joseph Levenson's interpretation of the development of modern Chinese philosophy.[36] Levenson seems to apply a kind of psychoanalysis to all great modern Chinese philosophers, who have been described as attempting to rationalize things and to save the Chinese ego when in fact the Chinese civilization was plunging into a sea of disasters. Apparently Levenson

fails to make a distinction between the psychological reaction of man in an age of crisis and the truths he may be compelled to learn in an age of crisis. Levenson's theory may eventually lead to a complete relativism which denies that man, Eastern and Western alike, has the ability to learn truths.

(3) For over two thousand years the Confucian tradition has transmitted a metaphysics of creativity and a way of realizing the original mind. Although metaphysics is denounced by most Western philosophers today, Confucian metaphysics is different from the kind of metaphysics that we find in the Western tradition. Since this Confucian tradition has lasted so long, and some of the insights of the school are defended by some of the most brilliant Chinese minds today, one suspects that there may be some true ingredients in it. Therefore, I propose to suspend judgment and to start with a purely phenomenological description of the metaphysical principle of creativity and the original mind. Then we may test whether it has any existential relevance whatever; and finally, we may attempt to evaluate what are the true ingredients in this philosophy and give our own interpretation of it.

(4) Methodologically speaking, objective understanding always precedes genuine synthesis. I certainly do not mean that we must wait until we know everything before we attempt any synthesis. Life itself is an ongoing synthesizing process. But great synthesis comes only after we can truly transcend our own tradition and enter into other traditions. Using this as a criterion, I must say that Northrop's bold attempt to synthesize the East and the West is not a complete success, although I appreciate his pioneering work in the field of comparative philosophy. Northrop fails to identify important differences between Confucianism, Taoism, Buddhism, and Hinduism, and lumps all Oriental philosophies together. He also fails to make the important distinction between immediate apprehension of an undifferentiated space–time continuum and intuitive realization of the metaphysical principle. Northrop's synthesis of East and West appears dubious.[37]

(5) The need for a meeting of East and West is more urgent than ever before. Some Westerners realize the limitations of their culture and they are learning about the wisdom of the East. People who do not have peace of mind turn to Zen. People who are concerned with ecology are eager to learn about the Confucian organistic philosophy. In such an atmosphere it may be profitable to introduce some of the Chinese efforts to construct a synthesis of traditional insights and what has been learned from the West.

NOTES

1. In ancient times, there were the so-called Logicians, who were much like the Greek Sophists. But they were not sceptical philosophers in the proper sense, and they were never popular with Chinese people. See Wing-tsit Chan (Ed.), *A Source Book in Chinese Philosophy*, Princeton University Press, Princeton 1963, pp. 232–43. Wang Ch'ung (27–100?) in the Han dynasty was sceptical of many of the premises of his contemporaries. But he was a naturalist rather than a sceptic (ibid., pp. 292–304). When Buddhism first came to China, the Buddhist assertion that the world is fictitious did cause some disturbance in the intellectual world. But Buddhism is not scepticism. Moreover, the Chinese schools of Buddhism, such as T'ien-t'ai, Hua-yen, and Ch'an (Zen), have shifted to a more positive outlook on life and made important compromises with the Confucian tradition on the practice of Confucian moral principles. Even so, orthodox Confucian scholars still denounced the negative outlook of the Buddhist philosophy (ibid., pp. 396–449, 646–53).
2. Within the Confucian school the famous dispute on *ko-wu* between the school of Chu Hsi and the school of Wang Yang-ming may be interpreted as an epistemological dispute. But the emphasis was laid on the dispute between the different interpretations of the goal and the method of *The Great Learning* (ibid., pp. 84–94, 654–67).
3. This trend of thought urges people to renounce the traditional values and to place their hopes on a wholesale Westernization of China by way of adopting the Western values of democracy and science without reservation. Hu Shih, a disciple of John Dewey, was the leader of the famous cultural movement in 1919. Today, however, pragmatism is somewhat eclipsed by her remote cousin, logical empiricism. Ying Fu-shen, the leader of the young logical empiricist group, died of cancer recently. He was famous for his political dissension with the authorities.
4. Hsiung Shih-li was born in 1883. Both Wing-tsit Chan and O. Brière listed Hsiung as being born in 1885. See Chan, *Source Book*, p. 763; see also O. Brière, *Fifty Years of Chinese Philosophy 1898–1948*, trans. by Laurence G. Thompson, Frederick A. Praeger, New York 1965, p. 152. After the extensive correspondence I have had with Hsiung's disciples and friends in Hong Kong, it becomes clear that 1885 is an erroneous date. In his correspondence to me Professor Chan agrees that 1883 is a more acceptable date. In his early years Hsiung participated in revolution. Then he decided that revolution in ideas is even more important. He studied under Ou-yang Ching-wu at the Institute of Buddhism in Nanking. Soon he became dissatisfied and turned to Confucianism. He was a professor of philosophy at Peking University. After the Communist takeover, he stayed on the Chinese mainland. He died on 23 May 1968. Chan has included a chapter on Hsiung Shih-li in his *Source Book*; he also wrote a general introduction to Hsiung's thought in his *Religious Trends in Modern China*, Columbia University Press, New York 1953, pp. 33–34, 126–35. I have published an article, 'Hsiung Shih-li's Theory of Causation', in *Philosophy East and West*, Vol. XIX (October, 1969), pp. 399–407. It is reported that several dissertations on Hsiung Shih-li are in the process of preparation.

5. Mou Tsung-san (1909–) is now in his early sixties. He graduated from Peking University, and taught at various universities on the mainland before the Communist takeover and then in Taiwan. Now he is a senior lecturer and Chairman of the Department of Philosophy at New Asia College, The Chinese University in Hong Kong. Mou is virtually unknown in the West. Brière barely mentions his name in his *Fifty Years of Chinese Philosophy*. But most of Mou's important writings were published after the period Brière covered in his volume. He was one of the four professors who signed 'A Manifesto for a Re-appraisal of Sinology and Reconstruction of Chinese Culture', which is included as an appendix in Carsun Chang, *The Development of Neo-Confucian Thought*, 2 Vols., Bookman Associates, New York, 1957–1962, Vol. II, pp. 455–83. Recently I published a review of Mou Tsung-san's monumental work on Sung neo-Confucianism, *Hsin-t'i yü hsing-t'i* [*Mind and Human Nature*] in *Philosophy East and West*, Vol. XX (October, 1970), pp. 419–22. I believe this is the first time that Mou's epistemological thought has been introduced to a Western audience.
6. Hsiung Shih-li, *Hsin wei-shih lun* [*New Consciousness-Only Doctrine*], Commercial Press, Shanghai 1947, p. 2. This book has several versions. I am using the most popular one.
7. Ibid., p. 3. For the benefit of Western readers, I would like to suggest that the alienation of the senses from the original mind reminds one of the Hegelian dialectic, and that the construction of an external world through habit reminds one of Hume's philosophy.
8. Ibid., pp. 4–6.
9. Hsiung Shih-li, *Shih-li yü-yao* [*Important Sayings by Hsiung Shih-li*] (Reprinted by Kuang Wen, Taipei 1962, four volumes in one), Vol. II, p. 12.
10. Hsiung, *Hsin wei-shih lun*, p. 2.
11. Hsiung, *Shih-li yü-yao*, Vol. II, pp. 16–18.
12. Ibid., Vol. II, p. 16.
13. Ibid., Vol. II, pp. 18–19.
14. Ibid., Vol. II, p. 12.
15. Ibid., Vol. II, pp. 14–16.
16. The stanza was taken from a poem by a Sung poet, Hsin Ch'i-tsi. It is customary for Chinese philosophers to appeal to poems to illustrate the philosophical message revealed to them through theoretical reflection and moral practice.
17. Mou Tsung-san, *Jen-shih-hsin chih p'i-p'an* [*A Critique of the Cognitive Mind*], 2 Vols., The Union Press, Hong Kong 1956–1957.
18. Mou Tsung-san, *Hsin-t'i yü hsing-t'i* [*Mind and Human Nature*], 3 Vols., Cheng Chung, Taipei 1968–1969.
19. Mou, *Jen-shih-hsin chih p'i-p'an*, Vol. I, pp. 5–8.
20. Ibid., Vol. I, pp. 45–60.
21. Ibid., Vol. I, pp. 116–34.
22. Ibid., Vol. I, pp. 135–7.
23. Ibid., Vol. I, pp. 60–68.
24. Ibid., Vol. I, pp. 68–94, 166–83.
25. Ibid., Vol. I, pp. 128–33.
26. Ibid., Vol. I, p. 119.
27. Ibid., Vol. I, pp. 349–408, 435–78.
28. Ibid., Vol. II, pp. 228–45.

29. Ibid., Vol. II, pp. 251–7.
30. Ibid., Vol. II, pp. 257–91.
31. Ibid., Vol. II, pp. 292–334.
32. Mou, *Hsin-t'i yü hsing-t'i*, Vol. I, pp. 8–11, 115–90. For a penetrating understanding of the Confucian ways of thinking, all three volumes of *Hsin-t'i yü hsing-t'i* should be consulted. In the introductory part of the book, Mou contrasts the main types of Chinese ways of thinking with the main types of Western ways of thinking. Then he takes great pains to lay bare the structure of thought of prominent Sung neo-Confucian philosophers such as Chou Tun-i, Chang Tsai, the Ch'eng brothers, Hu Wu-feng, and Chu Hsi. I have introduced the general ideas of the book in the review article referred to in Note 5.
33. Mou, *Jen-shih-hsin chih p'i-p'an*, Vol. II, pp. 297–313.
34. Ibid., Vol. II, p. 313.
35. Hsiung Shih-li and Mou Tsung-san are probably the two most important contemporary neo-Confucian thinkers who have made significant contributions to the development of a neo-Confucian epistemology. There are other important contemporary neo-Confucian thinkers who have made significant contributions to a reconstruction of Confucian insights in the modern world. Within the limitations of space, however, I have discussed these two thinkers as being, in my view, more or less representative of the trend.
36. Joseph R. Levenson, *Confucian China and its Modern Fate*, University of California Press, Berkeley 1958.
37. F. S. C. Northrop, *The Meeting of East and West*, Macmillan Co., New York 1946.

ANTONIO S. CUA

III. *The concept of paradigmatic individuals in the ethics of Confucius*

This essay deals with one basic feature of Confucian ethics as an ethics of flexibility by way of examining Confucius's concept of paradigmatic individuals (*chün-tzu*). Part I attempts a critical reconstruction and assessment of this concept. Part II takes up a feature of the account of *chün-tzu* in terms of the problem of rules and exceptions. It is suggested that the problem is best dealt with by making a distinction between normal and exigent moral situations — a distinction that appears to be implicit in the Confucian doctrine of *ching-ch'üan*. Viewed in this light, the flexible character of Confucian ethics can be seen to have an important bearing on a problem in moral philosophy.

The ethics of Confucius contained in the *Analects*, a major authoritative source of Chinese moral education, does not present a systematic scheme for conduct. There is a lack of an explicit and coherent ordering of moral ideas. This unsystematic character in part reflects its concern with and emphasis on the concrete and the particular.[1] In this respect the ethics of Confucius is an ethics of flexibility that attempts to mould and adapt to the changing scenes of human life. In the words of a recent historian, 'the chief strength of Confucianism is its flexibility, a remarkable quality that enables it to resist all pressures and to face all adversities'.[2] This quality of Confucian ethics, I believe, is best understood in terms of Confucius's notion of *chün-tzu* as a notion of a superior man who functions as a paradigmatic standard for practical morality.[3] My aim in this essay is to inquire into the plausibility and significance of this notion as an underlying theme of Confucian ethics.[4]

I

Although Confucius believed that only a *sage* (*shêng jên*), divinely inspired and intuitively wise, can envision and establish a harmonious social order, the ideal of sagehood was not regarded by him as practically attainable by ordinary moral agents. He once remarked that he could not ever hope to meet a sage (*shêng jên*), but only a *chün-tzu* (VII,25).[5] The ideal of sagehood, in his mind, functions more like a supreme but *abstract* ideal of a perfect moral personality, as a standard of inspiration rather than as a standard of aspiration.[6] Thus he more often discoursed on the conduct and quality of *chün-tzu* than on the nature of sagehood. In general, the notion of *chün-tzu* is a notion of a man of moral excellence, of a paradigmatic individual who sets the tone and quality of the life of ordinary moral agents. A *chün-tzu* is a man who embodies *jên* (human-heartedness) and *li* (propriety). As a guiding paradigmatic individual, every man can strive to be him rather than *Siao-jên* (inferior man). There are of course degrees of personal achievement depending on the situation, character, ability, and opportunity of moral agents. The translation of '*chün-tzu*' as 'superior man' forcefully brings out the *chün-tzu*'s superiority of moral character and aptitude.[7] The translation of '*chün-tzu*' as 'true gentleman' focuses on *chün-tzu*'s relation with the cultural setting of his actions, his ability to satisfy, so to speak, the stylistic requirements of a form of life.[8] A *chün-tzu*, in this sense, is an embodiment of a 'cultural life style'.

The varying remarks on *chün-tzu* in the *Analects* may be regarded as setting forth the different requirements or qualities for a life of moral excellence. A *chün-tzu* is, first of all, a man of moral virtues pervaded by an affectionate concern for *jên* or humanity.[9] He is a man of propriety (*li*) and righteousness (*i*); of catholicity and neutrality in whom words and deeds are in harmony. The discussion that follows relates to these prominent features of the concept of *chün-tzu*.

(i) *A man of moral virtues* (*jên*)

There are remarks of Confucius that portray *chün-tzu* as a man who possesses various virtues pervaded by the ideal of *jên* (human-heartedness). Confucius said, 'If a superior man abandon virtue (*jên*), how can he fulfil the requirements of that name? The superior man does not even for the space of a single meal act contrary to virtue (*jên*). In moments of haste, he cleaves to it. In seasons of danger, he cleaves to it' (IV,5).[10] *Jên* is Confucius's ideal of an inclusive end that embraces the realizations of particular moral dispositions or virtues. Confucius, on one occasion responding to an inquiry about *jên*, said that a man of *jên* practices five things: 'gravity, generosity of *soul*, sincerity, liberality, and kindness.' His reasoning consists in a series of hypothetical propositions: 'If you are grave, you will not be treated with disrespect. If you are generous, you will win them all. If you are sincere, people will repose trust in you. If you are earnest, you will accomplish much. If you are kind, this will enable you to employ the services of others' (XVII, 6). The consequents in these hypothetical propositions appear to be rooted in the notion of avoidance of undesirable states of affairs. If this interpretation is correct, particular moral virtues cited, with others such as knowledge and courage (XV, 17) are recognized as having moral values insofar as they promote the realization of a life of *jên*. They are virtues in the sense that the absence of them would lead to undesirable consequences which hamper the realization of *jên*-morality. The reasonableness of accepting the form and content of this argument thus rests on an appeal to reflective desirability.[11] This teleological structure has been recognized. In examining the use of hypothetical sorites in Confucian classics, Mason-Oursel points out that the relationship between means and ends is not founded on identity, but on something like 'a stream of action' that extends over heterogeneous terms. 'Their order cannot be altered without rendering the reasoning impossible.'[12] In the words of *The Great Learning*, 'Things have their root and their branches. Affairs have their end and their beginning. To know what is first and what is last will lead near to what is taught in *The Great Learning* (i.e. a life of illustrious virtue).' It is sufficient to note for our present purpose that a *chün-tzu* cultivates the particular virtues for the purpose of attaining to a life of *jên*. This purpose requires knowledge of reflective desirability of actions and human affairs.

(ii) *A man of propriety (li) and righteousness (i)*

Although *li* (propriety) and *i* (righteousness) are traditionally regarded as moral virtues, they received special attention in Confucian ethics. Our discussion in the preceding section on *jên* and particular moral virtues may be regarded as dealing with the internal aspect of *jên*-morality. The accent here is on self-cultivation rather than the outward form of conduct. As Confucius remarked, 'What the superior man seeks, is in himself. What the mean man seeks, is in others' (XV,20). *Li* and *i* relate more to the *style* and manner of moral performance. They are characteristics, so to speak, of the correctness of performance as governed by the social matrix and the appropriateness of these to concrete situations.

Confucius said, 'The superior man, extensively studying all learning, and keeping himself under the restraint of the rules of propriety (*li*), may thus likewise not overstep [the boundary] of what is right' (VI,25). This passage and many others suggest that *li*, as a body of ritual rules, functions as a restraining orbit of moral actions. *Li* appears to be the *convention* that defines the form and possibility of moral actions. In this sense, *li* defines the conventionally accepted *style* of actions, i.e. the form and possibility of moral achievement within the cultural setting, or what may be termed 'cultural lifestyle'. *Li*, unlike *jên*, does not define the nature of morality, but only the limiting form of execution of moral performance. In a more contemporary idiom, we may express this idea in terms of the *tie* or *contact* of an individual agent's actions with the cultural form of life which gives them the locus of identification and the possibility of moral achievement. An appropriate action, as conforming to the ritual requirements of *li*, may be identified as a moral action insofar as it is pervaded by a concern for *jên*. If one wants to lay more stress on the importance of *li*, then one may say that particular moral actions are partial exemplifications of a cultural lifestyle. However, without a persistent regard for *jên*, ritual observances would amount to mere formal gestures vacuous of moral essence. The *chün-tzu*'s respect for *li* or cultural lifestyle is at the same time a respect for the reality of the situation, the background and possibility that furnish the contexts for successful moral performance. This emphasis on *li* is one possible justification for the Confucian homage to the concrete. Every action, on this view, has a *conventional* aspect for understanding its normative meaning and import. Whether or not we accept this stress on *li*, some sort of convention for identifying the normative import of action must be an essential element in any moral theory that aims at an assessment of actions in terms of right and wrong.

The other aspect of action relates to the importance Confucius assigned to the role of the concept *i* or righteousness. 'The superior man holds righteousness (*i*) to be of highest importance' (XVIII,23).[13] *I* is contrasted with profit (IV,16). This contrast brings out the Confucian distinction between morality and egoism. The notion of *i*, not elucidated in the *Analects*, is a difficult notion. It may be variously rendered as 'righteousness', 'right conduct', 'moral principle or standard', or 'the doing of what is right'. All these renderings perhaps suggest different aspects of *i*. Insofar as *i* is opposed to profit, *i* may be taken as characterizing the Confucian Moral Point of View. *I*, like courage, knowledge, and others previously mentioned, would also seem to be a particular virtue (i.e. righteousness) that results from the correctness of moral performance. If *li* defines an aspect of right act in *jên*-morality, it is an emphasis on the *tie* between actions and the cultural lifestyle. *I*, on the other hand, gives us a sense of rightness as relating to the concrete problematic situation that calls for moral action inspired by *jên*. In the language of Professor Fung, 'righteousness (*i*) means the "oughtness" of a situation. It is a categorical imperative. Everyone in society has certain things which he ought to do, and which must be done for their sake, because they are the morally right thing to do'.[14] However, the 'oughtness' of the situation, though a characteristic of obligatory actions, has its central focus on the right act as appropriate to the particular situation confronting a moral agent. Doing what is right in a situation is not just a mere matter of conformity with moral and ritual rules, but also conformity to a *judgment* of the relevance and vindication of these in actual situations. *I* is another focus on an aspect of the concrete. If *li* is the emphasis on the contact between *jên*-morality and the cultural lifestyle, *i* is that on the contact between *jên*-morality and actual situations. Thus, the judgment of what is to be done is reserved to the moral agent. Confucius remarked, 'The superior man *in everything* considers righteousness (*i*) to be essential. He performs it according to the rules of propriety (*li*). He brings it forth in humility. He completes it with sincerity. This is indeed a superior man' (XV,17). This passage brings out the relationship of *li* and *i*. Our exposition of *i*, if it is correct, focuses on a view of the nature of moral action as an action in accordance with a judgment of the relevance of moral rules to concrete situations that occur within the setting of a cultural lifestyle.

We may sum up the significance of the preceding requirements for *chün-tzu*. A *chün-tzu* is a man of *jên*, *li*, and *i*. The concept of *jên* is the concept of an ideal of moral excellence. It is the *jên*-quality that pervades the life of a *chün-tzu*. This is the focal point of his paradigmatic function as a standard of aspiration for ordinary moral agents. *Jên* and other particular virtues portray the inner aspect of Confucian ethics. This focus gives us a pervasive and underlying feature of Confucian morality. The focus is on man himself and what he can morally accomplish in relation to others. This latter emphasis deals with the social and cultural setting of moral performance — the ritual context (*li*) in which human transactions occur with varying import of interests and motives. *Li* gives the moral action a locale of normative identification and an orbit of restraining conditions for the proper achievement of the moral ideal. Actions that conform to *li* requirements may be said to be in contact with the cultural lifestyle — the Confucian form of life. If *li* focuses on the *tie* of individual actions to culture, the freedom of a moral agent is radically limited in what he *can* do and accomplish. However, the restraining function of *li* defines only the *form*, not the *content*, of this freedom. The emphasis on *i* as a requirement of being a *chün-tzu* preserves a great deal of latitude in action. Just as *jên* cannot be practiced without *li*, the cultural setting, so *jên* cannot be realized without *i* or judgment of the relevance of *jên* and *li* to concrete situations of moral performance. It is *i* that establishes the contact between actions and the actual situations that confront the moral agent. Our next two sets of descriptions of *chün-tzu*, together with the present account, explain in large part this flexible and adaptable feature of Confucian ethics.

(iii) *A man of catholicity and neutrality*

'The superior man is broadminded and not partisan; the inferior man is partisan but not broadminded' (II,14; also VII,30). The superior man is not like an implement (II,12), 'which is intended only for a narrow and specific purpose'. Instead, 'he should have broad vision, wide interests, and sufficient ability to do many things'.[15] He is a man of moral integrity that exemplifies itself even in the face of great emergency (VIII,8). He aims at 'the higher things or principles' (XIV,24) and is 'dignified without being proud' (XIII,26).

The above remarks on the aptitude and broadmindedness of *chün-tzu* are quite naturally expected in view of Confucius's emphasis on *jên*, *li*, and *i*. If *jên* consists in the affectionate concern, in varying degrees, for humanity, it requires from the moral agent the ability to 'know men' and sympathize with the being and predicaments of other moral agents. However, the ability to execute one's moral intentions within ritual contexts is also important. If *i* is required to give an actuating import to *jên* and *li*, then *chün-tzu* must exercise that 'secret art' that gives practical effect to his moral nature as an exemplary guide to the conduct of other agents. This theme of the contagion of the *chün-tzu*'s conduct in Confucius's thinking is perhaps best expressed in the *Chung Yung*: 'The way which the superior man pursues, reaches wide and far, and yet is secret. . . . The way of the superior man may be found, in its simple elements, in the intercourse of common men and women; but in its utmost reaches, it shines brightly through heaven and earth. . . . The superior man can find himself in no situation in which he is not himself.'[16] Although the *chün-tzu*'s way is secret and capable of effusive influence in the lives of ordinary moral agents, he does not remain a mere spectator of human behavior, for he '*seeks to* perfect the admirable qualities of men, and does not *seek to* perfect their bad qualities' (XII,16). Being a man of *jên*, he wishes to establish his own character and also the character of others. Confucius said, 'to be able to judge *of others* by what is nigh *in ourselves*; — this may be called the art of virtue (*jên*)' (VI,28).

This 'secret way' or art of *chün-tzu* is not a mere matter of actions as intellectually determined by moral and ritual rules. If a *chün-tzu* has a natural preference for *jên*-morality, this preference does not commit him to specific courses of actions prior to a confrontation with an actual moral situation. Thus Confucius said of himself, 'I have no course for which I am predetermined, and no course against which I am predetermined' (XVIII,8).[17] Moral actions, in concrete contexts, are not a straightforward deduction from given moral rules. The mere intellectual determination of the morality of action does not suffice in the assessment of moral performance. For the relevance of moral and ritual rules has to be assessed in concrete situations. This flexible and varying function of *i* accounts for the *neutrality* of *chün-tzu*'s attitude, or lack of commitment to specific courses of action. The actual assessment of moral and ritual rules is at the same time a way of vindicating their actual importance in human life. This act of assessment requires the neutral attitude. It is also this neutral attitude of *chün-tzu* that gives scope to the exercise of *i* in novel and abnormal situations. Thus a *chün-tzu* 'in the world, does not set his mind either for anything, or against anything: what is right (*i*) he will follow' (IV,10). He is said to be 'satisfied and composed' (VII,36) and free from anxiety, fear, and perplexities (XIV,30; XII,6). Being a man of *jên*, he is free from anxiety about acting contrary to morality; being a man of courage, he is free from fear; being a man with knowledge of human affairs, he is free from perplexities (XIV,30). His *easeful* life is more a matter of attitude and confidence in his ability to deal with difficult and varying situations, rather than an exemplification of his infallible judgment and authority. This aspect of the notion of *chün-tzu* poses a problem in Confucian ethics. How can a man of virtue (*jên*) and moral integrity be indifferent to specific courses of action that follow from his espoused set of moral principles and rules? If a moral agent is to serve as a paradigmatic guide for actual conduct, it seems reasonable and proper to expect from him specific commitments to what he will do in accordance with moral rules. In Confucian ethics, moral rules and expected types of obligatory actions are by and large a matter of social roles within the cultural lifestyle (*li*). If *chün-tzu* is a man of *li*, it seems reasonable to expect from him at least a commitment to the application of these moral rules in concrete situations. I shall reserve the exploration of this problem for Part II of this essay.

(iv) *A man of his words and deeds* (*yen*)

The neutral attitude of *chün-tzu* is related to Confucius's special emphasis on the harmony of words and deeds. If morality deals with the relations between men, as the character '*jên*' suggests, living in accordance with *jên*-morality requires the knowledge of men. And 'without knowing the *force* of words, it is impossible to know men' (XX,3). Thus the harmony of words and deeds is a frequent theme of Confucian ethics. A *chün-tzu* must act in accordance with what he professes (VIII,32). Even Confucius himself disclaimed being a *chün-tzu* in this sense. He said, 'In letters I am perhaps equal to other men, but *the character of* the superior man, carrying out in his conduct what he professes, is what I have not yet attained to' (VII,32). This doctrine of words and deeds, to borrow a phrase from Austin, may be said to be a case of 'suiting the action to the word'.[18] This sort of action, in real life, is difficult to accomplish, not only because of the formidable strength of character required, but also because of the dynamic diversity of human situations that vary a great deal in their normative import. To preserve *chün-tzu*'s freedom to adapt to changing and varying circumstances, Confucius laid more stress on the importance of *suiting one's words to the action*. Thus Confucius remarked that a *chün-tzu* 'acts before he speaks, and afterwards speaks according to his actions' (II,12; also IV,22 and XIV,21). 'He is modest in his speech but exceeds in his actions' (XIV,29). Ideally a morally correct speech corresponds to a morally correct performance. A *chün-tzu*, therefore, does not engage in moral discourse for its own sake. He attempts to *suit* his words to actions performed. Conversely, his actions must, in other cases, conform to his words. This is particularly true of evaluative labels with which others endow him. He must live up to his title of being a *chün-tzu* (IV,5). Our present discussion is intimately related to the famous Confucian doctrine of rectification of *names* (*ching ming*), for words of honor and morality have their normative import. The names or titles of persons and their roles in society pragmatically imply certain obligatory types of actions as befitting these names. To rectify names (*ming*), or moral words, is to conform in action to the normative implications of these names.[19]

The notion of correct speech and action is important in Confucian ethics, not only for conduct in accordance with *jên*-morality, but also for the successful execution of moral intentions within the form of a cultural lifestyle (*li*). Moral words and actions are embedded in ritual contexts. The significance of this *performative* aspect of *li* has been emphasized by Professor Fingarette. In stressing this aspect of *li*, he brings the Confucian view closer to the Austinian insight on the significance of the forces of speech-acts.[20] It is a *chün-tzu*, as we have previously mentioned, who is aware of the *forces of speech*. And from the standpoint of Confucian morality, a *chün-tzu* provides a moral exemplar in both his words and deeds. Suiting one's words to one's actions, of course, presupposes the satisfaction of the requirements of *jên*-morality.

In sum, the notion of *chün-tzu* is Confucius's ideal of a paradigmatic individual who functions as a guiding standard for practical conduct. In Confucius's view ordinary moral agents may not attain to sagehood (*sheng-jên*). However, they can look to a *chün-tzu* for guidance and may become a *chün-tzu* themselves. The notion of *chün-tzu*, though an exemplary model for practical conduct, is not an ideal of a perfect man, but an ideal of a *superior man* who embodies the various qualities we have discussed.

II

One problematic feature in the preceding account relates to *chün-tzu*'s neutrality, or absence of commitment to specific courses of action. I have suggested that this neutral attitude is essential to one aspect of *i* (righteousness), i.e. to the exercise of judgment on the relevance of moral and ritual rules to concrete situations. However, *i* has also the plausible meaning of being a standard of righteousness. Confucius's remark on the neutrality of *chün-tzu* in relation to *i* can thus be plausibly rendered in two different ways. In Legge's translation, quoted previously, the text runs: 'The superior man (*chün-tzu*), in the world, does not set his mind either for anything or against anything; what is right (*i*) he will follow' (IV,10). The same text has been rendered by Professor Chan as: 'A superior man (*Chün-tzu*) in dealing with the world is not for or against anything. He follows righteousness as a standard (*i*).'[21] Legge's translation suggests the view that a *chün-tzu* acts according to what he *thinks* is right in any circumstance in which he finds himself. His neutrality is, in this respect, a necessary prerequisite to his flexibility and adaptability to varying situations. In Professor Chan's translation, the passage suggests the view that a *chün-tzu* does follow a moral standard, but he does not hold to any specific course of action prior to a judgment on the relevance of the moral standard. To hold righteousness as a standard is to hold fast to the Confucian moral point of view, for *i*, as we have seen, is contrasted with profit — a contrast that I regard as a contrast between morality and egoism. The two interpretations jointly are consistent with what I believe to be the plausible feature of Confucian ethics.[22] A *chün-tzu* does what is right from the moral point of view in the sense of acting independently of personal interest or profit. However, adopting the Confucian point of view does not by itself dictate specific courses of action prior to an encounter with actual situations. The *chün-tzu's* neutrality is his freedom of action, although this freedom is radically limited by the restraining orbit of his cultural lifestyle (*li*). In other words, a *chün-tzu* remains free within the ritual scheme of conduct. He can succeed or fail to realize *jên*-morality within this ritual universe.

However, there is also a sense of *chün-tzu's* freedom in the judgment and interpretations of moral rules. In this regard, the *open-texture* of moral rules is recognized in Confucian ethics. Moral and ritual rules retain their normative force in *normal* cases. But exigent circumstances may arise that alter their force or appropriateness. In commenting on Confucius's remark (IV,10), Professor Chan instructively reminds us that

> This is a clear expression of both the flexibility and rigidity of Confucian ethics — flexibility in application but rigidity in standard. Here lies the basic idea of the Confucian doctrine of *ching-ch'üan*, or the standard and the exceptional, the absolute and the relative, or the permanent and the temporary. This explains why Confucius was not obstinate, had no predetermined course of action, was ready to serve or to withdraw whenever it was proper to do so, and according to Mencius, was a sage who acted according to the circumstance of the time.[23]

However, the doctrine of *ching-ch'üan* rendered as the doctrine of 'the standard and the exceptional' may be quite misleading. The relevant meaning of '*ching*', for our present purpose, is 'an invariable rule, a standard of conduct; constant, recurring'; that for '*ch'üan*', 'exigency, circumstances; that which is irregular, and opposed to *ching*, that which is constant or normal — from this comes, therefore, the idea of temporary, etc.'[24] The doctrine of *ching-ch'üan* can also be interpreted, more plausibly and significantly for moral philosophy, as a doctrine of the *normal* and the *exigent*, or the normal and the exceptional. We may speak of 'the normal', from the moral point of view, as an invariable rule in the sense of a rule regularly and invariably applied to situations or actions that fall within the scope of its application. From this point of view, moral rules are regularly observed if they are to have the force of normative rules. This regularity is tied to their application to normal and clear-cut cases. The notion of *ching*, in effect, points to an aspect of our moral experience — the aspect of stability. Moreover, in real life one may confront situations that appear to fall outside the scope of the application of rules. These situations may be termed 'abnormal' or 'exigent' situations. '*Ch'üan*' focuses on this sort of case.

I should like now to apply the above version of the doctrine of *ching-ch'üan* to two perplexing passages in the works of Mencius.[25] The King Hsuan of Chi asked Mencius, 'May a minister put his sovereign to death?' Mencius replied:

> He who outrages the benevolence (*jên*) *proper to his nature*, is called a robber; he who outrages righteousness (*i*) is called a ruffian. The robber and ruffian we call a mere fellow. I have heard of the cutting off of the fellow Chau, but I have not heard of the putting a sovereign to death, *in his case*.

Legge comments on this passage that 'Killing a sovereign is not necessarily rebellion nor murder'.[26] This is, no doubt, Mencius's point. But this sounds like double-talk, unless we understand the force of the implicit rule 'Do not kill a sovereign'. I believe that Mencius's point is that this rule does not apply to a case of this sort. The rule is judged to be irrelevant. When a person with the name (*ming*) or title of 'sovereign' outrages *jên* and *i*, he is no longer deserving of that title. Here 'sovereign' is an evaluative term. In the discourse, the sovereign is stripped of his *name*. To be a sovereign is to live up to what the *name* implies, to the requirements of *jên* and *i*. In this discourse of Mencius we do not have a case of an exception to a rule, but rather a judgment, or better, a *ruling* that the implicit rule does not apply to this sort of case. This ruling may function as a rule in future cases of the same sort as Mencius seems to suggest in his view on the justification of revolution.

Reflections on another passage in Mencius, quite disturbing to logically minded readers, will perhaps bring out the doctrine more clearly. The discourse runs as follows: Shun-yu Kwan said,

> 'Is it the rule that male and female shall not allow their hands to touch in giving or receiving anything?' Mencius replied, 'It is the rule'. Kwan asked, 'If a man's sister-in-law be drowning shall he rescue her with his hands?' Mencius said, 'He who would not so rescue a drowning woman is a wolf. For males and females not to allow their hands to touch in giving or receiving is the *general rule(li)*; when a sister-in-law is drowning, to rescue her with the hand is a *peculiar exigency (ch'üan)*.[27]

What Legge translates as 'general rule' is actually the word '*li*'. It would be better rendered in this discourse as 'a ritual rule'. Note that in this discourse a ritual rule is explicitly stated. The sort of situation is also described quite clearly. Mencius did not recommend in the present case that we break the rule, but rather that we act according to *ch'üan*, or the *exigency* of the situation. An exigent situation is a situation that demands urgent and swift attention. It is a pressing situation that calls for behavior appropriate to the circumstance. To regard a situation as exigent does not necessarily imply that we are called upon to revise our rules by making an exception to it. Rather, we are to attend to what the situation demands. The situation may be said to be *exceptional* in the sense that it does not appear to be covered by our normal application of the rule. It is an exception to the rule only in the sense that the rule, deemed apparently relevant, does not apply to the situation of this sort. We are in effect making a *ruling*, a judgment that the apparently relevant rule does not apply to the present case. Mencius could have said, analogously to the first discourse examined, that we do not call that situation of saving a drowning woman 'touching hands' at all. The rule forbidding males and females from touching hands applies to the relations among men and women in normal social intercourse, but does not extend to the situation in question. A ruling of this sort may be a guiding paradigm for future situations. In a non-Confucian legal-like morality, the ruling is bound to be regarded as a 'built-in' exception to the rule.

This emphasis on the significance of ruling is, I think, one major contribution of Confucian ethics. In Confucian ethics, there is no straightforward application of moral and ritual rules. There are neither 'rules of relevance' nor 'rules of inference' for concrete moral performance.[28] For pedagogical purposes we teach a body of rules, but in the dynamic situations of human life we need to make rulings even in the absence of given rules. This is the logic of *chün-tzu*. A *chün-tzu* is an exemplary moral agent who embodies *jên* and *li*. He is a paradigmatic guide for ordinary moral agents by virtue of his ability to cope with the changing circumstance within the Confucian moral point of view. By his neutrality of attitude toward specific courses of action, he preserves his freedom of action. The significance of the Confucian notion of *chün-tzu* thus lies in its suggestion of a conception of a reasonable moral agent who lives within a common form of life. Confucian ethics is, in this sense, an ethics of flexibility. I hope that the present essay succeeds in conveying this important feature.[29]

NOTES

1. For a recent study of this conceptual feature in the *Analects*, see my 'Logic of Confucian Dialogues' in J. K. Ryan (Ed.), *Studies in Philosophy and the History of Philosophy*, Vol. 4, The Catholic University of America Press, Washington, D. C. 1969, pp. 15–31.

2. Wu-chi Liu, *A Short History of Confucian Philosophy*, Dell Publishing Co., New York 1964, p. 11. See also James R. Ware's Introduction to his translation, *Analects, The Sayings of Confucius*, New American Library, New York 1955, p. 7; H. E. Creel, *Confucius and the Chinese Way*, Harper & Row, New York and Evanston 1960, p. 137; Arthur Hummel, 'Some Basic Moral Principles in Chinese Culture' in R. N. Ashen (Ed.), *Moral Principles of Action*, Harper & Brothers, New York and London 1952, p. 601; Yu-tang Lin, *The Pleasures of a Non-Conformist*, William Heinemann Ltd., London, etc., p. 109; and Yu-lan Fung, *A History of Chinese Philosophy*, Princeton University Press, Princeton 1952, Vol. I, p. 74.

3. For an exposition of this notion and its importance for moral philosophy see my 'Morality and the Paradigmatic Individuals', *American Philosophical Quarterly*, Vol. 6 (1969), No 4. In 'Reflections on the Structure of Confucian Ethics', *Philosophy East and West,* Vol. 21 (1971), No. 2, I have attempted to exhibit the role and function of *chün-tzu* as a paradigmatic individual in Confucian ethics.

4. Hereafter, I shall use the term 'Confucian ethics' and the 'ethics of Confucius' interchangeably. The present study restricts its account to the *Analects*, but with a little modification, I hope, my essential points apply also to other Confucian thinkers, particularly Mencius and Hsün-tzu. For a justification of this methodological approach, see my 'Some Reflections on Methodology in Chinese Philosophy', *International Philosophical Quarterly*, Vol. 11 (1971), No. 2.

5. Unless otherwise indicated all references in the text of this essay are taken from the *Analects* translated by James Legge, *The Chinese Classics*, Vol. I, Clarendon Press, Oxford 1893.

6. For this distinction, see H. J. N. Horsburgh, 'The Plurality of Moral Standards', *Philosophy*, Vol. XXIX (1954), No. 111.

7. This is Legge's translation. See also W. T. Chan (Ed.), *A Source Book in Chinese Philosophy*, Princeton University Press, Princeton 1963. I have adopted this rendering of '*chün-tzu*' as 'superior man'.

8. See Arthur Waley, *The Analects of Confucius*, Random House, New York 1938.
9. I have used 'humanity' and 'human-heartedness' as translations for the concept of *jên*. A detailed study of the functions and relations of the concepts of *jên*, *li*, and *chün-tzu* may be found in the second essay cited in Note 3 above. On the whole I much prefer to leave these concepts untranslated. English equivalents given are intended only as focal points of reference. For a justification of this methodological approach, see my 'Some Reflections on Methodology in Chinese Philosophy', forthcoming in *International Philosophical Quarterly* (March, 1971).
10. See also *Analects*, XVIII, 16; I, 14; V, 15; VI, 28; XV, 17; and XVII, 16.
11. I have attempted to sketch the relationship between these Confucian notions of reasonableness and reflective desirability in 'Ethics and the Use of Dialogues', forthcoming in *International Logic Review*.
12. P. Mason-Oursel, 'La Demonstration Confucéene: — Note sur la Logique Chinoise Prébouddhique', *Revue de l'Histoire des Religions*, Vol. 67 (1913), pp. 52–53. See also, M. D. Resnik, 'Logic and Methodology in the Writings of Mencius', *International Philosophical Quarterly*, Vol. VIII (1968), No. 2.
13. For other remarks on *i* or righteousness, see *Analects*, I, 13; VII, 3; XII, 20; XIII, 4; XV, 16; XVI, 10 and 11.
14. Yu-lan Fung, *A Short History of Chinese Philosophy*, Macmillan Co., New York 1950, p. 42.
15. I here follow Professor Chan's translations and commentary. See Chan, p. 24. Also, IX, 6.
16. *Chung Yung*, Chs. 12 and 14. See Legge's *Chinese Classics*, Vol. I.
17. The complete passage runs as follows: 'The men who have retired to privacy from the world have been Po-î, Shû-chî, Yü-chung, Î-yî, Chû-chang, Hûi of Liû-hsiâ, and Shâo-lien. The Master said, "Refusing to surrender their wills, or to submit to any taint in their person; — such, I think, were Po-î, and Shû-chî. It may be said of Hûi, of Liû-hisâ and of Shâo-lien, that they surrendered their wills, and submitted to taint in their persons, but their words corresponded with reason, and their actions were such as men are anxious to see. This is all that is to be remarked in them. It may be said of Yü-chang and Î-yî, that, while they hid themselves in their seclusion, they gave a license to their words; but in their persons, they succeeded in preserving their purity, and, in their retirement, they acted according to the exigency of the times. I am different from all these. I have no course for which I am predetermined, and no course against which I am predetermined"' (*Analects*, XVIII, 8).
18. J. L. Austin, *How to do things with Words*, Clarendon Press, Oxford, and Harvard University Press, Cambridge, Mass. 1962, pp. 81–82.
19. See *Analects*, XIII, 3 and *Hsün-Tzu: Basic Writings*, trans. by Burton Watson, Columbia University Press, New York and London 1963, pp. 139–56.
20. Herbert Fingarette, 'Human Community as Holy Rite: An Interpretation of Confucius' *Analects*', *Harvard Theological Review*, Vol. LIX (1966), No. 1. Reprinted in *On Responsibility*, Basic Books, New York and London 1967.
21. Chan, p. 26.
22. If my present reconstructed account is correct, the Confucian moral point of view may be formally characterized as a morality of righteousness (the basic meaning of *i*) as contrasted with egoism, but substantively defined in terms of the ideal of *jên*.

23. Chan, p. 26; cf. Fung, Vol. I, p. 74.
24. These renderings for '*ching*' and '*ch'üan*' are taken from *A New Complete Chinese–English Dictionary*, Chung Chien Co., Hong Kong n.d.
25. I have taken some liberty in presenting this doctrine of *ching-ch'üan* with a view to making this doctrine more plausible and interesting for moral philosophy. I hope that reflective Confucian moral agents who, like myself, were reared in the tradition that places its major emphasis on the *Analects*, will agree with this manner of presenting what I regard as one major insight of Confucius into the nature of moral experience.
26. *Mencius*, Bk. I, Pt. II, Ch. 8. See Legge's *The Chinese Classics*, Vol. I, p. 167.
27. *Mencius*, Bk. IV, Pt. I, Ch. XVII.
28. For this distinction, see Paul Taylor, *Normative Discourse*, Prentice-Hall, Englewood Cliffs 1961.
29. I am indebted to Dr. Alastair Hannay for both critical and editorial assistance in preparing this essay for publication.

TANG CHUN-I

IV. *The spirit and development of neo-Confucianism*

The ideal of human life as a life of sagehood is the core of Confucian thought. In neo-Confucianism the stress is on the self-perfectibility of man, and the central concern of neo-Confucianist thinkers has accordingly been with the question of how man can cultivate his own potentiality to be a sage. The different answers they give are in the form of teachings about the 'way', these teachings incorporating different philosophical views of mind, human nature, and the universe. The author outlines the views of successive neo-Confucianists and their versions of the 'way', seeing their teachings as developments towards the doctrine presented by Wang Yang-ming (b. 1472), whose thought can be seen in particular as a synthesis of the views of Chu Tzu and Lu Shiang-shan.

I. INTRODUCTION

The year 1972 is the five-hundredth anniversary of the birth of Wang Yang-ming. Wang's teaching is generally considered to belong to the school of Lu Shiang-shan and to be opposed to that of Chu Tzu. This view is less than adequate. In two recent articles[1] I have traced the origins of Chu Tzu's and Lu Shiang-shan's thought to their different answers to the common problem of how to acquire sagehood, answers which incorporate different concepts of the human mind and of human nature. There I insisted that Wang's thought actually developed from the teaching of Chu Tzu, but that it ended in certain agreements with that of Lu. In the present article I shall take the self-cultivation of sagehood to be the central spirit of neo-Confucianism as contrasted with preceding Confucianism. I shall take the problems of this self-cultivation as a continuous thread in order to point out the development of neo-Confucianism through the key ideas in its exponents' thoughts about the problems. And I shall end with a brief summary of my former two articles.

II. The Creative Ideas of Ancient Confucianism,
the Idea of the Sage in Han-Confucianism,
and its Transition to Neo-Confucianism

All the main Confucian ideals of life and culture and the central Confucian view of the universe were originally propounded by Confucius, Mencius, and Hsün Tzu, or occur in the commentaries on the *Book of Changes* and in chapters in the *Book of Rites*. Thus, Confucius himself taught the idea of *jên*, or humanity, and other virtues, and man's duty to revere the decree of Heaven; the ideas of man's difference from the animal, of human nature as essentially good, of the spiritual stages towards sagehood, of man as *tien-ming*, or cosmic citizen, and of the life of the sage as also a holy life and confluent with the life of universe, were all taught by Mencius; the ideal of a cultural society or kingdom, the social-cultural-political responsibilities of different classes of men, and the ways for transforming man's evil nature to fit the needs of society and to be worthy, or a sage, were propounded by Hsün Tzu; the metaphysical ideas of the cosmos as the expression of eternal *tao* in creative change and as permeated with cosmic spirituality, are explained in the commentaries on the *Book of Changes*; the spirit of rites, music, and other human cultures, as identical with the spirit of Heaven and Earth, is explicated in chapters of the *Book of Rites*; and finally the identity of Heaven's decree and human nature, the realization of them in the authentic or real manner of human life, and the adoration of the sagehood of Confucius as conforming to the creativity of Heaven, were systematically expounded in the *Chung Yung*, one chapter of the *Book of Rites*. Thus practically the whole of the central core of Confucianism was laid down by the Confucianists two thousand years ago. There is no question that these ancient Confucianists were the most original and creative contributors to the tradition.

The ancient Confucianists were idealistic philosophers in Plato's sense. They aspired to be sages themselves, admired the sage-kings of the past, and wished to teach the princes to be sage-kings. Very lofty ideals certainly, indeed so much so as to appear unattainable in practice. Confucian scholars of the later Han dynasties were accordingly more realistic in their political and ethical thinking. They did not deny the existence of the ancient sages, but were content to revere and worship them in a religious spirit. The people of the Han dynasties had faith in God or gods. In the apocryphal classics, forgeries by

Han's scholars, Confucius as a sage is sometimes worshipped as an incarnation of a god descended from Heaven. This thought was rejected by rationalistic Confucian scholars and Confucius did not emerge as an incarnation of God, like Jesus Christ. Nevertheless Confucius, as a sage, and all the sages of the past were still generally considered to have been born in Heaven and to have descended from above, because no ordinary men could compete with their supreme virtues and talents.

The religious ideas of 'heaven' and 'the sage' held by Confucian scholars in the Han dynasties had very important practical significances in Chinese history. The idea of Heaven as identified with one God, the great-grandfather of all men, as in Tung Chung-shu's thought, greatly helped to establish the sense of the unity of Heaven as a model of the unity of the imperial kingdom on earth, as also the sense of God's way of sovereignty in Heaven as something to be followed by the imperial emperor. The idea that gods in Heaven, sometimes taken as five in number, with five kinds of divine virtue, reigned in rotation over definite periods of time justified the Confucian idea of political evolution and revolution, and the division of political powers among different officials. As gods have different divine virtues and powers, so different officials need different kinds of moral virtues and different talents or abilities in order to fulfil their different functions in government, and an individual man need not become a sage, that is, possessed of all virtues, talents, or abilities. Thus human nature, as generally considered by Confucianists of the Han dynasties, is not the same for all men, as Mencius or Hsün Tzu thought, but is classifiable into many kinds according to men's born abilities and dispositions for virtue. The realistic understanding of differences in human nature, and of their different functions in the whole human community, became the important thing for Confucian scholars of the Han dynasties. A scholar of these times did not need to ask how he could become a sage like the Confucius he worshipped, because he may not have been born with abilities and dispositions corresponding to those of Confucius.

However, after the Han dynasties, some thinkers from the Wei-Chin dynasties believed it possible for man to become a sage through the Taoistic contemplation of life and the universe. Buddhism brought from India the new gospel of man's ability to become a sage like Buddha. From the Wei-Chin to the so-called five dynasties the main current of Chinese philosophical thought was Buddhism. Confucian scholars continued to write many commentaries on the Confucian classics, but without making any philosophical innovations. It was the neo-Confucianism of the Sung-Ming dynasties which raised again the problem of the cultivation of sagehood.

III. The Spirit of Neo-Confucianism Compared with the Confucianism of the Han Dynasties and Ancient Confucianism

In contrast to the Confucianists of the Han dynasties, we should say that neo-Confucianists, generally speaking, do not believe that sagehood is beyond the ordinary man; they believe that an ordinary man can become a sage from within, and ascend from below, to acquire virtues of a divine status. This is because the differences in man's natural dispositions are not taken by them to be differences of essential human nature, which, being pure, good, and the same for all men, is the real ground for man's development through inner spiritual cultivation; and also because they generally consider the differences in men's abilities or talents to do things in the external world to bear no essential relation with man's development to sagehood. Hence, actually to become, and not just to worship, a sage became the aim of Confucian scholars or students at the very beginning of neo-Confucianism, as finally, for Wang Yang-ming and his school, it became that of all laymen in their different professions in the human community. Hence the saying that 'those who fill the street are all sages (in potentiality)'.[2] This is rightly conceived as a revival of the Confucian faith in man, as it had been propounded by Mencius and Hsün Tzu, and was implicit in Confucius's teaching — a faith which had been lost to Confucianism since the Han dynasties.

Yet this revival of Confucian faith was no mere repetition of earlier Confucian thought. The ideal of human life as a life of sagehood, the central core of Confucian thought as it had been provided by ancient Confucianism, remained generally accepted by neo-Confucianists. However, in regard to the 'way', or *tao*, for one's spiritual cultivation, there were many problems that had not been discussed by the ancients. The Confucian thinkers of the Han dynasties had pointed out that man has a temperamental nature which may be partial and not good. The neo-Confucianists, though denying that man's temperamental nature is his essential human nature, could not deny its existence. For them, in order to realize the goodness of this essential human nature, man must confront his temperamental nature, which, being partial and biased, may hinder his advance to sagehood. And there are also other obstacles, such as emotions, selfish desires, personal habits, subjective opinions, unconscious inclinations, and so on, which one has to confront on the way. All these negative factors stand, literally, in the way of man's realization of his positive ideal of sagehood. The ancient Confucianists, however, did not take these factors seriously. I would maintain that the central spirit of neo-Confucianism, on the other hand, is acceptance of the need to face all the negative factors and to find a way which is the negation of these negations of the possibility of realizing the positive ideal. In the following sections I shall support the above thesis by means of illustrations of the main teachings of the greatest neo-Confucianists on the ways in which man can acquire sagehood, in relation to their most important philosophical ideas about man's nature and mind, and the universe.

IV. Shao K'ang-chieh's Ideas of Contemplation of Things and the Sage as Man of Men

I begin with Shao K'ang-chieh, Chou Lien-ch'i, and Chang Heng-ch'u, as thinkers of the first period of neo-Confucianism. In the first period, Heaven still tends to come first and man second. Man, however, is able to improve his position and to identify himself with Heaven by acquiring the virtues of the sage through a proper spiritual cultivation.

I take Shao K'ang-chieh first in this period because he is senior in age to the other two. Shao has not been recognized as an orthodox Confucianist, because his attitude to life is too artistic and self-indulgent, like a Taoist, and his interest in the esoteric knowledge of numeralogy is also unorthodox. Yet he is an avowed Confucianist, and his ideas about the contemplation of things may also be taken as the first stage of development in the growth of neo-Confucianism.

I wish to explain only one, central idea of Shao's, in his book on the contemplation of things. This is the idea that man's emancipation from his subjective viewpoint, whereby he sees things through his own emotions, and his acquiring a way of contemplating things as they are objectively are the way to realize his essential human nature. Here it is the subjective emotions that are taken as the obstacles to progress to sagehood. The positive contemplation of things objectively includes also the contemplation of man as a thing in the natural world. Man differs from other things because, with his free activity of mind,

he can know the beings of other things and then, as it were, absorb
or comprise their beings in his own being. Hence man is defined as 'a
thing of all things'. Here, man as a thing is taken as originally standing
on the same level with other things, and then as ascending above other
things as a thing of all things. Shao also takes the sage, as a man, to
stand originally on the same level with ordinary men. The sage, however, is a man who has universal wisdom and universal sympathy with
other men's minds. The mind of the sage, then, is 'a mind of all minds',
and hence the sage is defined by Shao as 'a man of all men' above the
ordinary man. Having universal wisdom and sympathy, the sage may
also be considered as having a universal mind co-extensive with all
the minds of all men without any self-limitations. Thus his knowledge,
speech, and actions all represent the doings of Heaven, and his virtue
is actually identified with that of Heaven. This type of thought, without going into details, is clearly quite different from the Confucianism
of the Han dynasties in which the sage is regarded not as man-made
and to have ascended from below, but as Heaven-born and to have
descended from above.

V. Chou Lien-ch'i's Idea of Heaven as the Ultimate
Original Source of Things and the Establishment
of the Way of Man's Becoming a Sage
as Man's Ultimate Goal

Chou Lien-ch'i, considered an orthodox Confucian, differs from Shao.
In Chou's teaching the extensive contemplation of things, man, and
sagehood is not considered essential for spiritual development. Man's
own intensive aspiration to sagehood is considered to be the basic
requirement. This intensive aspiration is called 'chih' or the 'resolute
aim of man'. Chou said that 'the sage aims to be Heaven, the worthy
aims to be the sage, and the scholar aims to be the worthy'.[3] The
ladder for man's ascent to Heaven is the steadfast resolve of his inner
mind. In Chou's thoughts we find an inner world of moral or spiritual
cultivation with height and depth. He did not, in his metaphysics,
conceive of Heaven as a mere totality of infinite things in a horizontal
sense, but as the ultimate, real, and original source of the creation of
infinite things successively, in a vertical sense. This original source,
being creative, was called 'kan-yüan', and being ultimate and infinite,
'tai-chi', or the 'infinite-ultimate'. As a universal and eternal 'way' for
the creation of things it was called 'tao'. And *tao* as the reality of

the infinite creation is called 'chen'. Man, as a creature, has his original source within his mind, which is his nature, and the sage is the man who reveals and realizes his nature from within, through his creative wisdom and action in response to the outside world. Thereafter, the sage also realizes the ways of *jên-chi*, or 'man's ultimate', 'corresponding to the 'infinite-ultimate' of Heaven, and acquires the very same virtues as real, universal, and eternal, which Heaven has as the original source of all creation. Chou may not deny that Heaven's manifest virtue is greater, in creating infinite things, than the virtue of the sage whose life is short and creations limited. Yet the question of virtue is not to be considered in relation to its outer manifestation, and the quantity of the products of a virtue is not a standard for estimating the value or essence of that virtue. As we said before, the sage is not defined by neo-Confucianism as a man superior to other men by virtue of his talents or abilities; so Heaven, or God, despite having infinite creative power to create infinite things, is not necessarily superior to the sage, who has qualitatively the same virtue. This idea is also common to all later neo-Confucianists, and must be borne in mind, otherwise all their pronouncements about the identity in virtue of man and Heaven will have no meaning and should be taken to express an impossible ideal.

Chou saw clearly that the inner nature of man originates from the ultimate source of Heaven with its *tao* of creativity, and took this as the metaphysical ground for man's capacity for sagehood. Yet he also recognized that there are obstacles in the way of man's actually becoming a sage. In his view, however, it was not only the subjective emotions that man must emancipate himself from, as Shao Kang-chieh thought. Rather it was the desires that form the background of emotions, and which come from a partiality in the orientation of the mind and disturb its tranquility, that he considered to be the real obstacles to man's realizing his true nature in an upright, i.e. not partial or biassed, response to things, and to lead man astray and make him evil. Thus he taught of being 'without desires to keep the tranquility', and of there being tough-minded evil connected with tough-minded good, and soft-minded evil connected with soft-minded good.[4] The mind has to be 'void' when it is quiet, so that it can be enlightened and transparent. It must respond to things uprightly when it is active, so that it can be impartial and universal.[5] Voidness of the mind is the prior condition for the realization of its nature in its response as impartial and universal, so that the heavenly virtues of the sages, such as universal love, universal justice, universal righteousness, and so on, can be cultivated.

Chou was always considered the first founder of neo-Confucianism, and was admired by almost all the later Confucianists. All his writings are very short, yet rich in meaning. I cannot discuss all of them, but the above rough outline of his thought of the 'way' is enough to justify our talking of him as the orthodox representative of the spirit of neo-Confucianism.

VI. CHANG HÊNG-CH'Ü'S IDEA OF THE UNIVERSE AS A COMPREHENSIVE HARMONY AND OF MAN'S BECOMING A SAGE AS FILIAL PIETY TO THE *TAO* OF HEAVEN AND EARTH

Compared with Chou Lien-chi, Chang Hêng-ch'ü is a more systematic and articulate thinker. Here I shall mention only the central thought of his metaphysics in connection with his ideas about the 'way' of spiritual cultivation. This central thought is of the universe as 'tai-ho', or 'comprehensive harmony', from both the horizontal and the vertical point of view. In this metaphysics the discrete things of the universe only *appear* to be discrete. In reality they are composed of 'chi', which is the 'being' of things and has voidness within itself, an inner space which extends an invitation to other beings and through which it lets itself be transformed or recreated into a new being.[6] Hence the principle, or *tao*, of transformation and creativity subsists in *chi* itself. *Chi*'s voidness and its extending an invitation to other beings is called its 'shen' or 'function of spirituality'. *Chi*'s function of spirituality is then the principle of unity of different beings and of different things. Seen through their 'spirituality', all the discrete things of the universe made of *chi* are mutually immanent, and the universe has to be thought of as a comprehensive harmony which is full of spirituality in one great process of the transformation and creativity of things into a unitary whole. This harmony as it originates from the mutual immanence of things has a horizontal aspect, while as a whole above discrete things, it has a vertical aspect.

From the above metaphysics, man's perception of external things is nothing but a function of his spirituality as one who invites other beings or things to come to the voidness of his mind. Yet the voidness of man's mind is not finite, for it can allow the perceived object to be forgotten and superseded, and it then transcends the limitation of perception and enlarges itself infinitely, extending its invitation for all the things or persons of the universe to be known with wisdom and sympathized with love, and so on. Hence man's spiritual virtues, when fully developed, are the spiritual virtues of the sage, which are identical with the spiritual virtues of the universe as a comprehensive harmony.

In the process of the development of his spiritual virtue, man, as a child of the universe, gradually creates his new virtues, realizing his nature and also extending his filial piety to the 'principle of creativity' of the universe, or 'kan', the 'principle of Heaven', as his father, and 'principle of realization' of the universe, or 'kun', the 'principle of earth', as his mother, in order to continue the life of the universe as a great family, with 'all men as brothers' and 'all things as companies'. This is the world of man as seen through the eyes of the developing sage.

Chang's philosophy is something more than just a beautiful picture. He too knew of the obstacles to be encountered on the 'way'. Although man has a nature that is directed towards the universal principles of the universe, which he called the nature of Heaven and Earth, as ground for his possibility of becoming a sage, he also has a 'nature of chi-chih', a 'temperamental nature', or 'material nature', which is directed only to particular things in the world, and may be self-limited and self-closed to these particular things, and from this stem men's selfish desires and evil as obstacles to sagehood.

The self-limitation or self-closedness of man is a solidification of his being, as if it lacked voidness. The solidification of his being is also its materialization. Chang did not deny this tendency to solidification of man's being in his material nature, which makes him become self-limited and self-closed, then selfish and evil. Man who aspires to go the way to sagehood must come face-to-face with this nature of his and transform it. To do this is to open the closed, to transcend the limitation, or to make the solid fluid; it is to increase the spiritual voidness in his mind, to enlarge his mind so as to comprehend the things of the universe and the realization of his nature as the nature of Heaven and Earth. As it is possible for man to do all this, his material nature can in principle be transformed without residue, which is also proof that his material nature is not his real or essential nature, but just a natural obstacle to one who, while aspiring to realize his essential nature as a potential sage, is at a stage where this is still only his potentiality. At this stage he is in inner conflict. His life in itself is not harmonious, nor is it in harmony with the universe. And here he may also doubt that the universe really is a comprehensive harmony. Yet when he becomes a sage, all the obstacles and conflicts are gone, the universe as a real harmony is verified in his very life. Chang's metaphysics is therefore in fact the description of the world of the sage, though it still seems that he thought of his metaphysics as primary and his idea of the sage as secondary, as if the former was not simply a description of the life of the latter. But whatever inadequacy we may find in *his* exposition of the relation of man to universe was avoided in the further development of neo-Confucianism.

VII. CHENG MING-TAO'S IDEA OF MAN'S MIND WITH ITS NATURE AND UNIVERSE AS WITHOUT DUALITY AND HIS WAY OF SPIRITUAL CULTIVATION FOR BECOMING A SAGE

Cheng Ming-tao's thought, as a further development of Chang Hêng-chu's, began from seeing the universe as the outer side of man, and man's mind, with its nature, as the inner side, and the two sides of man as counterparts of one whole. Heaven is not thought of as primary and man as secondary, and the metaphysics of Heaven was actually taken as the description of the sage's world; this description being nothing else than the revelation of the reality of Heaven.

Cheng Ming-tao wrote very little, though his sayings were recorded by disciples. Here I shall refer only to one of his short letters to Chang Hêng-chu,[7] concerning the problem of how to make mind and nature as peaceful and constant as a sage. In this essay, Cheng said that the sage's mind is itself wide open and universal, without partiality, and that when it encounters things it responds spontaneously and concurrently with 'that with which the thing should be responded to'. Thus the sage delights because the thing should be delighted in, or is angry because it calls for anger, and when the thing is gone nothing is left. The sage's mind and its nature are then open, universal and without partiality, and at the same time always peaceful and constant. Now in Cheng Ming-tao's thought, the thing is no more than the object of the sage's response, and whether his response is delight, anger, or something else, is determined by 'that with which the thing should be responded to'. The thing as such is objective, though the actual response is subjective. The objective and subjective are two sides of the mind of the sage which arise simultaneously and then sink into silence, again simultaneously. Thus the mind of the sage is always responsive and always peaceful and constant.

Yet Cheng Ming-tao, too, fully recognized the difficulties or obstacles in the way of becoming a sage. He said, in the same letter, that the ordinary man usually has two attitudes, involving respectively a subjective and an objective bias. When he confronts things as objective, he usually turns his consciousness outward, using his intellect to grasp and attach to them and so losing it in the objective things. This is called 'yung-chih', or 'using intellect'. When thinking about his subjective response, on the other hand, he usually turns his consciousness backward to possess his response, and becomes self-centered and self-closed in his already existing response. This is called 'tsu-szu', or 'selfish'. The ordinary man is either using his intellect to grasp and attach himself to things, or he is self-possessed and becomes selfish, and is constantly running first in the one and then in the other of these two opposite ways.

Both ways lead man away from the proper middle way of the sage's mind, which is open, without self-possession, and responds immediately and spontaneously to things in the right way, and without attachment.

Cheng Ming-tao's views on how to become a sage are congenial and intimate to man's present experience. This is a way which every man can go immediately, if he wants. It does not depend on any established system of truths about the universe, which is seen simply as the outer side of man, and as unified with his mind and its nature as his inner side. Through man's right response the universe and man's mind, with its nature, can be seen as an undifferentiated and integral whole without separation or duality. Hence the sense of communion of feeling of all men and of all things in the universe as 'i-t'i', or 'one body', can be generated as the ground of all virtues. Cheng Ming-tao has also many sayings, full of metaphysical significance, on what the reality of the universe which is revealed as 'one body' consists of, but this I shall not discuss here. I would maintain, however, that all these sayings have to be understood as the description of the world of the mind of the sage, and not only as a metaphysics of this world as a reality immanent in the mind of the sage.

VIII. CHENG I-CHUAN'S IDEAS ABOUT THE PRACTICE OF
REVERENCE AND INVESTIGATION OF THINGS AND THE SEARCH FOR *LI*
AS TWO PARALLEL WAYS FOR MORAL PRACTICE

Taking many of his elder brother's ideas about man and the universe for granted, Cheng I-chuan knew, as a teacher, even more of the obstacles and hindrances to the realization of sagehood. For example, he saw that 'selfishness' and 'using intellect to grasp things', mentioned

by Cheng Ming-tao, are actually the 'habitual ways' in which ordinary man takes both things and himself. Man's actions are controlled
by habit, which is formed by his whole past life, and also stems from
unconscious desires and animal instincts, which are included in the
concept of 'temperamental nature', as Chang Hêng-chu and the Cheng
brothers all agree. The habits and temperamental nature of man are
burdens and irritations in the background of his present immediate
experience. His striving for sagehood in this present experience is like
sailing in an ocean full of waves. The neo-Confucianists were always
heroic in not praying for salvation from a transcendent God, but
there were still these more immediate difficulties to face, without self-
deception, on the way. In talking more than did his brother about
the moral practices for remedying moral sickness Cheng I-chuan went
one step further in the development of neo-Confucianism.

The ways of moral practice, as Cheng I-chuan taught them, are
divided according to the inner side and the outer side of man. In
the inner side, the idea of reverence, already proposed by Cheng Ming-
tao, was stressed still more by Cheng I-chuan, and replaced Chou
Lien-chi's teaching of tranquility. The idea of reverence is subtle. It
is not necessarily a reverence for any definite object, such as man or
a god, but a reverence that subsists whether one is doing things or
doing nothing. In either case, one can acquire a spiritual state of
reverence which is not merely a state of tranquility. The mental state
of tranquility may be thought of as static and flat. The mental state
of reverence, as living and always growing, Cheng I-chuan thought
of as dynamic and like a round sphere of mental light surrounding
things and the mind itself, making the mind self-enlightened and
open, both in knowing and in doing things with concentration and
without self-closure. It can also be explained as a state of constant
wakefulness where the mind is neither crowded by selfish desires nor
sunk into the things which it is concentrated in knowing and doing.
The predominance in the mind of such a state of reverence is called
'chu-ching'. *Chu-ching* is a way in which the mind keeps itself awake,
and therefore existing, and it goes by the name of 'han-yang', which
may be translated as 'self-immersion and self-nourishment' of the
mind.

Another teaching of Cheng I-chuan's is the investigation of things
with a view to knowing their *li*, for the realization of our knowledge
of them. The idea of *li*, or Heaven-*li*, was also proposed by Cheng
Ming-tao, but he usually meant by it a universal principle of the uni-

verse, where Cheng I-chuan usually took it to mean principles of particular or individual things. 'Li' is a word without a definite translation. It may be rendered in English as 'principle', 'law', 'form', 'essence', 'pattern', 'rule', 'regulation', or 'maxim'. In connection with 'mind', it may also be translated as 'reason'. *Li* may be universal or particular, or the property of a unique or individual thing. It may also be what things actually are, shall be, or ought to be. The word's etymology is from the regulation of fields and the polish of jade, and it later came to mean the line of jade. The line of jade is the smoothness one can feel by passing one's hand from one part to another of a piece of jade after it has been polished. *Li* may be synonymous with *tao*, which originally means 'way' or 'road'. The line of jade can be thought of as the way or road of jade, and the way or road can be thought of as the line on Earth. Because the line in jade is smaller, and the way or road is larger, so *tao* is the *li* of larger things, and *li* may be the *tao* of smaller things. As the line of jade may be seen once for all as an object, so *li* is more objective, while the way or road is what man has gone through, and is therefore more subjective. Yet *tao*, when objectively thought, is *li*, and, *li*, subjectively considered as what man thinks and acts through, is *tao*. So although there are differences in these two terms, they are nevertheless mutually implicated in each other, and can be used synonymously. However, *li* or *tao*, as the line or way of men's thinking and acting, has a more important meaning in Chinese thought. The *li*, if translated as 'objective principle', or 'natural law', is also to be taken as the way or road of man's thinking about specific things, and not merely as objective Platonic ideas before the subjective mind. The *human* law, rule, regulation, or personal maxim is the right way for man's action. Every *thing* may also be taken as formed according to its process of formation, so man can *think* through a process in order to know the form, and the form here is then nothing else than that course which man's thinking takes. When the essence or pattern of a thing is taken as man's thinking of it, or acting with regard to it, then it is also precisely the way or road man has to pass through to complete his knowledge and action. It is a pity there is no English word corresponding to 'li' or 'tao' meaning just that which 'man's thinking and acting can pass through', like the line, way, or road, and with the same richness of meaning.

As *tao* or *li* means the way man's thinking or acting can take, then any *tao* or *li* which man cannot take, or which leads only to an impasse, is not a real *tao* or *li*. The error or falsehood of an idea or proposition is found where thinking is unable to continue. When ideas are self-contradictory, or fail to correspond with the facts, thinking reaches an impasse. Similarly the evil or wrong in our action is found where an action is unable to continue because it conflicts with other things or with the ideals of the mind. The action which is morally good and right is the action which can really be carried on indefinitely from the present to the future, from oneself to other men, and from the human world to the natural world, and to heaven, without meeting any impasse. Here we have the criterion of 'real' *tao* or *li*. Real *tao* or *li* is the way man should go, and also the only way man *can* really pass along and through. The 'ought to be' of man is what, in the end, he 'shall be' and 'actually can be'. So the Chinese philosopher always uses the same word, 'li' or 'tao', for the universal way of human life, including all acting and thinking. As one's universal way of acting and thinking, *tao* or *li* is one's reason, so the word 'li' may be translated as 'reason' when it is thought as something immanent in one's actual thinking and acting. And as such *li* is also called 'human nature'. Man has an innate capacity to think and act with his reason as an embodiment of *li*. Cheng I-chuan's saying that '(human) nature is *li*' was admired by Chu Tzu as putting what no one before him had said so definitely.

Although *li* may be a universal, a particular, or simply a property of an individual thing, when Cheng I-chuan talked about *li* he was more concerned with the *li* of particular and individual things in ordinary life than with the universal principle of the universe as a whole. Here Cheng I-chuan paid more serious attention to the fact that our ordinary life takes place in concrete situations composed of particular things. So man has to search for and grasp the forms, patterns, principles, and laws of these things as their *li*'s, and the rules, regulations, maxims, and laws, as the *li*'s of his own thinking and acting which are necessary for his having true knowledge of these things, and for his right and good action in terms of the proper response to these things. In doing so, man realizes his human nature as reason or *li*, which means that he then has virtues. When the virtues are genuine and perfect then man can be a sage. There is no short-cut to sagehood by merely thinking the spiritual mentality of the sage or the metaphysical universal principle of the universe, and neglecting knowledge of particular things in everyday life. This is because, lacking this knowledge, he will not know what the proper response to things is. He will have made a cleavage between the outside part and the inside part of himself as man, and he can never attain to sagehood, for the sage is a man of the world as well as of Heaven, a man who realizes his human nature in every concrete situation of his life.

The two parallel 'ways' of Cheng I-chuan's teaching, the insistence on reverence as a subjective way for moral practice, and the investigation of things in a search for their *li*'s and the *li*'s of our responses, as an objective way, are of equal importance. The practice of reverence, in opposition to man's private desires, habits, and his temperamental nature, for the purification and constant wakefulness of mind, is certainly a difficult matter. So also is the investigation of things, in view of their multitude; indeed one might even say that due to their great, even infinite number, the investigation of all things is an impossible requirement for sagehood.

However, this does not necessarily follow from Cheng I-chuan's view. If man's investigation of things in his search for their *li*'s was merely a quest for theoretical knowledge of objective things themselves, as for the scientist, then it surely would be an endless enterprise. But if it is for the purpose of knowing the *li*'s of our right and good responses to things in concrete life-situations, it is not a hopeless matter. The things a man encounters in concrete situations are limited, and the *li*'s of right and good response that he should know may be even less. For example, the colours I see in a situation may be many, yet the right and good attitude in seeing them may be just one. The people I meet in a room may be many, but my respect for them may be one. The problem of our moral action in regard to things only arises where a number of different actions or responses seem right and good, and then to help our choice and define what is really right and good in the very situation, we have to study the things in the situation and to know what they really are. This, too, is not a hopeless matter. Even in a situation where two possible actions conflict and both are equally right and good, one can still refrain from doing either. In an extreme situation, one may even commit suicide in order to preserve his reverence for both. To commit suicide in such a case is right and good, according to Confucian teaching. Cheng I-chuan also said that the scholar should see only the right and good and nothing about his living or dying. Whether an action or response is right and good or not, the standard is in man himself. In a particular situation, there must be a particular right or particular good, which can be searched out. Hence the investigation of things with a view to finding their *li* is what man *can* and *should* do.

In the thought of the Cheng brothers, problems about the ways for cultivating sagehood were not discussed objectively on the basis of a general metaphysical or cosmological idea of the universe and man. Their teachings were addressed to their disciples as individuals. Each individual had to think for himself how to relate his mind to his nature and things, including other men. When the Chengs died, scholars of this school came to hold different ideas about such questions as the meaning of reverence, the meanings of *jên*, the real difference between the mind of the sage and that of ordinary people, whether a state of reverence or of tranquility should be cultivated first, what is contemplated in a state of tranquility, what the relation of nature or *li* is to mind, and whether mind is merely a function, and its nature, or *li*, its reality or substance, or whether mind is itself the reality or substance. Some of these questions were raised by disciples of the Cheng brothers, but their masters gave ambiguous or unsatisfactory answers. Some of them were not discussed by the Cheng brothers at all. Discussions of them by the scholars of the whole Cheng school were very subtle and the scene became rather confusing, especially since all the problems centered on something so elusive as the inner mind. But about a hundred years later there came two great thinkers, Chu Tzu and Lu Shiang-shan, to dissolve the confusion, each with a metaphysics of mind as the foundation of the practical attainment of sagehood. Since the thought of Lu Shiang-shan is the more simple and somewhat like the elder Cheng's, I shall deal with him first, though Lu is in fact younger than Chu by about ten years.

IX. Lu Shiang-shan's Idea of Original Mind and Man's Self-Establishment

The most important contribution of Lu's thinking is that he revived Mencius's idea of 'pen-hsin', or 'original mind'. Lu taught that the original mind and its nature as *li* are identical in being and that it is good in an absolute sense as the origin of all moral virtues. Cheng I-chuan, and some scholars of his school, thought that although the 'nature' of mind, as its substance or reality, was good, the conscious mind, as merely an expression or function of that nature, may be morally neutral. They did not take 'nature' here to mean the very nature of original mind. In Lu's thought, the original mind is not always expressed wholly and fully. This is so with the mind of ordinary man. But it *can* be wholly and fully expressed, and this is so with the

mind of the sage. There are only differences of degree in expression of
the original mind between the ordinary man's and the sage's mind.
Therefore when the ordinary man is fully self-conscious of his original
mind as the root of his present mind, which is true equally for him and
the sage, he can find his way to sagehood even without studying the
sayings of sages, or thinking of the sage as only an ideal. Man, as he
stands in the universe, can attain to sagehood with his own resources.
Yet Lu knew as well as other neo-Confucianists of the need to overcome
impediments to the original mind's full expression. Man is dependent
upon external things for his existence in the universe. So his mind is
always directed and attached to things, and can entertain selfish
desires for them. When it does that, it is bent down towards those things
and man is no longer able to stand up in the universe, his mind now
being separated from its root, namely the original mind. And again,
although the mind, as that which thinks, can acquire real knowledge
of things, it can also inject its thought with prior conceptions, thus
constructing opinions about real things which do not amount to real
knowledge. Even real knowledge of certain things when used out of
context constitutes wrong opinion. So a man who attaches himself to
his knowledge as if it were a constant possession, unaffected by context or occasion, is always transforming it into wrong opinion.

Lu Shiang-shan is remarkable among neo-Confucianists for his
view that opinions are more detrimental than selfish desires to man's
mind, because opinions are a systematic net formed by the mind as
its own snare. Selfish desire is bad, in his view, but desire as such is
not bad, and sympathy with men's desires and their fulfilment is good.
Opinions, on the other hand, are bad; though knowledge itself is not
bad and thinking liberated from opinion is good. When one is liberated
from one's opinions and selfish desires, one's mind is without attachment either to things or to one's knowledge, and one's knowing and
thinking then become a pervasive light shining upon the whole
world of one's knowledge or thought. This light is coextensive with
one's world or universe, and the universe then becomes the embodiment of the light of mind; hence Lu's dictum: 'the universe is my
mind, my mind is the universe.'[8] In such a state of mind, a man will
take all that should be done in the universe as all that he should do
for himself. If he acts from a sense of responsibility, he will have no
sense of self-possession, and this is the properly spiritual state of sagehood accessible to anyone who can liberate himself from the bondage
of his mind and stand up in the universe as an independent man.

X. Chu Tzu's Thoughts about Mind and Moral Practice as a further Development of Cheng I-chuan's Thoughts

Chu Tzu was considered the most systematic thinker and versatile scholar among neo-Confucianists of the Sung dynasty. However, what his main contribution to neo-Confucianism is and how his thought differs from that of Lu Shiang-shan are controversial questions. I myself, after many years of hesitation,[9] would now say that his main contribution is in his thought about mind. Chu Tzu was for a long time perplexed at the confusing ideas of mind held by scholars of Cheng's school in his youth. And even just a few days before he died, ill as he was, he was correcting sentences in his commentaries on the chapter of 'making the (moral) will real' in *The Great Learning*. Throughout his life he anxiously sought the right way to sagehood through an understanding of mind, and changed his views on mind many times. But his conclusive and central idea seems to have been that mind has its substance or reality in itself and its functions in its response to things.

The substance or reality of mind itself comprises, for Chu, all its *li*'s as its inner nature. When no *li* or nature is expressed, the substance or reality of mind itself is just a pure consciousness, void, serene, transparent, and luminous. But when mind is affected by things inner or outer, it functions through its knowing, feeling, willing, and acting in response to them, and therein *realizes* its nature or *li*. The mind's response as an actual occurrence is composed of *chi*, or substance, just as any actual thing. When *li* or nature is not realized, it is prior to *chi*. It is then not something that 'is', but merely what 'ought to be', i.e. a 'way' the mind's actual responses must take in the process of becoming.

Mind as a pure consciousness which is void, serene, transparent, and luminous is the possession of every man. However, since it can be clouded and concealed by selfish desires and man's temperamental nature, the corresponding way for its recovery and purification is called the 'chen-yang', or 'self-preservation and self-nourishment', of mind, i.e. the maintenance of the state of reverence taught by the Chengs. Yet for Chu Tzu the state of reverence is not just an outcome of man's own practice, it is the mind's real and original state. Its reality as void, serene, transparent, and luminous is always flowing and growing silently. Since the state of reverence itself, however, is the same as that taught by Cheng I-chuan, Chu Tzu may be thought

simply to have made explicit what was implied in the teaching of the
Chengs. But in fact he has gone a step further.

The reality of mind, or pure consciousness, as void, serene, transparent, and luminous, was also in Chu Tzu's view a pure subject of
its functions and never an object. When affected by things, the mind
functions by knowing, feeling, or willing in regard to them, and then
it is directed beyond itself. Hence, to want to know the mind as an
object, and to direct our knowing backwards upon its origin, is to
become involved in an endless circle, and one that is 'selfish' in a very
subtle sense. One reason why Chu Tzu opposed Lu Shiang-shan's
teaching is that Chu thought Lu's teaching about 'the self-conscious-
ness of the original mind' to be enjoining man to know and grasp
his mind as an object. Here Chu may have misunderstood Lu to
some extent. Still, he saw clearly that man may direct his knowing
backwards to its origin and think of his mind as an object, thus becoming selfish in this subtle sense, and this is a profound insight into a
potential error of the mind's ways. The right way of seeing the mind
as it is is not to know it as an object, but simply to let it reveal itself in
its self-preservation and self-nourishment.

Of course, we have a word 'mind' to express or denote the existence
of mind; we can therefore refer to its existence by this word, and the
word itself may be an object. But what it expresses is only a subject.
The particular functions of mind may also be thought of as inner
objects, in the self-reflection of consciousness, but the consciousness
which reflects is not an object. Inferring from the word and the particular functions of mind as objects to the conclusion that mind or consciousness is itself an object is just an extension of our habit of grasping
external things. It is an illegitimate procedure.

The knowing mind, when not turning in upon itself, is directed to
things in order to acquire knowledge of them. The investigation of
things with a view to finding their *li*'s is no artificial matter, but necessary to a mind whose nature is to address itself to things. Besides
Cheng I-chuan's teaching of the practice of reverence, then, Chu also
accepted his teaching of the investigation of things, but found, in
two directions, a wider significance in 'investigation of things'. In
one direction, Chu Tzu did not think of the investigation of things
so much in terms of uncovering the principles of particular things.
For him there is a general scheme of all things in the universe, and this
can be investigated and known as their universal principle or *li*. Thus
Chu Tzu has his metaphysics or cosmology of nature.[10] In this, even

man's mind can be seen objectively as a combination of *li* and *chi*, and since he can know the most general scheme of objective nature, as its *li*, his mind may pass through the general scheme or *li* to comprehend the natural universe as a whole. The mind extends to the whole universe. On the basis of this knowledge of nature man can then realize the dignity of his mind.

In the other direction, Chu Tzu found a further significance in the investigation of things in relation to inner spiritual cultivation. According to Cheng I-chuan, the purpose of the investigation of things is to know the *li*'s of things themselves, and then also the *li*'s which man should follow to make his response to them right and good. But how is it possible for the response to follow the *li*? Why do many people know the *li* yet fail to follow it? Here Chu Tzu had to go a step further. Following the book of *The Great Learning*, he took the response of man to outward things to originate from will and feeling. If we want our response to be right and good, we have to take the *li* which we know and should follow as a standard for making our will good, and then the will can be directed to the good alone. That is, we must first have a will which actually likes good and dislikes evil. Liking good and disliking evil are feelings accompanying the will directed to the good when the mind knows the *li* and takes it as a standard. Through liking good and disliking evil, the positive good is posited, and the negative evil is negated; and then our will is directed only to the good, and becomes itself a really good will. This teaching of *The Great Learning*, known as 'making the (moral) will real', Chu Tzu adopted as the next step of moral cultivation after man's realization of his knowledge about the *li* which he should follow.

However, merely 'making the will real' is not enough. The will springs from the mind. If the direction of the mind is partial and wrong, the will may not be directed only to the good. Here *The Great Learning* has a teaching about how to correct the direction of mind, called the 'rectification of mind'. In it, the causes of partiality of mind are discussed. It is said that our natural feelings or emotions such as anger, delight, or fear, which attach to things, have particular directions and the mind's own activity may limit it to a particular direction and make it partial or biased. Therefore 'rectification of mind' is meant to put the mind in its right place and point it in the right direction as master of its feelings or emotions, so that the will, springing from mind, will then be directed only to the good, and have that moral feeling which is its liking good and disliking evil, as noted above. And then from this will, which conforms to the *li* which man knows and should follow, will naturally be generated, by our mind and body, the right and good response to outside things, which in turn means that the *li* which is the inner nature of our mind is also realized. Through one's body one is connected with other men, of one's family, country and the whole world under Heaven. In *The Great Learning* there are also teachings about how to train the body, regulate the family, govern the country, and maintain peace and justice in the world. All these Chu Tzu adopted as connected with the doctrine of the investigation of things and the realization of knowledge as the first two steps in *The Great Learning*.

Although these two steps also came into the teaching of Cheng I-chuan, the latter did not connect them specifically with 'making the will real' and 'rectification of mind', or 'practice of reverence', as ways of inner cultivation. Chu Tzu in effect bridged the two sides of Cheng I-chuan's thought. When Chu talked about reverence as inner cultivation, he knew that the mind should not grasp *itself*, and that the knowing function of mind is naturally directed towards things, as we have explained. And when he talked about the investigation of things and the realization of knowledge, he knew also that they are connected with inner cultivation. Thus the two sides of Cheng I-chuan's teaching can be seen as mutually implicated and connected. It is clear that Chu Tzu's thought centered on the 'mind' with its 'li'. So, on the one hand, the investigation of things is a search for the *li* which man has to follow as an inner standard for 'making the will real' and 'rectification of mind', while, on the other, 'rectification of mind' or 'practice of reverence' is necessary for the realization of the *li* which is our inner nature. That is, while, on the one hand, the *li* of objective things, as it is known through the realization of the mind's knowing function, is also immanent in this very function, so that when the *li* is known from outside things we can say that it has also been revealed from the mind inside,[11] so, on the other hand, when man practices the 'rectification of mind' or 'reverence' to purify his mind and preserve it as a void, serene, transparent, luminous reality, it is precisely in order to keep open the door of mind, and to let the *li*, as its nature, be the more easily revealed and realized. Hence the two ways of Cheng I-chuan mutually help one another to make the *li* known or be revealed to and followed by the mind in its knowledge and actions; which then makes the mind reasonable, and brings man to the 'way' which leads to sagehood.

When mind is not knowing or acting, it is still a mind and remains in a state of reverence; and Chu Tzu explained the *Chung Yung*'s teaching of 'ch'en tu', or 'self-care in solitude', as differentiated into two kinds of inner reflection. One is when a certain idea motivates one's action and one has to examine whether it tends to be, or is, good or evil, right or wrong, and then likes or dislikes it accordingly. This corresponds to the way of 'making the (moral) will real' in the *Great Learning*. The other is when there is no idea motivating action, and there is therefore nothing to occasion either like or dislike. Here too the mind should be in a state of self-care, to prevent evil or wrong ideas arising unconsciously.[12]

Chu Tzu's thought about the mind and moral cultivation is subtle, profound, and generally sound. However, he took *li* merely to reside *within* the mind, and thus to be distinguished from it. And he further distinguished between mind's reality, or substance, as static or tranquil, and its function as dynamic or effective. In Chu Tzu's cosmology, too, the 'mind', as a synthesis of *li* and *chi*, is in an ambiguous position. How to unite the dualities of *li* and *chi*, of mind as reality, or substance, and as function, and of mind and its *li*, remained outstanding problems. For although Chu explained how 'investigation of things', 'realization of knowledge', 'making the moral will real', 'practice of reverence' and 'rectification of mind' were related to one another, these still remained distinct ways of moral cultivation. A unitary way was still to be found. So Chu Tzu's teaching is not so simple as Lu Shiang-shan's who saw that the mind with its *li*, or nature, is simple, that the mind, whether static or dynamic, is the same moral mind, and that there is only one way for moral cultivation, i.e. knowing the original mind and encouraging its self-enlightenment. The differences between Chu Tzu's teaching and that of Lu had also to be unified. This was the achievement of Wang Yang-ming.

XI. Wang Yang-ming's Realization of Liang-chih or Conscientious Consciousness as both a Function and the Substance or Reality of Mind — a Synthesis of Chu Tzu's Dualism and Lu Shiang-shan's Teaching of Original Mind

Wang Yang-ming has generally been taken to belong to Lu's school. This is not quite right. Of course Wang admired Lu, and his thought is an attempt to unify the dualities in Chu Tzu's teaching. It was also his view that the mind of the sage and that of the ordinary man do not differ in kind, but only in degree of enlightenment. All this is close to Lu. Yet Wang's learning began with his study of Chu Tzu, and all his problems and key ideas stem from Chu. Wang admired Lu as a successor of Mencius, but he was a greater admirer of Yen Tzu, whom Chu Tzu also admired. Wang said that he was grateful to Chu Tzu as to his parents or Heaven. Whenever he found that he differed from Chu Tzu, he was most anxious to find sayings in Chu that minimized the difference, and he edited a book of Chu's sayings, entitled *The Conclusive Thesis of Chu Tzu's Late Age*, which was taken to represent his own thought. Which all shows that Wang's learning originated from Chu Tzu even though its conclusions were closer to those of Lu Shiang-shan. So I take his teaching to be a synthesis of Chu Tzu and Lu Shiang-shan.[13]

From his study of Chu Tzu, Wang evolved a development of the former's theory of the investigation of things. According to Chu, the investigation of things and search for their *li* culminate in knowing the *li* of our response to objective things. But this response is something man can investigate directly. So Wang thought that the word 'thing' in the *Great Learning* should be understood to refer to that ('thing') which man does to the so-called objective thing, where the 'thing' he does can include the so-called objective thing as an ingredient. For example, where the doing in question is seeing something, that doing includes colours as its ingredients; similarly hearing can include sounds as its ingredients. The moral problem is connected with the doing as a whole. There are moral problems about the ways of seeing and hearing, for they can be right or wrong, and good or evil, but not about the colours or sounds themselves. The right and good way of our doing is the *li* which we have to know in order to make the thing which we are doing right and good. This is the only *li* which has to be known when we want to be a moral being or a sage. Hence Wang interpreted the realization of knowledge as realization of knowledge about the *li* of our doing, or of our response to so-called objective things. This constituted an important break with Chu's view, even though it was a development of Chu's rather than of Lu Shiang-shan's teaching.

According to Wang, then, our universe is a universe which we act upon and respond to, and we know it only through our acts and responses. My own universe of things and men, therefore, extends no further than the range of my affections and responses. It is a kind of idealism, though not a theoretical idealism supported by metaphysical or epistemological arguments. Rather, it is simply a vision of man as capable of immediate knowledge of the universe through his own actions and responses.

As the *li* connected with morality, or with the ideal of sagehood, is the *li* of our doing or response, and our doing or response is in the self and known by the mind, then all the *li*'s have to be reached and known in the mind. There is no *li* of doing or response outside the mind and belonging to so-called objective things alone. For example, the *li* of filial piety is in our minds when we act with regard to our parents, not in the parents themselves. The same is true of all *li*'s. The *li* in our mind is at the same time the mind's *being* conscious and the *li* that we are conscious of. Yet when the *li* is conscious, mind or consciousness are also *in* the *li*, as well as the *li* being in that very mind or consciousness. Here the identity of mind and *li* can be directly confirmed and intuited if man reflects upon the relation of *li* and mind or consciousness as they really are.

If we agree that the *li* is in our mind as consciousness, and the mind as consciousness of *li* is also in the very *li*, we still have to ask how the consciousness of *li* functions in relation to the other parts of the mind as a whole. That the *li* is what should be followed is the common teaching of neo-Confucianism. Yet Chu Tzu granted that the *li* may not actually be followed. In that case, the *li* is transcendent or only subsists in the substance or reality of mind as its nature, and is not actually expressed in the mind. However, if the *li* which 'should be' is taken as transcendent, then the consciousness of its transcendence is a transcendental consciousness, and the *li* which 'should be' is not transcendental to *this* consciousness, but immanent in it; and so the *li* should not be taken as merely transcendent, as Chu Tzu thought. Of course, the *li* may very well not be expressed in the mind, and when that is so it can be taken as only subsisting in the reality or substance of mind as unexpressed and unrealized. But in this sense the 'consciousness of the very *li*' is also unexpressed. The expression of *li* and the expression of the consciousness of *li* are always simultaneous, never separate. Thus there is an existential identity of *li* and the mind as consciousness of *li*, which should be referred to by one term. Wang calls it 'liang-chih', which may be translated 'conscientious consciousness of mind', and its content is the moral *li* which should be and actually is followed when it is realized. In the teaching of Wang Yangming, every man has *liang-chih* because he has a consciousness of some *li*'s which should be followed, and thus has some knowledge of what should be, whether he actually tries to bring it about or not. We

need not know all of what ought to be, or all *li*'s. They will be revealed
gradually in the process of our lives. We are ordinary men not because
we have no knowledge of what ought to be, but because we do not
act fully upon the knowledge we have. We are not responsible for the
'should be's' we do not know. Our responsibility consists in responding
to any 'should be' that is immediately expressed, revealed, and known.
This is quite enough for our immediate moral practice. Therefore
to say that the *li* is one thing and practice another, as Chu Tzu, Lu
Shiang-shan, and others taught, does not do justice to our moral consciousness. Moreover, the very inadequacy of the notion is a hindrance
to our efficiency in moral practice. We have to understand that this
consciousness of *li*, or *liang-chih*, is originally both knowing *and* feeling.
The fact is that when *liang-chih* knows the right or good, a feeling of
liking it arises simultaneously, as does, when *liang-chih* knows the wrong
or evil, a feeling of disliking it. Chu Tzu did say that liking or disliking
is connected with our knowledge of good or evil, but he still thought
the realization of knowledge to be only the first step in moral practice,
and disliking evil and liking good to be the next step. This is an inadequate understanding of the consciousness of *li*, or *liang-chih*, as moral
consciousness. The adequate understanding is that the feeling of liking
good comes no later than knowing good, and feeling of disliking evil
comes no later than knowing evil. The knowledge of *liang-chih* includes
the feeling of like or dislike; and the will to do or undo subsists in the
feeling. So *liang-chih*'s knowledge and its action are taken as one thing
and not two. 'Realization of knowledge' and 'making the (moral) will
real', as taught by the book of *The Great Learning*, and which Chu Tzu
interpreted as two steps or two ways of moral practices, Wang conceived as but one single step, or one way. In Chu Tzu's thought the
rectification of mind is yet another step, or way, of moral practice.
For Wang, however, the consciousness of *li* as *liang-chih* is the very
being of the moral mind. When a man realizes his *liang-chih* as liking
and doing good, and disliking and undoing evil, then his mind is already on the right way and in the right place. So the 'rectification
of mind' is included in the realization of *liang-chih*. Furthermore, when
whatever is good for my body-behaviour, my family, my country,
and the whole world, is done, and whatever is evil for all these is
undone, then my body is trained, my family regulated, my country
governed, and the world's justice and peace attained. So all the teachings of *The Great Learning* which Chu Tzu interpreted as separate are included in one teaching of the 'realization of *liang-chih*'.

The above concerns realization of *liang-chih* when there are things for the mind to like or dislike. But what about the mind when it has nothing special to like or dislike, when it is in a quiet, tranquil, and static state, and all mental activity is unexpressed? Now Wang Yang-ming certainly agreed that there is such a state of mind, and indeed that one must have it in order to keep the mind, as Chu Tzu said, void, serene, transparent and luminous. And Wang Yang-ming also agreed with Chu that even in such a state the mind is not just idle, but still exercises self-care against the possibility of evil or wrong ideas being motivated from the depths of unconsciousness. But Wang did not agree with Chu that because nothing is known in this state, then it is a state of 'no knowing'. He asked: If it is a state of 'no knowing', then who is exercising self-care? The mind's, or *liang-chih*'s, knowing must always exist, whether there are things or ideas to be known or not. The state in which things or ideas are known and that in which nothing is known are in fact mutually implicated. When ideas or things come to consciousness, then the *liang-chih* must know immediately whether they are good or evil, right or wrong, and therefore whether liking or disliking, and willing to do or willing to undo, is the appropriate expression of its activities for its self-realization. Through its self-realization its own activities are carried on and fulfilled. When evils are removed and good attained the mind as *liang-chih* reaches a state beyond good and evil. It returns to the state in which it was prior to its expressive activity. But because *liang-chih*'s activities themselves originate from a state prior to their being expressed and have to return to that state, there can be no separation of the state in which its activities are expressed from that in which they are not.

Moreover, when *liang-chih* is not prompted by evil or good, but is in a 'pre-expressive' state, it continues to safeguard itself for its own self-realization. Nor is it really without expression in this state. For the state of self-care is a state of knowing which is also a state of bliss and liberation from any limitations of mind, and this is itself an expression of *liang-chih*, even though it has no particular object in view.

From the above two paragraphs, it is clear that, contrary to Chu Tzu's view, we must say that the mind as *liang-chih* never exists either as a merely static substance or reality without expression of its function, nor as a merely dynamic function without expression of its substance or reality. When the mind does not express itself in ordinary activity, its function of knowing is still expressed in its substance or reality, and when it does express itself in ordinary activity, the latter expresses the state of rest in which the mind's reality or substance, though un-expressed, still remains. So the mind as *liang-chih* is always both dyna-mic and static, always creating or acting and always tranquil or at rest. It is a pure knowing or conscientious consciousness, and can never be posited as an objective being. It can only be enjoyed subjectively as a kind of transparent spiritual light always in process of self-creation out of a state of 'self-rest'.

In Wang Yang-ming the dualities of *li* and mind, of the substance, or reality, and function of mind, of the external investigation of things and the internal ways of spiritual cultivation, were all unified into one integral doctrine of the realization of *liang chih*. His doctrines of the unity of mind and *li* and of mind as both static and dynamic are precisely those of Lu Shiang-shan, though, as we have said, many of Wang's key ideas and problems stem from Chu Tzu. His idea of *liang chih* as conscientious consciousness is also very similar to Lu's idea of original mind as a unity of *li* and mind, though *liang chih* is always concerned with particular things, and must realize itself in its response to things in concrete situations. Wang's 'liang chih' is more in-timate to our immediate experience than Lu's 'original mind', which is always spoken of as identical with the universe as a whole. There is an analogy between the practice of realization for *liang chih* and Cheng I-chuan and Chu Tzu's investigation of things, in that both involve consideration of individual cases on their own merits.

Because *liang-chih* concerns present concrete situations, it is possible to know the existence of *liang-chih* in any present situation, given immediate self-reflection. The realization of *liang-chih* is a way to sagehood because every man has it in himself to be a sage. We could even say that in the depth of every man's heart there lies hidden a sage waiting to be revealed when the closed door of the mind is opened. Because it taught that every man can be a sage, Wang's teaching flourished in the late Ming period and its influence was felt throughout the whole Chinese community. Many of Wang's disciples developed his thought to a very high level. But his teaching was also perverted because people assumed that, being potential sages, they were as good as sages already, and therefore in no need of spiritual cul-tivation or moral practice in confronting actual or possible hindrances to spirituality and morality. This, of course, was not Wang's teaching, but merely a degeneration of the spirit of his doctrine of 'becoming a sage through the self-transformation of one's life'. When this degen-eration reached its lowpoint in late Ming, there was a movement by great thinkers to revise Wang's teaching, and also an anti-Wang movement which ended in a movement opposed to the neo-Confucianism of the Sung-Ming dynasties as a whole.[14] Hence the main currents of thought from the Ching dynasty to present-day China are not in line with the development of neo-Confucianism. It is regrettable that the spiritual depth and moral grandeur of the neo-Confucianists, and the significance of their thought, have so often been forgotten or misunderstood, and still await revival and new understanding.

NOTES

1. Tang Chun-i, 'An Evaluation of the Similarities and Differences between Chu Tzu and Lu Shiang-shan's Thoughts as Seen from their Origin', *New Asia Journal*, Vol. VIII (1967), No. 1; and 'The Learning of Wang Yang-ming and a Re-evaluation of Similarities and Differences between Chu Tzu and Lu Shiang-shan's Thoughts', *New Asia Journal*, Vol. VIII (1967), No. 2, and Vol. IX (1969), No. 1.
2. Wing-tsit Chan (Trans.), *Instructions for Practical Living (Ch'uan hsi lu)*, Columbia University Press, New York 1963. See pp. 193, 194, 239 and 240.
3. *T'ung shu*, Ch. 10.
4. Ibid., Ch. 7.
5. Ibid., Ch. 20.
6. Cf. my 'On Chang Hêng-chu's Theory of Mind and its Metaphysical Basis', *Philosophy East and West*, Vol. VI (1956), Nos. 1 and 2. I discuss the meaning of 'chi' for the benefit of Western readers.
7. *Ming-tao-wen-chi* (Essays of Cheng Ming-tao) Vol. III.
8. *Shiang-shan-chuan-chi* (Complete Works of Lu Shiang-shan), Vol. 36.
9. Cf. Sec. 5 of my 'An Evaluation of the Similarities and Differences...', op. cit.
10. In this respect he accepted Chou Lien-chi's ideas about the origin of the universe as infinite-ultimate, Chang Hêng-chu's ideas about *chi* as the real being of things, and Shao Kang-chieh and the Han dynasties' scholars' ideas about number, *ying* and *yang*, the five activities, and the eight diagrams. Chu Tzu used all these ideas to construct his metaphysics of objective nature.
11. Cf. Ch. 2, Sec.4 of my 'The Learning of Wang Yang-ming and a Re-evaluation ...', op. cit.
12. This is the innermost practice of the moral mind in man's solitude. It is also the most serious experience in the mind's inner life at the transition between consciousness and unconsciousness, and also between consciousness's *function* of knowing and the knowing itself. This doctrine of Chu Tzu's should actually be included in the doctrine of 'rectification of mind' in the *Great Learning*.
13. Cf. Ch. 3, Sec. 1 of my 'The Learning of Wang Yang-ming and a Re-evaluation. ...', op. cit.
14. Cf. Ch. 15 of my *The Development of the Ideas of Human Nature in Chinese Philosophy*, New Asia College, Hong Kong, and my 'The Development of the Concept of the Moral Mind from Wang Yang-ming to Wang Chi', in *Self and Society in Ming Dynasty Thought*, Columbia University Press, New York 1970.

PAUL WIENPAHL

V. Ch'an Buddhism, Western thought, and the concept of substance

The article relates Ch'an Buddhism to Western thought via the philosophy of Spinoza, in particular through the concept of substance. It shows that Spinoza abandoned this concept as a fundamental metaphysical one. The consequent re-use of 'substance' requires a re-examination of the concepts of property and identity. It is seen that Spinoza made this drastic break with Western tradition by experiencing egolessness, the psychological basis for his metaphysical moves. The move is illustrated by the development of quantum physics. Egolessness and a rethinking of identity are basic to a feeling for, if not an understanding of, Ch'an Buddhism.

It is with reluctance that I add to the verbiage about Ch'an and Zen Buddhism. For this Far Eastern form (of thought) is essentially a practice or psycho-physical exercise in which one works toward a kind of clarity of mind (reflected in a simplicity of life) in which concepts and ideas no longer have us enthralled but in which they are under control.

> I said this as a temporary expedient, but you are building up concepts from it. — Let there be silent understanding and no more. Away with all thinking and explaining.[1]

*

The central concept in Western scientific and philosophic thought is that of substance. It appears in common sense in the notion of an individual thing. Being, what is, was divided by the Greeks into substances and accidents, the latter later to be called actions, properties and qualities. What is, is things (substances) which have attributes. The substance of a thing gives it its continuity in space and time, and accounts for its having an identity. Without substance the world seems insubstantial, like a chimera, illusory, mere appearance, and individual things without identity.

Because of this substance–attribute outlook, Western thought has found Ch'an Buddhism esoteric and either difficult or impossible to understand. Probably the earliest recorded reaction to Ch'an by a Westerner in modern times was that of Pierre Bayle, the French encyclopedist. He described 'the theology of a sect of the Chinese' who based their outlook on the incomprehensible notion of nothingness. It is clear when you read his description that he was reporting on Jesuit accounts of Ch'an Buddhists or, as they called them, the followers of Foe Kaio (No-man).[2] Bayle's treatment of this sect appears in his entry on Spinoza whose 'monstrous hypothesis' he found to resemble closely the views of the followers of Foe and the heart of which helps to relate Ch'an to Western philosophy.

I shall examine the basis of Spinoza's thought briefly to expose what caused Bayle to see that which is in fact more than a resemblance between this philosophy and Ch'an Buddhism. The interest here lies not in an historical fact, which is albeit consumingly intriguing, but in the fact that Spinoza had gone completely counter to the Western tradition. In doing so he opened new vistas for the West which are being realized today in the 'new consciousness', in the theoretical foundations of quantum mechanics, and in our notions of identity. More importantly for our purposes in the present article, Spinoza laid the ground by these means for an understanding by Westerners of one of the great spiritual developments of the Far East, Ch'an Buddhism. We shall see that he came to abandon the concept of substance, or to give 'substance' a quite new usage which corresponds to the Buddhist's 'no-substance', and which brings attention to identity in a fashion characteristic of the latter. I shall then indicate that Spinoza came to his great break with our past by a deep turning to experience uncharacteristic of even the most empirical of our philosophers, and finding in himself what the practitioner of Ch'an finds: egolessness.

In psychological terms, Spinoza's 'metaphysics', in which the concept of substance dissolved, is an expression of egolessness, emptiness, or nothingness, the notion central to any discussion of Ch'an Buddhism.[3]

> and whatever has form is illusory ... but whosoever perceives a self in matter is travelling the wrong path ...

I

Spinoza's correspondents found his metaphysics (i.e. Part I of the *Ethics*) the only difficult part of his philosophy. They repeatedly, as men have since, returned to the facets of one problem which they expressed in different questions. This problem centered around the major insight in Spinoza's philosophy. We shall see why he never settled it, even for the most sympathetic and acute of his friends, and why he remains a solitary figure without followers. It is necessary to have the insight before us to do this.

The questions raised by Part I of the *Ethics* are, for example:
(1) How can you prove God's existence from the idea or definition of Him? (2) Why is there only *one* substance (God), or why is God unique? (3) How can existence and essence be the same in the case of a substance or God? (4) Does Spinoza's determinism not excuse all wickedness? (5) Why can two substances not have the same attribute, or an attribute in common?[4]

The central thesis of Spinoza's metaphysics is expressed in Prop. V, Part I, *Ethics*: 'In the nature of things there cannot be two or more substances of the same nature or attribute.'[5] The demonstration or explanation of this proposition is that things are distinguishable from each other only by differences of attributes (Prop. IV) because the attributes give the essence of the thing (Def. IV). Thus, if two things (substances) have the same attributes they must be identical. Or, what comes to the same, there cannot be two things of the same nature or attribute.

Prop. V implies that there cannot be two or more substances, that is, that there can be only one (Demonstration, Prop. V).

> By saying that they are all of one substance, we mean that their names and forms, their existence and non-existence, are void ... All these alike ... from the Buddhas to the meanest of crawling reptiles or insects ... are all of the substance of the One Mind.[6]

This is readily seen by the following argument. Suppose that there were two substances. Call them *A* and *B*. However, the conception of *A* (any description of *A*) would involve (mention of)*B*. For example, to understand *A* you would have to know that it is different from *B*. But that would mean that *A* is not a substance because a substance is (by Def. III) that the conception of which does not involve the conception of anything else. Thus, the hypothesis that there can be two substances is reduced to an absurdity.

One must understand Prop. V fully to see its crucial nature. Thus, it must be seen that asserting it is equivalent to saying that *a substance is identical with its attributes.* Since men have read him, you find that there is something fundamental in Spinoza's thought which we either miss or are kept from recognizing by an attitude deep within us. We have in this equivalence a way of putting the difficulty. Western thought has been traditionally based on the *distinction* between substance and attribute, a thing and its properties. Grammatically the distinction is that between subject and predicate. Spinoza had abandoned the distinction as a metaphysical one.[7]

> Anything possessing *any* signs is illusory ... Just as apes spend their time throwing things away and picking them up again unceasingly, so it is with you and your learning. All you need is to give up your 'learning' and 'enlightened', 'pure' and 'impure', 'great' and 'little' ... Such things are mere conveniences ... really you must give them up!

A deeper aspect of Prop. V is that it leads us to saying that a substance must exist, that it necessarily exists, that the essence of a substance includes its existence. Thus, having identified God as the one substance, when Spinoza 'proves' that God exists he is simply *explaining* the basis of his outlook.

Because of ingrained prejudices this is difficult to see. However, a glimpse of it comes with Spinoza's distinction between modes and substances or attributes. Given that there is only *one* substance, there cannot be separate things or substances in the world. Therefore, Spinoza describes what we ordinarily call 'things' as *modes* of what is, or being. The ancient division of being into substance and attributes is completely changed. Being is now divided into modes. This enables Spinoza to see and claim that 'existence' as it applies to being has a usage different from that which it has when it is used for ordinary things. Therefore, when Spinoza says that being exists he is saying something different from that when we say that a table exists or Paul exists.[8] What he is saying in effect is that what has been called 'substance' is its attributes, which comes to saying that being is divisible into modes which are what we ordinarily call individual things. To say that a certain individual 'thing' (mode) exists is to make an existence-claim of the ordinary sort.

Additional help with the identification of substance and attribute, or the introduction of the new notion of 'mode', and therefore with the virtual identification of essence and existence, comes with observing that there *is* a distinction between so-called substance and attribute but it is a *grammatical* one. It is the difference between the uses of 'substance' and attribute'.[9] In like fashion, when Spinoza says, 'God exists', he is using 'exists' in a way grammatically different from its use in 'dogs exist'. He is saying that God or Being is its attributes and that its essence is to exist. And, indeed, the essence of being is to exist. To be is to be. Being *is* existing. 'Being' means 'existing'. This, you may feel, turns existence into a property. But it is rather that Spinoza is using 'exists' *nominally* instead of *verbally* in God's case (as a noun instead of a verb, if you wish). And, if God *is* his properties (one of which is that he is self-caused), then He 'exists'. *Nominally*, God or Being *is* existence.

It is of great importance to realize that *this manner of speaking* is Spinoza's way of putting his fundamental insight across. We return to the matter later when we will be speaking psychologically rather than metaphysically. However, *Webster's International Dictionary* (2nd ed.) is of further assistance in the present vein. 'Existence' is defined as 'a state or fact of having being'. Note that existence is to *have* being. The definition also says of existence that it is 'reality as opposed to appearances, obs.'. And Spinoza *is* saying that reality *is* appearance. (*That* is another version of 'substance and attribute are identical'.) The definition further refers us to the word 'essence'. 'Essence', def. 4, is existence. Essence is also described, def. 1, as 'an equivalent of Aristotle's category *ousia* (more commonly translated *substance*)'.

> There's never been a single thing;
> Then where's defiling dust to cling?[10]

II

That a thing is *not* its properties seems so natural as to be necessary and, in Wittgenstein's phrase, our language repeats it to us inexorably. We say, '*he* does *this*', '*it* does *that*', '*Paul* is *tall*'. However, there are several ways of seeing that at the heart of Spinoza's outlook there is the identification of substance with attribute (property), which comes to abandoning the former as a metaphysical concept and consequently redefining the latter.[9] The first of these is in the demonstration of Prop. V (if two things differ 'only by the difference of their attributes, it will be granted that there cannot be more than one with identical attributes'). The demonstration, that is, comes to an expression of the principle of the identity of indiscernibles, that two things cannot differ solely in number (*solo numero*). If two things have the same property they are identical. To count them you would have to be able to distinguish them which is impossible if they have identical attributes. The principle amounts to identifying a thing with its properties.

The principle has a long history in Western thought and is closely related to another which has been absolutely fundamental: the logical law of identity, A = A.[11] Employment of the principle has been extremely confused because of two ambiguities in it. The one lies in the Western concept of identity itself. The other in the question of what is to count as an individual thing, and is based on confusing application of the law of identity on the one hand to things and on the other to their properties.

The ambiguity in 'identity' is reflected in all our dictionaries. The word 'identify' means, on the one hand, to be separated out as an individual, to be distinguished from other things and thus to be nameable. On the other hand, it means to become one with another, to lose identity in the first sense. The second ambiguity may be seen as follows. Two men can be the same in the sense that they are both rational, that is, if we count their properties as essential for saying that they are the same. On the other hand, Spinoza cannot be the same individual as the man who made an attempt on his life. That is to say, if you regard them as individuals, regardless of the sameness of some of their properties, they cannot be one but must be two. If, however, an individual is regarded as a collection of properties, then, if two have the same properties, they are the same. In other words, if the distinction between individuality (being a substance or thing) and property or qualification is broken down, our conventional way of looking at both *and* at identity of individuals takes on a basically new aspect. The conceptual foundations of Western thought quiver.

A development of this sort has occurred outside of philosophy in physics. In Aristotelian and Newtonian physics it was assumed that there is identity of individuals, that is, that individual things can be distinguished from each other and that they can be because they are in fact individual. However, an important break occurred between Aristotelian and Newtonian physics which made the latter possible. This is that, whereas Aristotle had accepted all properties or qualities as of the same kind, Newton employed the distinction between what were being called primary properties and secondary qualities. The basis for the distinction is that secondary qualities are relative to the observer. Primary properties are not. Thus odor depends on who is doing the smelling. Weight does not depend on who is doing the weighing. Newtonian physics, however, continued to accept the identity of individuals, that is, that in addition to his properties an individual was composed of a substance which remained unchanged however much his properties might change. Weight does not depend on who observes or measures it in a thing, but it may change in the same individual.

Certain observations began to appear which eventually produced further changes in the conceptual foundations of physics. For example, it was found that light behaved in ways which could be accounted for by assuming that light is propagated in waves. It was also observed that light behaves at times as though it were particles. The wave and the particle theories of light resulted, an unsatisfactory situation in which incompatible theories accounted for the same, or identical, phenomenon.

Later in the development of atomic physics it was observed that it is impossible to specify both the position and velocity of an elementary particle at the same time. Physicists began to talk of indeterminacy, and to realize that an observation affects what is observed. In other words, the distinction between primary properties and secondary qualities began to blur.

In this situation, and working in quantum mechanics, Niels Bohr finally resolved the physicists' multiplying dilemmas by introducing in 1925 the idea of complementarity. Non-physicists see its force most easily in relation to the opposition between the wave and particle theories for which it was in fact proposed. The idea is that the two theories complement each other. Therefore, let us in theory as well as in practice accept both.

The momentous step here is that, philosophically speaking, the physicists had come to abandoning the distinction between a substance or thing and its properties. Light came to be regarded no longer as some thing in nature which will be finally identified either as wave or as particle. *It* came to be seen as wave or particle, that is, as these *properties* or those, depending on how we wished to treat it, that is, upon the context in which we are dealing with them (not it). In Jammer's words, the 'language of contemporary physics' ceased to be one of individuals with properties and became one of *'processes'*. The whole idea of property has been re-constituted and with it, of course, that of individuality (or substance). In turn this means that our idea of identity had also been *loosened*. We can now no longer speak strictly of identifying elementary particles.

The physicists came to take this momentous step only with dragging feet. Their reluctance was monumental. One can see why when one reflects that it required not merely a change in the conceptual foundations of physics. It implied or went with a similar change in our notions of what it is to be a person, of personal identity. The physicist had been faced not merely with an irrationality. He had been faced with a destruction of his own individuality. Or, at the very least, with his *idea* of it. If we must accept the fact that we can no longer identify elementary particles, the basis itself of the material world, so we must face the fact that personal identity (identification) has also just been a way of looking at our lives. As we must come to treat physical particles statistically, that is, only in large numbers, so we must come to see individual persons as no longer individuals, but *really* (metaphysically) as not distinguishable from the mass of people.

We are now in a position to see more clearly what it was that Pierre Bayle had called Spinoza's 'monstrous hypothesis' comes to and why Bayle could have called it *monstrous*. We see, further, why people shrank from Spinoza's views, though when they knew him personally they loved him as a man.[12] What Spinoza had seen was that there is the other way of identifying. We can become separate individuals and be named. But we can also lose this identity and merge with the world. We can identify with Being. This Spinoza called the union which the mind has with the whole of nature. When he called it this in the *Essay on the Improvement of the Understanding* he also said that it is our highest good, and contrasted it with money, fame, and sensual pleasure as the goals of men. In the *Ethics* he called it the understanding Love of God and spoke of it as our highest virtue, or our greatest strength.

> The very nature of the Great Way is voidness of opposition. Bodhidharma firmly believed in being *one with the real 'substance' of the universe in this life*! – The moment of realizing the unity of Mind and the 'substance' which constitutes reality may truly be said to baffle description.[13]

III

We may now move further into Spinoza's insight expressed in Prop. V and come thereby to other ways in which he prepares us for understanding Ch'an Buddhism. Spinoza had found 'substance' useless and in effect re-examined identity. This may be further appreciated by seeing that Spinoza's whole philosophy unfolds from it or becomes understandable by means of it. The identification of substance and attribute is equivalent to saying that there is only one substance and this is equivalent to saying that there are no substances, that is, that we can abandon the concept, at least as a fundamental one. In Buddhist terms, Spinoza came to the idea of no-substance, or to no-substances. In Western terms again, this is to abandon metaphysics, for the concept of substance is the basic concept of metaphysics.

Whoever perceives a self in matter is travelling the wrong path.

Help in seeing this is provided by some medieval terminology which Spinoza employed. It depends on distinguishing between modal distinctions, real distinctions, and distinctions of reason. Modal distinctions are those between a substance and a property or between two properties. Real distinctions are those between two substances. Distinctions of reason are those *we make* in order to be able to think or talk about things. For Descartes, for example, there were real distinctions between God and the world, between mind and matter, and presumably between minds. The fundamental point of Spinoza's philosophy is that *there are no real distinctions*. There are only modal distinctions and distinctions of reason. From this all the rest unfolds.

> The substance of the Absolute is inwardly like wood or stone, in that it is motionless, and outwardly like the void, in that it is without bounds or obstructions. — (This) is a warning against conceiving of entities as existing or not existing and thereby falling into the error or special separateness.[14]

A table is not really distinct from a chair, or you from me. Consequently all the so-called real things in existence are simply modes of being. They do not have an existence on their own. Substance, now with a capital 'S' for it is another name for God or Being, is their immanent cause not their transeunt cause. That is, Substance *is* the so-called things. It follows that God and Being are one, and the Appendix to Part I of the *Ethics* is a denunciation of anthropomorphism.

> Learn not to pay attention to any distinctions between this and that arising from your sensations, thereby purging your bodies of *useless* discernments between one phenomenon and another.[14]

And so all the distinctions go except in so far as they are distinctions which *we* make for our purposes. The distinction between mind and body, our minds and our bodies, your mind and mine. The distinction between subject and object goes, except in so far as we make it. The distinctions between good and evil, and between willing and understanding. All *dualism* goes.

> A perception, sudden as blinking, that subject and object are one will lead to a deeply mysterious wordless understanding. — Transcending the Three Worlds connotes rising beyond the dualism of good and evil. Buddhas appear in the world in order to make an end of desire, of form and of formless phenomena.[15]

Making the distinction between minds, between persons, real, creates the problems of solipsism and other minds, as well as the problem of proving God's existence in the ordinary sense of that term. If there are no separate things, except modally, these problems do not arise. Hence, too, Spinoza's assurance that God exists and his abandonment of metaphysics. Nor are any of these problems puzzles for the Ch'an Buddhist. Their absence in discussions of Ch'an and the absence in it of any metaphysics account in part for the feeling of strangeness a Westerner has with Ch'an, which is correctly but misleadingly expressed by saying that Ch'an is not a philosophy at all but a way of life.

One of the things the Ch'an Buddhist tries to get rid of in the practice of *Ch'an* or meditation, to quiet our 'monkey minds', is philosophical speculation. The Buddha responded to metaphysical questions by refusing to answer them, and urging the questioner to forget them and to get on to something important.[16]

— It should be emphasized here that what distinguishes Ch'an from other forms of Buddhism is the practice of Ch'an or meditation. 'Ch'an' means meditation. This consists in going beyond words and all speculation. For this we have no equivalent in current Western 'thought', though Spinoza speaks of something like it as a method of improving the understanding, and it is in the neo-Platonic tradition. —

> 'Subhuti, what do you think? Are there many particles of dust in the universe?' Subhuti replied: 'Many, Honored One!' 'Subhuti, the Tathagata says these particles of dust are not (real), (but) are (merely) *called* particles of dust.'[17]

The denial of real distinctions also requires an epistemology unique in Western thought except perhaps for Plato, and for the neo-Platonists. Thus Spinoza described what might be called three levels of awareness. On the first we are aware of 'things' (perception). On the second we are aware of, or establish, relations between them. We do this by means of ideas or concepts and on this level it is, strictly speaking, the concepts of which we are aware (opinion and reason). On this level a distinction between things is made *and* a distinction between things and us, the so-called subject–object distinction. However, since no distinctions are real, there must be a third level of awareness, that is, a level in which the distinctions, particularly that between subject and object, disappear. Spinoza calls this 'science intuitive'. It is very hard to talk about because mostly when we talk, at least *about* things, we are trying to be rational, which means that we are employing the subject–object distinction. For this reason much mystery has been made of Spinoza's science intuitive and the Buddhists' Awakening or Enlightenment.

> Give up those erroneous thoughts leading to false distinctions! There is no 'self' and no 'other'.[18]

Out of all this comes Spinoza's determinism. If nothing in the world is really distinct from anything else, then everything is related. This acceptance of determinism in turn leads to Spinoza's notion of freedom, which is the crux of the ethical portion of his outlook. Freedom cannot consist in anything like freedom of action which implies a free agent, for there are no *agents* (substances). Freedom lies in intuitive understanding, where there is no distinction between knowing and doing.

> There are three kinds of relinquishment. When everything inside and outside, bodily and mental, has been relinquished; when as in the Void, no attachments are left; when all action is dictated purely by place and circumstance; when subjectivity and objectivity are forgotten — that is the highest form of relinquishment.[19]

IV

There is yet another way of understanding Spinoza's identification of substance and attribute and his consequent abandonment of the concept of substance. This way lies through the man's life. On it we come more practically and less abstractly to the resemblance between Spinoza and the Ch'an Buddhist. It has been said of Spinoza's philosophy, the *Ethics*, that it has a unity which no other philosophical work has. This unity was characteristic of the man *and* his work, of the man as well as his work. The *Ethics* is Spinoza in words.

There is logic behind the abandonment of substance and the new talk of modes. But there is a force far more compelling. For Spinoza it was so overwhelming that it made his written work take the deductive form, the most certain we have for presenting ideas. For it seemed to Spinoza that what he was saying was absolutely necessary. It was inconceivable that it could be otherwise. It had to be.

The force here was the force of Spinoza's life itself. The force of experience. More than intellect was driving him to say what he did. His whole being was. For in saying that there are no *substances*, Spinoza was expressing his own *egolessness*. He was expressing his detachment, his *sense* of wholeness and his wholeness. His conception of God is a description of himself. It is a paradigm of self-knowledge. Just as God is not *a* substance, so was Spinoza not an agent in his own eyes. The egoless man *is* what he does. He has seen through the idea of self or ego (the agent), which in metaphysics is the idea of substance.

Lest this seem far-fetched we have only to look at Spinoza's list 'of the other attributes of God' in, for example, Letter XXXV. It comprises the properties of an egoless man. God, it is said, is eternal, has no parts, is unlimited (infinite), indivisible and perfect. When these terms are 'translated' psychologically they give the picture of the egoless man familiar to any reader of the literature of Ch'an Buddhism. He is untroubled by thoughts of the past and the future, he is out of time (eternal); he contains all that is necessary to him (unlimited); he is simple (has no parts); he does not have contra-dictory impulses (is indivisible); and he has no imperfections (is perfect). — It is advisable here to add that egolessness is a matter of degrees. In this too Spinoza and the Ch'an Buddhist are in agreement. It is not an absolute condition. One becomes egoless and there is no end to the becoming except death, the only final union.

In grounding Spinoza's 'thought' thus in experience rather than logic, I am simply reporting what he himself tells us. Throughout the *Ethics* he stresses the importance of experience. And, like Wittgen-stein who repeats, 'Don't think, but look!', Spinoza approaches the end of the *Ethics* with an admonition that clearly could come only from a man who was not speculating but was putting experiences into words. 'For although I showed generally in the First Part that all things (and consequently the human Mind also) depend on God with respect to essence and existence, yet that demonstration, though legitimate and placed beyond all chance of doubt, nevertheless *does not so affect our Mind as when* the same thing *is concluded from* the essence itself of *some single thing*, which we say depends on God.'[20]

Elsewhere, in Letter XII, Spinoza wrote, 'but we can only explain the existence of Substance by Eternity, that is, the infinite enjoyment of existence or (in unwilling Latin) *essendi*'. He apologized for the gerund, but he wanted, as I have suggested, to speak *nominally* of existing and had, therefore, to use a noun form of a verb which is rare in classical Latin and which the ancients themselves found difficult.

We have struggled metaphysically with the involvement of existence in essence in God's case. Let us now look at it experientially. Look at the metaphysical equivalence 'a substance is its attributes' = 'no substances' = 'God exists' from the aspect of a man growing egoless. One of his early feelings in the process he may express with the cry, 'I am'. This is the cry of *being*. With this step he may think, too, that he *does* after all have a soul, that he has a will of his own, that the talk of free will *has* been true. With this step he feels alone, individual and strong; capable of independent action. 'God exists!' expresses the next step. It is the cry of further awakening. He may have been told by a mentor to feel the strength of the world behind him. He now sees that the new strength he feels *is* the strength of the world (or God, in another manner of speaking; Huang Po called it One Mind). It just seemed to be his when he first felt it and cried, '*I* am'. (If you want explanations here, perhaps it seemed to be his because its locus, when first felt, was [in] him.)

'God must exist' is a fuller expression of egolessness that 'I am'. The man who cries thus is seeing through his agency. And, seeing, he is relinquishing it (or the idea of it, for that is all that it is). He then comes to accept everything. He *is what* he is. 'Is' and 'what' are identified.

The next step is not to speak at all. Or rather, it is to understand that egolessness is ineffable. This is when one sees through metaphysics. A further step is made when he is able to go back to using terms like 'God', but without being hung-up on them, as one is prior to any of these steps.

We are now in position to see again, but more fully, why Spinoza's readers, and now add 'of Ch'an', bog down in a single mire of difficulty with these thoughts. There are two reasons, a philosophical and a psychological one. The first is that they are trying to understand and accept a proposition which is in opposition to the heart of our traditional metaphysical outlook, the proposition that a thing *is* its properties and actions, that there are no things, no substances. They are being asked to abandon metaphysics, which is endemic, particularly to Western thought though it affects all who speak and must grow up to be individuals before they can find union with others.

The second reason is better regarded as a cause of his readers' inability to understand Spinoza, which is precisely comparable to the Westerners' inability to understand Ch'an Buddhism. Spinoza could accept the abandonment of substance. Because of his own egolessness he could accept the relinquishing of substance, of personal identity, and his own union with the other. Indeed, the abandonment is an *expression* of this egolessness. Ironically it was this at bottom which led men to speak of his 'monstrous hypothesis' and which made it impossible for even those who knew him to understand Spinoza, *though they loved him.* For to understand him they had to be as egoless as he (Axiom V, Part I: 'Things which have nothing in common cannot be understood, the one by means of the other.'). And egolessness is barely, if at all, brought about by conversation. One comes to it by a variety of causes and circumstances. Talking may help, but only very little. Mostly it is a thing done on one's own. There may be helping hands, but, for example, you learn to stand and then to walk alone.

> And by this (wordless) understanding you will awake to the truth of Ch'an. When you happen upon someone who has no understanding, you must claim to know nothing. He may be delighted by his discovery of some 'way to Enlightenment'; yet if you allow yourselves to be persuaded by him, *you* will experience no delight at all, but suffer both sorrow and disappointment. What have such thoughts as his to do with the study of Ch'an? Even if you do obtain from him some trifling 'method', it will only be a thought-constructed dharma having nothing to do with Ch'an. Thus, Bodhidharma sat rapt in meditation (Ch'an) before a wall; he did not seek to lead people into having opinions.[21]

Spinoza's readers ask why there is only one God (Perfect Being). The answer is that there cannot be two things with identical properties because a thing is its properties. How can you prove a thing's existence from the idea of it? Because *in the case of a substance* to see that it *must* exist is simply to see that it is not distinct from its properties. Existence *is* a property (the word can be used as a noun), but only in the case of *speaking* of Substance. With modes the matter is different. And when speaking of them, too, we do employ the distinction of subject and object and on this level of understanding we then see men as agents of their actions. Then, too, the idea of wickedness is useful. But finally it is just a manner of speaking. Determinism does not *excuse* wickedness. It is rather that, properly (intuitively) understood, men's lives are not marked by wickedness (or right doing).

There are simply foibles and strengths. Finally, why can't two substances have the same attribute or an attribute in common? Because
a substance is its attributes or attribute. More basically, because
there is only *one* substance. And this we can now, I hope, see comes
to saying that there are no substances — which returns us to egolessness.

When viewed 'under the aspect of eternity', that is, as though he
were Substance, a man is seen as egoless. He is self-less. Such a man
no longer regards himself as the agent of his actions. Consequently he
accepts all things. Acceptance is being.

> ... when all action is dictated purely by place and circumstance; ...
> So they were called 'Sages, who, abandoning learning have come to
> rest in spontaneity (*wu wei*)'. ... just allowing things to take their
> course the whole day long as though you were too ill to bother.[22]

V

There is a difficulty with this presentation. How can we claim to
understand what others have not and thus seem to partake of the
egolessness of Spinoza? Several things may be said here.

The first is that egolessness is not new to the West. It is only relatively new to contemporary Western *philosophy*, for it can be decried
in neo-Platonism and the mystical tradition in the Christianity of
the Middle Ages. Secondly, in a curiously unofficial way it has been
part of our history. While intellectually not reputable since the rise of
modern science, it has been emotionally accepted in what we call
religion, though it has not been much lived in that area of our lives.
Thirdly, there is now a growing awareness of egolessness and hence
of Spinoza and Ch'an in our time. It is part of the new consciousness,
of the sometimes-called 'cultural revolution'.

Finally, as you become acquainted with Ch'an (meditation) and
with Spinoza's philosophy, you learn, as I have indicated, that egolessness (i.e. an aspect of Spinoza's science intuitive) is not some
absolute condition which you either have or do not have. It is a
matter of degrees. Further, it may start as an idea, as an awareness
of it. It may also start in our unconscious or as a part of our lives
without our being aware of it. Thus, readers will know what I am
talking about, in these times and with some of our history, and I can
talk about it without either of us being whole. As Spinoza has it, our
bondage lies in this that we can see the better and follow the worse.[23]
We can reason about egolessness without being egoless. Knowing is

easy. Being is hard. The *Ethics* closes with, 'All things excellent are as difficult as they are rare'. Huang Po said, 'Be diligent! Of a thousand or ten thousand attempting to enter by this Gate, only three or perhaps five pass through'.

NOTES

1. Huang Po. Quoted from *The Zen Teaching of Huang Po*, 'On the Transmission of Mind', trans. by John Blofeld, Grove Press, Inc., New York 1959, pp. 34, 53.
   To be as little misleading as possible in this article, and to accomplish my purpose, I shall intersperse it with quotations from Huang Po. The advice in those just quoted is crucial to Ch'an Buddhism. It is repeated throughout the recorded teaching of Huang Po, for example, pp. 27, 31, 33, 43, 55, 56, 67, 69, 79, 81, 89, and the last two, 131–2.
2. See *The Dictionary Historical and Critical of Mr. Peter Bayle*, The Second Edition, Volume the Fifth, London MDCCXXXVIII, 'Spinoza'. The Chinese name is Bayle's version. His account is based on reports by the first Westerners since the Middle Ages, the Jesuits, to bring us some information about Far Eastern philosophy and religion. Their reports were published in Paris in the 1600s shortly prior to Bayle's work on his dictionary. These reports and Bayle's use of them have, to my knowledge, gone unnoticed in the literature on Ch'an Buddhism since interest in it developed during the past forty years.
3. The Buddhist terms 'ego' and its variants like 'egolessness', which appear in this article, are unrelated to the Freudian 'ego', though they approximate our ordinary use of 'ego'. Following is a definition of 'ego' in the Buddhist sense:
   'Ego: according to Buddhism, the notion of an ego, i.e., awareness of oneself as a discrete individuality, is a delusion. It arises because, misled by our bifurcating intellect into postulating the dualism of "myself" and "not myself", we are led to think and act as though we were a separated entity confronted by a world external to us. Thus in the unconscious the idea of "I" or self-hood, becomes fixed, and from this arises such patterns as "I hate this, I love that", "This is mine, that is yours." Nourished by this fodder, the ego-I comes to dominate the mind, attacking whatever threatens its domination and grasping at anything which will enlarge its power. Antagonism, greed and alienation culminating in suffering, are the inevitable consequences of this circular process.' Philip Kapleau, *The Three Pillars of Zen*, John Weatherhill, Inc., Tokyo 1965, p. 239. This has been re-issued in the United States by Harper & Row.
   Egolessness, or being free of the ego, is also called enlightenment or awakening. The word 'Buddha' comes from a Sanskrit root which means 'to awaken'.
   The 'self' in the quotation from Huang Po, p. 73, which follows, corresponds to our 'substance'. Mainly when the Buddhist talks of human experience he talks of sentient beings, i.e. psychologically rather than metaphysically. Thus the less animate analogue of 'self', 'substance', is less likely to appear in his teaching.
4. Spinoza had a technical and a non-technical use of 'attribute'. The technical is given by Def. IV, Pt. I. According to this, an attribute is a mode of perception. His non-technical use was the common one of his and our day. Ac-

cording to it, an attribute is like a property or quality of a thing. It differs from these in being more general. Thus, redness is a property of some things. Extension is an attribute of the whole physical world. In Prop. V the use is closer to the non-technical than the technical. Spinoza's thought had moved from dualism, characteristic of the West, to what is styled non-dualism by the Ch'an Buddhist. In this shift, as we shall see, the concept of substance is abandoned or becomes unimportant. Consequently the terms 'attribute', 'property' and 'quality', traditionally defined in terms of 'substance', acquire new uses. Spinoza outlined this in his technical use of 'attribute' which he defined as 'that which the understanding perceives of a substance, *as if* constituting its essence' (Def. IV, italics added). Because his thought was sharply transitional he was hampered by customary terminology. He employed the terms (to be understood at all), but they were given a new usage in the context of the *Ethics*. Thus with 'property' and 'quality'. The subject is important and requires much space. Fortunately for our purposes we do not have to enter into it.

5. Any edition of the *Ethics*. Translations are mine. Spinoza's thought is set forth in the order: definitions, axioms, propositions, demonstrations, and scholia. The so-called 'demonstrations' are rather explanations of the propositions which expand the definitions with the aid of the axioms. The scholia are further unfoldings.

6. Huang Po, pp. 87, 109.

7. Early on in his work Spinoza was aware of the difference between grammatical and metaphysical, or, as we shall also call them, real distinctions, and the trouble confusion between them can cause. 'However', he wrote, 'I do not wonder that philosophers sometimes fall into these verbal and grammatical errors. For they judge objects from names and not names from objects.' *Cogitata Metaphysica*, in *The Principles of Descartes' Philosophy*, trans. by H. H. Britan, The Open Court Publishing Company, La Salle, Illinois 1943, p. 117. The quotation following in the text is from Huang Po, p. 71.

8. This is a bit careless, but care on the point is beyond the scope of this article. 'Exist' goes improperly with proper names. However, 'being' becomes, as will be seen, a proper name.

9. As we have noted, if you re-use 'substance' you must re-examine 'attribute'. And Spinoza did redefine the latter as referring to a mode of perception (instead of an aspect of a thing). Further, in the early days, 1663, he wrote: 'I wish you to understand by substance and attribute the same ... except that it is called attribute with respect to the understanding, which attributes such and such a nature to substances.' Letter II, *The Correspondence of Spinoza*, ed. and trans. by A. Wolf, Russell & Russell, New York 1966. Cf. '*Essence* is expressed by grammar'. L. Wittgenstein, *Philosophical Investigations*, Blackwell, Oxford 1958, § 371.

10. Huang Po, p. 110.

11. For this history see Max Jammer's *The Conceptual Development of Quantum Mechanics*, McGraw-Hill Book Co., New York 1966, Secs. 1.1, 4.2, 7.2, and 'Concluding Remarks'.

12. Bayle, by the way, attacked Spinoza precisely at the point of Prop. V. However, the consequences of the abandonment of the concept of substance as a foundation of our thinking, which we now see as an abandonment of a funda-

mental notion of identity, is apparent in all the rest of Spinoza's philosophy. He had himself to call special attention to these consequences with the full awareness that they went counter to our basic ways of looking at things. Thus, for example, when he said that the foundation of virtue itself is self-interest and that virtue is its own reward, he had to admit how contrary to the conventional outlook both of these results of his thinking are. See Props. XVIII, Scholium, Pt. IV, and XLI and XLII, Pt. V.

13. Huang Po, p. 70. Spinoza criticized the traditional goals of men on the basis that we become attached to them. They enthral us. Like the Ch'an Buddhist Spinoza prized detachment. See P. Wienpahl, 'Spinoza and Wang Yang-ming', *Religious Studies*, Vol. 5 (October, 1969) No. 1, pp. 19–27. Spinoza might as well have been compared to Wang Yang-ming for our purposes as to Huang Po. However, Chinese scholars are inclined to list Wang Yang-ming as a neo-Confucian rather than a Ch'an Buddhist. This inclination is based, I think, rather on historical details and understandable prejudice than empirical data. Wang Yang-ming could not have spoken as he did without the experience of Ch'an (meditation).

14. Huang Po, pp. 32, 74, 199 (italics added). But see also pp. 35, 68, 70, 71, 72 and 81–82. Spinoza defines real, etc., distinctions in Ch. I of the *Cogitata Metaphysica*, pp. 115–21.

15. Huang Po, pp. 86, 92.

16. See, for example E. A. Burtt, *The Teachings of the Compassionate Buddha*, Meridian Books, New York 1955, p. 34.

17. *The Diamond Sutra*, trans. by Lu K'uan Yü, in *Ch'an and Zen Teaching*, Rider & Company, London 1960, Series One, p. 178, italics added.

Spinoza's reference to his method, which is enormously important and largely ignored in accounts of him, is in Letter XXXVII. The translations of this are crucially faulty, having 'conceive' where Spinoza had 'perceive'.

18. Huang Po, p. 88. As noted, 'Buddha' means 'awakened'. Spinoza was fond of comparing ordinary experience to dreaming with our eyes open. See, for example, end of Scholium, Prop. II, Pt. III. The metaphor also occurs in a footnote in the *Essay on the Improvement of the Understanding*.

19. Huang Po, p. 49.

20. Scholium, Prop. XXXV, Pt. V, italics added. The phrase 'the essence of' is Spinoza's way in the *Ethics* of calling attention to a single thing independently of its relation to others, to the, paradoxically, existential thing, or the thing as existing. In the *Essay on the Improvement of the Understanding* he employs the phrase 'uncreated things' for this purpose.

The quotation from Wittgenstein is § 66 in the *Philosophical Investigations*.

21. Huang Po, pp. 92–93. I have substituted 'Ch'an' for 'Zen' in the translation because we have used the Chinese word for the original Sanskrit 'dhyāna' throughout. I cannot stress too strongly that 'Ch'an' means meditation. To understand it, therefore, you have to do it. Beyond this there is nothing. See P. Wienpahl, *The Matter of Zen*, New York University Press, New York 1964, and *Zen Diary*, Harper & Row, New York 1970.

22. Huang Po, pp. 45, 56, 90.

23. Scholium, Prop. XVII, Pt. IV. The final quotation is from Huang Po, pp. 131–2, which end the record.

WILLIAM L. CHESHIER

VI. The term 'Mind' in Huang Po's text Huang Po Ch'uan Hsin Fa Yao

For the Western philosopher the most difficult idea to understand is the Zen (Ch'an) notion of 'Mind', which is a key to understanding Zen Buddhism. In order to transmit the idea of 'Mind' Huang Po suggests that the only successful method for understanding it is intuition. Perhaps the difficulty for the Western philosopher arises from his compulsion to analyze and his wholesale rejection of intuition as a valid method of understanding. For the Zen Buddhist, 'Mind' is a sea in which men float expecting to know it as a whole by analyzing every droplet.

Huang Po (Obaku), philosophically an important figure in Ch'an (Zen) Buddhism, uses the term 'mind' no less than two hundred and seventy times in the very short work, *Huang Po Ch'uan Hsin Fa Yao*.[1] Throughout the work he attempts to distinguish between the greater *Mind*[2] and the lesser *mind*.[3] The distinction is difficult to recognize. The problem, therefore, may be stated: Is there a difference between *Mind* and *mind*? And, if there is one, what is it?

The customary approach taken by Zen Buddhists in explaining their philosophy has been implicit and suggestive, rather than explicit and expository. Huang Po puts it:

> Thus, those who seek the goal (*Mind*) through cognition are like the fur (many), while those who obtain intuitive knowledge of the Way are like the horns (few).[4]

Therefore, as Huang Po views it, it is intuition rather than analysis that will lead us to an understanding of the idea of *Mind*. Henri Bergson has been one of the leading exponents of intuitive knowledge in Western philosophy. So, perhaps presenting Bergson's views at this point may help the reader understand Huang Po more easily. In *An Introduction to Metaphysics* he writes:

... an absolute could only be given in an intuition whilst everything else falls within the province of analysis. By intuition is meant the kind of intellectual sympathy by which one places oneself within an object in order to coincide with what is unique in it and consequently inexpressible. Analysis, on the contrary, is the operation which reduces the object to elements already known, that is, to elements common both to it and other objects. ... All analysis is thus a translation, a development into symbols. ... But intuition ... is a simple act.[5]

Bergson maintains that analysis employs concepts to express intuition. But the former cannot really transfer the essence of the latter. For conceptual analysis is the employment of symbols which are substituted for the intuition, and require no more intuitive effort from the one it is directed at. Analysis attempts to *compare* one thing with another thing that resembles it. Even when many concepts of the same thing are put together they are symbols only of 'impersonal aspects' of the object. They give us only a shadow of the object.[6] As Bergson puts it: '... the error consists in believing that we can reconstruct the real ... diagrams.' And, he continues, 'from intuition one can pass to analysis, but not from analysis to intuition'.[7]

But, we may ask: How does one induce intuitive knowledge? Bergson suggests that the only method for relaying intuition is through images. Thus he says:

No image can replace the intuition ... but many diverse images, borrowed from very different orders of things may, by the convergence of their action, direct consciousness to the precise point where there is a certain intuition to be seized. By choosing images as dissimilar as possible, we shall prevent anyone of them from usurping the place of the intuition it is intended to call up, since it would then be driven away at once by its rivals.[8]

Bergson goes on to explain that we may not be sympathetic to anything except what comes from within us. Thus the object for intuition is the inner dynamic process of the self. Here Bergson makes it quite explicit:

There is one reality, at least, which we all seize from within, by intuition and not by simple analysis. It is our own personality in its flowing through time — our self which endures. We may sympathize intellectually with nothing else, but we certainly sympathize with our selves.[9]

The method of intuition is the use of images. Bergson holds that analysis can only give one an artificial, constructed notion of the object.[10] The second way (intuition) is the only way one may achieve a 'real' understanding of the object.

Huang Po believes that intuition, which implies an abandonment of structured reason, is the only way one will achieve an understanding of *Mind*. It appears that Huang Po and Bergson are both agreed regarding the role of intuition in knowing the self.

In attempting to explain *Mind*, Huang Po makes much use of imagery. However, the task of this paper is not simply to indicate and justify Huang Po's use of imagery; rather, it is to explain what the very term that Huang Po is attempting to point to means. To explain what *his* term *Mind* means we must therefore abandon the analytical procedure which fails to capture the essence of the term. Instead of 'watering down' the explanation by providing the reader with an artificial reconstruction of the idea of *Mind* expressed by Huang Po, therefore, I will attempt to employ the same technique that we find in his text, namely explanation by imagery. There are two reasons for this choice: first, it is hoped that by using the same method as Huang Po, I will be able to transmit the 'flavor' of the term to the reader; second, I believe that if I tried to *analyze* the term, this paper would become merely another forgotten attempt to fit Eastern thought into a Western structure, accomplishing very little towards an adequate understanding of Eastern thought. Let us begin, then, by examining the first part of this text.

I. The Chun Chou Record[11]

We shall begin with some examples of the images used to explain the term *Mind*.

Huang Po begins his imagery by saying that, 'The Mind ... is not green nor yellow, and has neither form nor appearance' (p. 29). In attempting to express the limitlessness of *Mind*, Huang Po merely expresses it in terms of visual preception. If one is allowed to interpret *Mind* as having characteristics, one limits it.

In his second image Huang Po compares *Mind* to the sun by saying:

> Mind is like the void in which there is no confusion or evil, as when the sun wheels through it shining upon the four corners of the whole earth, the void gains not in brilliances; and, when the sun sets, the void does not darken. The phenomena of light and dark alternate with each other, but the nature of the void remains unchanged. So it is with the Mind ... and sentient beings (p. 31).

This image represents the difficulty confronting us. Huang Po believes that it is an error to suppose that the world exists in the duality presented by the image. Huang Po wishes only to express unity, something that transcends duality.

In the following image we begin to see how Huang Po attempts to identify *Mind* in a more positive way. For him, *Mind* is equivalent to the Absolute. Thus he says:

> The substance of the Absolute is inwardly like wood or stone, in that it is motionless, and outwardly like the void, in that it is without bounds or obstructions (pp. 31–32).

These images have not been enough to transmit a complete picture of what he means by *Mind*. Further on, he develops the image:

> It is pure Mind, which is the source of everything and which, whether appearing as ... the rivers and mountains of the world which has form, as that which is formless, or as penetrating the whole universe, is absolutely without distinctions, there being no such entities as self-ness and otherness (p. 36).

It is at this point we begin to get at the meaning of the term. Huang Po continues to explain that *Mind* is not any particular thing and that by attaching ourselves to anything we will never realize *Mind*. 'Above, below and around you, all is spontaneously existing, for there is nowhere which is outside the Buddha-Mind' (p. 37). Further, he says, 'to mistake material surroundings for *Mind* is to mistake a thief for your son' (p. 42).

We find Huang Po's next image brought out in answer to a question by one of his disciples.

> *Q*: Surely the void stretching out in front of our eyes is objective. Then aren't you pointing to something objective and seeing Mind in it?
> *A*: What sort of mind could I tell you to see in an objective environment? Even if you could see it, it would only be Mind reflected in an objective sphere. You would be like a man looking at his face in a mirror; though you could distinguish your features in it clearly, you would still be looking at a mere reflection (p. 60).

This image reaffirms the idea that *Mind* is part of everything, and if we attempt to talk about something objective we cannot help but approach it with *Mind*, which is both objective and subjective. It is quite obvious that *Mind* for Huang Po transcends either objectivity or subjectivity, yet embraces both.

Again, we return to the image of the sun when he says:

> You must get away from the doctrines of existence and non-existence, for Mind is like the sun, forever in the void, shining without intending to shine (pp. 61–62).

Finally, Huang Po's last image, directs itself to the idea of transcendent unity.

> You must see clearly that there is really nothing at all — no humans and no Buddhas. The great chiliocosms, numberless as grains of sand, are mere bubbles. All wisdom and all holiness are but streaks of lightning. None of them have the reality of Mind. The Dharmakaya, from ancient times until today, together with the Buddhas and Patriarchs, is One. How can it lack a single hair of anything? (p. 64).

What have all these images suggested? First, in truth, there is no real multiplicity. That we distinguish things as individual is an error produced by our own *mind* or a result of conceptual ways of thinking. It is a false or artificial construction of what we do not really understand. You might say that it is like the small boy who sees only a few blades of grass but is unable to appreciate the beauty of the lawn. Perhaps better, it is like the scientist attempting to find a drop of water in the sea.

Second, an adequate knowledge of *Mind* will not come from attaching ourselves to the universe as we have structured it. Further, how can we attach ourselves to the universe which is reached only through our own conceptual structure? The answer is, we cannot attach ourselves at all to the universe, for, by interpreting it we pervert it. Therefore we will never know the universe by attempting to be within it while *we are inclined to see it from outside*. It is only when one releases oneself from one's conceptual analysis of the universe that one will be allowed to exercise one's *mind* freely. It might be likened to the children's toy known as Chinese handcuffs. One inserts one finger from each hand into either end of a thin wicker tube. The harder the child pulls to get his fingers out, the tighter the tube grips. The solution is to relax and gently remove one's fingers.

If we stop here, we have only answered half of the question, for the initial question asks the difference between *Mind* and *mind*.

Let us now examine the term *mind*.

The term *mind*, as Huang Po uses it, is a personal idea. Perhaps it has an empirical meaning. Huang Po says, 'Away with all thinking and explaining. Then we may say that the Way of Words has been cut off and movements of the mind eliminated' (pp. 34–35). More evidence can be found that the term *mind* is used in an empirical sense if we pay attention to the following passage where he says:

> These six sense organs become severally united with objects that defile them — the eyes with form, the ear with sound, the nose with smell, the tongue with taste, the body with touch, and the thinking mind with entities (p. 51).

It is obvious that he is definitely attempting to make a distinction between the two terms (*Mind* and *mind*) because he says:

> If you hadn't mentioned ordinary and Enlightenment who would have bothered to say such things? Just as those categories have no real existence, so Mind is not really 'mind' (pp. 58–59).

So far we have seen that there is a significant difference between *Mind* and *mind*, and that the term *mind* has an empirical basis as opposed to the unlimited *Mind*. I believe that the term *mind* refers to the personal or empirical capacity for knowing *Mind*. *Mind*, for Huang Po, is free from concept. This is because if we conceptualize *Mind* we necessarily limit it, and Huang Po says *Mind* is unlimited. There are two reasons for suggesting that *mind* is the capacity for recognizing *Mind*. First, Huang Po would not have used the same term for both ideas unless there was some connection. Secondly, he says that *mind*-transformation is the way to achieve knowledge of *Mind*.

But let us examine a few more uses of the terms.

While criticizing the approach the Hinayanists take to reach the Absolute, Huang Po says, 'Srāvakas (Hinayanists) do not comprehend their own mind but allow concepts to arise from listening to the doctrine' (p. 39). In other words, these individuals do not understand how to achieve the maximum use of their *minds*, so they simply take the common way, namely, conceptualization.

Further evidence that the term *mind* is intended to have a personal meaning is found when we read Huang Po's answers to questions from his disciples.

> *Q*: But is the Buddha the ordinary mind or the Enlightened mind?
> *A*: Where on earth do you keep your 'ordinary mind' and your 'Enlightened mind'?
> *Q*: In the teaching of the Three Vehicles it is stated that there were both. Why does Your Reverence deny it?
> *A*: In the teaching of the Three Vehicles it is clearly explained that the ordinary and Enlightened minds are illusions. You don't understand. All this clinging to the idea of things existing is to mistake vacuity for the truth. ... All this amounts to beclouding your own minds! (pp. 57–58).

Huang Po holds that the *mind* should not be the focus of attention. The attention should be directed to *Mind*. But, as in the above example, the boy may focus his attention on the individual blades of grass so much that the beauty of the lawn is lost. It is the same with those who concern themselves with their *mind*, for it is only the capacity for realizing something so much greater. But Huang Po finds that 'Men are afraid to forget their minds, fearing to fall through the Void with nothing to stay their fall' (p. 41). Again he says:

> If you would spend all your time — walking, standing, sitting or lying down — learning to halt the concept-forming activities of your own mind, you could be sure of ultimately attaining the goal. Since your strength is insufficient, you might not be able to transcend samsāra by a single leap; but, after five or ten years, you would surely have made a good beginning and be able to make further progress spontaneously. It is because you are not that sort of man that you feel obliged to employ your mind 'studying dhyāna' and 'studying the Way' (p. 63).

What then is meant by the term *mind*? We may say that *mind* is used in an empirical sense. The *mind* deals with the world and is a part of it. Nevertheless, too often it becomes misdirected because it attempts to conceptualize.

Next, *mind* is intended to indicate something personal. Every individual at least has his own *mind* which he may use in whatever manner he chooses.

Finally, *mind* is used to mean capacity. Each individual is given the capacity to become aware of *Mind*. The error comes when the individual uses this capacity to conceptualize as opposed to allowing it to realize *Mind* freely.

If we look back, we can note how Huang Po distinguishes between *Mind* and *mind* by comparing them. There are many individual comparisons that he makes between these two terms, but they may be categorized into three main ways.

First, *Mind* is used to mean something greater than *mind*. It seems reasonable that since the *mind* is part of *Mind*, it would be less than *Mind*.

Second, *Mind* is transcendent unity and the individual *mind* is a personal thing possessed by each person.

Third, the individual *mind* is an avenue for realizing *Mind*. It is our capacity for achieving an understanding of this great *Mind*.

From the preceding discussion it will be evident that there is a difference between *Mind* and *mind*. However, the actual definition of *Mind* still remains somewhat unclear. Let us examine the second part of the text, and perhaps the definition will be made clearer.

II. WAN LING RECORD

In examining the Wan Ling Record, we find that Huang Po continues to distinguish between *Mind* and *mind*.

In order to stress the unity of *Mind* he says, 'There exists just the One Mind. Truly there are no multiplicity of forms, no celestial Brilliance, and no Glorious Victory or submission to the Victor' (p. 72). But, let us examine more carefully the notion of unity.

By unity does Huang Po simply mean a collection of individual things such as the pages in a book? Is it more than this? In another passage he says:

> ... we can encompass all the vast world systems, though numberless as grains of sand, with our One Mind. Then, why talk of 'inside' and 'outside'? Honey having the invariable characteristic of sweetness, it follows that all honey is sweet. To speak of this honey as sweet and honey as bitter would be nonsensical! (p. 108).

Perhaps even the term 'unity' is misleading. For it surely implies that there are things which are unified. It suggests a multiplicity of things, at least if we employ conceptual thinking. But for those who have realized *Mind*, multiplicity itself is recognized as false — an artificial construction due to our misguided ways of cognition. Therefore, the term 'unity' is employed as an intermediate notion to explain the illusion of multiplicity. But, for one who has realized enlightenment, this term is unnecessary.

Another point in discussing the term *Mind* is that we cannot attach ourselves to the universe *as we know it*. He says:

> With the practice of the Pure Land Buddhists it is also thus, for all these practices are productive of karma; hence, we may call them Buddha-hindrances! As they would obstruct your Mind, the chain of causation would also grapple you fast, dragging you back into the state of those as yet unliberated (p. 91).

What is meant by rejecting the world? Does this mean we should all attempt to take our lives so that we can escape from the world? This is not the case. Huang Po holds that since the world in which we live is a conceptualized structure formulated as a result of our *minds*, we cannot expect to know it. Therefore, rid your *mind* of all this clouded thinking and you will realize One *Mind*. As he puts it: 'Mind is filled with radiant clarity, so cast away the darkness of your old concepts' (p. 92). Putting it another way he says, '... let no activity be the gateway of my Dharma. Such is the Gateway of the One Mind, but all who reach this gate fear to enter' (p. 131).

So, rejecting the world is not intended to mean running away from it; rather, it means a rejection of concepts which are mistaken for reality. As Huang Po imagines it:

> Outside Mind, there is nothing. The green hills which everywhere meet your gaze and the void sky that you see glistening above the earth — not a hairsbreadth of any of them exists outside the concepts you have found for yourself! So it is that every single sight and sound is but the Buddha's Eye of Wisdom (p. 82).

Thus far, it appears that the term *Mind* is meant as the actuality of the world, or the proper way of understanding the world. But, again, what then is meant by *mind*?

According to Huang Po the *mind* contains the capacity to conceptualize the world. He says, '... Mountains ... rivers, the whole world itself, together with the sun, moon and stars — not one of them exists outside the mind' (pp. 81–82). In discussing the power of the *mind* to conceptualize he says:

> Develop a mind which rests on no thing whatever (p. 88).

or,

> Our bodies are the creations of our own minds (p. 89).

The question that arises from the idea that the *mind* conceptualizes is: Why does the *mind* conceptualize? If it is natural simply to allow your *mind* to realize *Mind*, then why do most men build concepts about the world? Perhaps it is because working with concepts is a lower level of spiritual activity. Therefore, we conceptualize simply because we fail to cultivate our *mind* adequately. Then, what is the right way to develop our *mind*? Here Huang Po suggests that he has found the right way to employ one's *mind* in recognizing the true state of nature. He gives us some ideas on how to approach the problem for ourselves. He says:

> When a sudden flash of thought occurs in your mind and you recognize it for a dream or an illusion, then you can enter into the state reached by the Buddhas in the past (p. 106).

or,

> Only when your minds cease dwelling upon anything whatsoever will you come to an understanding of the true way of Zen (p. 127).

After examining the images Huang Po has used to explain the terms *Mind* and *mind*, we find that the images from both parts of the text appear to be consistent with each other. In order to help the reader remember the basic images from both parts, they will be presented again briefly.

First, *Mind* is compared to the void, and sentient beings are compared to the sun lighting up the earth but not the void.

Second, Huang Po says that *Mind* is like wood or stone inwardly and like the void outwardly.

Third, he says that mountains and rivers along with all form and all that is formless, have their sources in *Mind*.

Fourth, asking whether one can find *Mind* in the objective is like looking at a man's face in a mirror. All you see is the reflection.

Fifth, he says that all that appears is not real, only *Mind* is real.

Sixth, he says that the *Mind* has no 'inside' or 'outside'. Just as it is ridiculous to talk about honey that is either sweet or bitter.

Seventh, and finally, Huang Po says that *Mind* is perfect clarity and that concepts are nothing but darkness.

Huang Po does not use much imagery when he discusses the individual *mind*. We find him somewhat analytical. He says that the *mind* is united with entities and these entities are concepts made up in the *mind* in order to understand the world. Also, the *mind* is a personal or individual thing. He says that it is our own *minds* that create our bodies. Further, it is our *minds* that provide the vehicle for realizing *Mind*.

While studying these terms through images, the basic idea that Huang Po was attempting to express stimulated me into an exploration of some original images. Perhaps the following will help the reader to understand Huang Po's terms.

To begin, we might say that *Mind* may be compared to air. Our *minds* are like the surface of a soap bubble floating in the air. The only way the air inside the bubble can know the air outside the bubble is through the surface. But, actually the air in the bubble is the same as the air outside the bubble. Therefore, there really is no inside and no outside. When the air inside the bubble realizes this, it will know all Air.

Asking what *Mind* is, is like asking where is the universe.

Our *mind* acts as a man walking down the street seeing another man. His first act is to describe the other individual according to color, race, nationality, etc., losing sight of the fact that it is first a man.

Finally, the *Mind* is like a home to a horse. Years ago horses were quite popular in the United States. When a farmer went for a ride in his horse and buggy, quite frequently on the return trip the horse was allowed to go without having the farmer hold the reins. The horse would invariably go directly home. But, if the farmer tried to hold the reins, the horse would baulk or react in an unexpected way. This might be compared to the relationship between *Mind* and *mind*. *Mind* is represented by the home and the individual *mind* represented by the horse. If we attempt to control our *mind*, it will begin to form concepts which will result in losing sight of the goal.

It is hoped that the reader has been stimulated into creating his own intuitive understanding of the terms *Mind* and *mind*. Also, perhaps we may have discovered that it is not necessary to be a member of a particular cultural tradition in order to understand its philosophy.[12]

NOTES

1. *Huang Po Ch'uan Hsin Fa Yao* has been translated into English by John Blofeld in his book *The Zen Teachings of Huang Po*, Grove Press, Inc., New York 1958. The difficulty with this translation is that Blofeld uses *Mind* and *mind* to distinguish between the general and individual use of the term. In the Chinese text *Hsin* was the only term used to signify both *Mind* and *mind*. The problem arises from the fact that Blofeld does not make the distinction explicitly clear.
2. Throughout this paper *Mind* will designate Huang Po's usage of the term as the experience of ultimate reality.
3. Throughout this text *mind* will designate Huang Po's usage of the term as the capacity to experience *Mind*.
4. J. Blofeld, op. cit., p. 32.
5. Henri Bergson, *An Introduction to Metaphysics*, Bobbs-Merrill Co., Inc., New York 1955, pp. 23–24.
6. Ibid., p. 28.
7. Ibid., p. 42.
8. Ibid., pp. 27–28.
9. Ibid., pp. 24–25.
10. *Object* is used here in its broadest sense, not necessarily of a material thing.
11. Quotations of Huang Po in this paper are all from John Blofeld's book, *The Zen Teachings of Huang Po*. References will be in parentheses by page number immediately following the quote.
12. This article is taken from a thesis submitted by the author to the faculty of Loyola University of Chicago in June 1970. Father Edward Maziarz and Dr. Joseph Wu directed the thesis and provided immeasurable assistance. Additional gratitude goes to Dr. Joseph Wu for his personal interest without which this paper would not have been completed.

LARS JUL HANSEN

VII. An analysis of 'Autumn Floods'
in Chuang Tzu

The present essay offers an interpretation and analysis of the theory of knowledge
and metaphysics expounded in the dialogue between the Sea-Spirit and the River-
Lord in Ch. 17 of Chuang Tzu's 'Autumn Floods'. Several possible systematic
interpretations are discussed. Considerable emphasis is put on clarifying Chuang
Tzu's arrangement of the arguments into groups, and the author traces out the
steps in the reasoning. The aim has everywhere been to indicate how the logical
deductions form a homogeneous whole, the subject-matter of which is to establish knowledge of 'The Great Principle'.

I. Introduction

The present essay is an attempt to give an analytical exposition of
certain fundamental ideas in the philosophy of Chuang Tzu, mainly
based on Chapter 17, called 'Autumn Floods' (*Ch'iu Shui*), of his work.
Despite the textual difficulties involved in such a task, I shall venture
an analysis of parts of this great prose writing in an attempt to arrive
at a possible interpretation of his thoughts.

My basic assumption will be that there is a coherent system of
thought behind the literary piece called 'Chuang Tzu'. A serious student, willing to lend a sympathetic ear to the master's words, must
recognize intuitively that there are certain fundamental concepts and
ideas guiding the author, despite the far from clear way in which he
expresses them. Everyone must admit that Chuang Tzu, the traditional author, is an extremely skilled artist, and the form and language
are undoubtedly used as tools in the artist's hands. The liberty of mind
which Chuang Tzu professes as a mark of the superior man, his ideal of
personality, is also the trademark of his own style. His prose is the

expression of a free-roaming spirit, but it is nevertheless a freedom
determined by an effort to shape a great system of thought. His work
is a well-wrought mixture, abundant in contradictions, plays upon
words, parables and well-balanced rhyme-prose. In addition, a playful
and easy-going style makes it all the more difficult to interpret him
systematically. However, it is impossible to dismiss the work as a mere
play of words, or an exercise in style. It remains a philosopher's
deliberate attempt to employ language as an instrument in the expression of profound reasonings.

With the work of Chuang Tzu, it seems plausible to take his language seriously, to look upon the apparent contradictions as deliberate rather than to dismiss them as nonsense.

Sinological research has established, apparently, that the literary
work called 'Tao te ching', or 'Lao Tzu', was already written, partly
or wholly, by the time that *Chuang Tzu* was in progress. Chuang
Tzu himself quotes *Lao Tzu* several times. We have certain explicit
statements in *Lao Tzu* on the properties of its language and style (e.g.
Chs. 70 and 81), expressing opinions as to how one should convey this
particular system of ideas. The ideas are clearly regarded as transcending the possibilities of straightforward speech and language. Although
the thoughts underlying *Lao Tzu* and *Chuang Tzu* need not be identical,
Chuang Tzu borrows the viewpoints of *Lao Tzu* as to the form of
language and its shortcomings in dealing with a certain kind of
philosophy. In its brevity, *Lao Tzu* is even more elliptical and esoteric
than *Chuang Tzu*, but the main features of the style and the reasons for
the specific form remain the same in both works. Needless to add,
Chuang Tzu, in the length and breadth of its prose, exemplifies a far
more developed stage of language.

Chuang Tzu himself gives a clue to his own style when in Chapter
27 he declares:

> Of my sentences nine in ten are metaphorical; of my illustrations seven
> in ten are from valued writers. The rest of my words are like the water
> that daily fills the cup, tempered and harmonised by the Heavenly
> element in our nature.[1]

In between the illustrations and metaphors, we find long argumentational sections furnishing us with simple, straightforward statements
pointing directly to the core of his philosophy. It seems natural to
take these sections as the primary sources for our analysis.

Our purpose is to find passages which present fairly long and unin-
terrupted sequences of thought which allow the deductions and con-

clusions to be traced, and so give us a logical structure to follow. The beginning of Chapter 17, the dialogue between the Spirit of the Northern Sea and The Lord of the Yellow River, looks like a coherent and representative exposition of certain basic ideas in *Chuang Tzu*. It is also perhaps one of the longest connected sections in the whole body of the work. Its style contains features commonly taken to belong to the specific literary form of *Chuang Tzu*, and it should be ascribed without reservation to the main author of the work.

Nevertheless, it remains but a small fraction in a great bulk of thought. The other parts cannot, of course, be disregarded, or overshadowed by this particular section. Yet the qualities of this dialogue make it a prime candidate for our choice of starting-point in understanding *Chuang Tzu*. I shall be satisfied if my interpretation is not explicitly contradicted by any other relevant section in the work.

The analysis is offered only as a *possible* interpretation, a possible and perhaps useful *clue* to the philosophy of Chuang Tzu. The history of sinology in Europe is a short one, and that of the systematic analysis of Chinese philosophy even shorter. Attempts at understanding must be permitted, however crude and unsatisfactory. So although it is impossible, for instance, to free oneself from the burden of Western philosophy, and likewise to eliminate the centuries lying between Chuang Tzu and ourselves, the fact that he touches some string in us is enough to show that it would be foolish to give up before we have even begun.

Except for the necessary philological notes, I have taken little notice of the abundant commentaries on *Chuang Tzu*. The first of importance was written as much as six hundred years after the death of Chuang Tzu, and then only by a famous philosopher himself, Kuo Hsiang. Nor have I been too much troubled with the authenticity of the text, its history, and the problems of authorship. It is a fact that the work has existed in its present form from the time of the Han dynasty, and it has thus been looked upon by several generations of Chinese as *the Chuang Tzu*, an object for interpretation and an exposition of early Taoist philosophy.

True, the work's structure is fairly loose, which might indicate that several authors, or pupils of one author, had compiled it, and thus it may be a product of several thinkers. But the homogeneity of the style points to one author of at least the major portions of the work.

There is no reason to believe that the author — let us call him Chuang Tzu — is an exception to the rule that a philosopher's ideas develop gradually and change through time. His work is probably a conglomerate of thoughts from different periods. We need not suppose these periods to be too long, say of 20 or 30 years duration, or too widely separated, which would imply important divergencies between the thoughts belonging to different periods; especially since the literary style remains largely unchanged throughout the book. It seems only natural to suppose that this piece of writing contains several layers of ideas thrown together. Contradictions in interpretation may thus be only on the surface, and without any real importance.

The editions of *Chuang Tzu* which have been of most value for this essay, are (1) *Chuang Tzu, Ssu-pu pei-yao* edition, and (2) *Chuang Tzu chi-chieh, Wang Hsien-chien chu*. The references are in all cases to *A Concordance to Chuang Tzu*, Harvard-Yenching Institute, Sinological Series.

Finally, I must add that the present essay is only part of a larger study dealing with the whole of Chuang Tzu's philosophy. Several problems are treated here somewhat cursorily, and some altogether disregarded.

Readers already familiar with the text are asked to excuse the frequent quotation and re-narration of its contents.

II. The Self-Knowledge of the River-Lord (42/17/1–42/17/7)

We are introduced to one of the main ideas of the dialogue at its very beginning, namely that of size or greatness (*dà*). A change in the natural circumstances conditioned by time (*shî*) has taken place to the effect that the river's current becomes so swollen that 'one could not distinguish between a horse and an ox' (42/17/1) from one side of the river to the other. This change in spatial dimensions involves a change in the empirical conditions for knowledge. From the outset we are confronted with the fact which Chuang Tzu wants to prove: namely, that empirical knowledge of the sensible world depends upon relations between the thing to be known and measured and those other things which go to make up the former's surroundings, i.e. which constitute the context of perception.

In the case of the Yellow River at the time of the autumn floods, the new distance between the observer and the things to be observed has the consequence that one cannot make a reliable judgment as to whether the object seen is *A* or *B*. Our vision has become blurred. Our knowledge and our power of discrimination and judgment have re-

vealed a dependence upon the dimensions which define the relations between object and observer. The field of observation has become wider
and the object has accordingly receded into the background.

It is primarily in Chapter 2 of *Chuang Tzu* (*Ch'i Wu Lun*) that the
epistemology of the philosopher is outlined in 'the theory of this and
that', and one is compelled to bear that passage in mind when studying
the present one. By using the verb *biàn* (*bù biàn niǔ mǎ* [42/17/1])
to denote the act of epistemological discrimination, the author has
indicated its connexion to his theory of this and that (*shì* and *bǐ*), as
well as to the key concept introduced below (in IV), namely that of
fēn ('difference' or 'part').

Time is responsible for the changes in nature mentioned above.
The place which time (*shí*) occupies in Taoist philosophy is later stressed
in IV, IX, and XII. Needless to say, it also has an important role to play
in Confucianism and in connexion with *I Ching* (the *Book of Changes*).

The Spirit of the Yellow River, the River-Lord, deveolps an attitude
towards himself of pride and pleasure. There is nothing to prevent
his firm belief that nothing can be greater or more beautiful than himself at this very moment. His self-regard is unlimited. He ascribes to
himself a superlative degree of beauty, saying 'all the beauty in the
world must be concentrated in me' (*yǐ tiān xià zhī měi wéi jìn zài jǐ*
[42/17/2]), the irony of which, in the author's mind, can scarcely escape
our notice. The word *jìn* means to 'exhaust' or to 'complete', pointing
to an idea of a totality, and this totality of beauty is supposed by the
River-Lord to be identical with his own self (*jǐ*), a finite part. He
regards himself as representing a totality and mistakenly thinks that
the part is identical with the whole exactly because he does not recognize anything of which he is part.

The self-regard of the River-Lord remains unchanged until he is
suddenly confronted with something decidedly bigger, namely the
Northern Sea, in comparison to which the Yellow River, even in a
swollen state, is without size or significance. Now he immediately
transfers his concept of what is superlatively big from one thing, himself, to another, the Northern Sea. He cannot possibly imagine anything
bigger than this immense amount of water around him. This marks
the new limit of his imagination and empirical knowledge, and consequently the boundaries of his judgments about quantities. His idea
of the superlatively big is now settled, and he measures everything else
in contrast to this Northern Sea. Surely this must be the totality he was
seeking!

The River-Lord gains a new self-knowledge and self-evaluation, an improvement of the understanding which is due to this way of being compared and contrasted with something else. This, as we shall see, is by and large the way in which the Sea-Spirit brings the River-Lord to a further comprehension of the world.

It is of interest to note the use of verbs in this opening section. (i) We are introduced to several verbs of visual perception and observation: *shì*, *jiàn*, *wàng* and *dǔ*. These are employed in describing how a subject perceives the world and acquires knowledge of it. The visual contemplation of nature, the mind's grasping of its change, movement, rest, and rhythm, in short the dynamism of the universe, is discussed elsewhere by Chuang Tzu (e.g. in Chs. 6, 7, 11, 12, 13, 14 and 18). Apparently, the known world is the one perceived by sight. Empirical knowledge is thus comprehension by visual comparison between sense objects constituting the world around me, leading to my judgments of quantity and quality, as was the case with the River-Lord. (ii) The author makes extensive use of putative verbs specific for the whole dialogue under discussion, indicating judgments about things issuing from the subject's apprehension of the world. For instance, the verbs *shǎo* ('to regard as few or insignificant') and *qīng* ('to regard as unimportant') are employed from the very beginning, and they constitute, together with *dūo* ('to regard as much or important'), *xiǎo* ('to regard as little or unimportant'), and *dà* ('to regard as great or significant') the stock set of verbs of judgment throughout the dialogue.

In connexion with *dà* and *xiǎo* below, it becomes apparent that there is a certain correlation between the mere perception of things' quantities, stated in judgments of size, and the valuation of these objects, stated in judgments of quality. An object is not solely looked upon as big or small in comparison with other objects immediately perceived in the same field of vision, i.e. in the context of perception; it is also directly valued as important or unimportant, to be respected or not. At this stage of thought, an association of this kind is likely to take place. This accounts for the pride and pleasure which the River-Lord feels when perceiving his own size.

Chuang Tzu cannot resist irony when he lets the River-Lord exclaim to the Northern Sea: 'Now, however, I have seen your unfathomable vastness.' [2] The expression *qióng* in *nán-qióng* ('unfathomable vastness') in its verbal meaning denotes the act of going to the extreme point or state or limits of something. In other words, the River-Lord cannot imagine anything capable of determining or setting a limit to the sea. In his eyes so far, it remains boundless. The Sea-Spirit reduces himself shortly afterwards to the size of a hair's tip in relation to the universe, thereby of course making the Yellow River even smaller than before. The text abounds in cases like this. Something just affirmed is afterwards either totally refuted or partially accepted and partially dismissed.

The Sea-Spirit offers three examples of a world-conception similar to that of the River-Lord before he met the Sea. Common to the well-frog, the summer-insect and the cramped scholar is their limited world of understanding and existence (42/17/5—42/17/6). This makes them incapable of dealing in speech or thought with any subject-matter that transcends their limits. The well-frog exists in a world determined by the limited *space* it occupies (*xù*). It is incapable of comprehending anything which goes beyond its experience and the sense-objects it has become acquainted with. The summer-insect is likewise determined by the limited *time* (*shí*) of its life-span. The human being, probably in addition to the limits forced upon it by time and space, is capable of becoming rooted in a doctrinally stated *world-view* (*jiào*). This world-view affects sets of values and attitudes which define the person.

The conclusion is evident. I can only understand what the mind can reach with the help of things already known. My world of thought and living is determined by my surrounding world of sense-experience, subject-matters in time and space, and my beliefs in regard to moral philosophy (*jiào*) (cf. IX–XIV below). It seems that Chuang Tzu has succeeded in mapping out a kind of 'Lebenswelt' theory, the world of my thought and existence.

The River-Lord has discovered that the boundaries of his world of existence have been wiped out and substituted by new ones in his encounter with the Sea-Spirit. His own bigness, the former superlative value of his world, which constitutes the circle defining his surroundings and values, is exchanged for a new superlative value, the vastness of the Sea. His world has been defined anew and another circle has been drawn, thereby forcing a new attitude and understanding upon him. He realizes his own shortcomings (*chǒu*). This self-acknowledgement is a condition for a further improvement of the understanding. The River-Lord has left his old values behind and is now prepared to gain new understanding. This knowledge is insight into what is called 'The Great Principle' (*dà lǐ*). *Lǐ*, principle, is not mentioned again until line 38 (43/17/38). The argument dealing with *dà lǐ* ends in line 48 (44/17/48), thus marking off the main argumentative parts of the dialogue as an exposition of The Great Principle.

III. The Self-Knowledge of the Sea-Spirit (42/17/7–42/17/15)

The opening sequence has provided a basis for the succeeding arguments. The connexion is clearly brought out by the use of the inchoative adverb of aspect, *jiāng*, and the final particle *yǐ* (42/17/7). The River-Lord may now be in a position to start on the ladder leading to a new conception of himself and the world.

The Sea-Spirit employs the method of comparison stated in the common comparing-formula of classical Chinese: *mò dà yú hǎi*, that is, in comparison with the Sea, nothing belonging to the category of water is great or big. The Sea has already been introduced above and even named the Great Sea, *dà hǎi*. In this comparison the Sea is clearly defined as the superlatively big. Denying to all other kinds of water the predicate 'big' establishes the uniqueness of the Sea. It alone remains worthy of being called 'big'. Everything else is small in comparison. It thus becomes the standard of size and measure in relation to which every other thing is measured.

The Sea is always being filled by all other floods and streams in the world, and afterwards emptied. This process will never stop. Yet the Sea may never be completely full (*yíng*) nor completely empty (*xù*). This image of the Sea is a suggestive and fascinating one, but an adequate discussion of it is unfortunately beyond our present scope. Its description as a well-balanced state of opposites inevitably calls Heraclitus to mind.[3] This balancing of opposites, conceived of as powers or entities, plays a well-known part in Chinese philosophy.

It seems natural to take the Sea in the parable above as a symbol for *tao*, the dynamic universe, its laws and structures. The predicates applied to the Sea correspond fairly closely with those frequently used to describe *tao* in early philosophical Taoism (cf. *Lao Tzu*, Chs. 4, 6, 8, 25, 45, 78).

The Northern Sea is further said to be uncorrupted by any changes in nature which in other cases usually influence things. Neither in spring nor in autumn is the Sea subjected to any alteration, in contrast to what happened to the Yellow River. *Tao* too, as we know from elsewhere in Taoism, is something which remains unaffected by variations and movements in nature.

The Northern Sea is basically different from all other kinds of water under heaven, different in quality and quantity (*cǐ qí gùo jiāng hé zhī líu* [42/17/8]). The degree to which it surpasses the other streams and floods is beyond the possibility of measure and number (*liàng* and *shù*). The Sea is evidently something totally different from everything else, and this can be understood in two ways:

1. What we cannot measure and count is this transcendence (*cǐ qí gùo*) implied by the use of *gùo* ('to surpass', 'to exceed'), and this perhaps points to an incommensurability between the Sea and rivers. Measures and numbers are inapplicable because the Sea may be reckoned as the totality transcending the parts, for instance as a whole not reached by the algebraical addition of parts, but something more even than all the parts together. Keeping in mind the possible parallels between the Sea and *tao*, this interpretation is not far-fetched. The use of *gùo* may indicate a transition from what may be counted and measured to that which eludes such quantitative judgments.

2. On the other hand, if we remember the context in which the image of the Sea is employed, it is improbable that a metaphor for *tao* should be introduced at this stage of the dialogue. The River-Lord's power of understanding is still undeveloped. For he deems the Sea to represent the outer limits of the world, or rather of *his* world at the present moment. The Sea-Spirit may therefore simply wish to stress what properties a totality like this world-concept must possess. The Northern Sea is thus described in such terms that it has qualities common both to *tao* in general, far beyond the present comprehension of the River-Lord, and to the Sea conceived of as the totality and the greatest at this level of insight. These attributes, e.g. the transcendence, must be borne in mind, as they state important facts about Chuang Tzu's world-concept. They may be freely used to interpret Chuang Tzu and his view of *tao* and the universe in relation to the rest of the world.

The basic concepts of counting and measuring are introduced. The words are used either verbally (*shǔ, liàng*) or nominally (*shù, liàng*) depending on the context.

The Sea-Spirit exhibits no pride and does not take himself to be very important or significant (*zì dūo*) because of his eminent qualities in comparison with other expanses of water. The reason for this is that he compares himself and his corporeality with another object of comparison, namely heaven and earth, or Nature. He is clearly conscious of his dependence upon *yin* and *yang*. Thus, analysis of his position in the universe (*tiān dì zhī jiān* [42/17/9]) shows his smallness to be like that of a little stone on a great mountain. How could he possibly regard himself as of any importance or size? He has no reason to take pride and pleasure in himself.

The Sea-Spirit has dismissed the view of himself as the greatest, or even as great at all. To perceive oneself in comparison with something else of greater importance makes it impossible to consider oneself as of any value. The field of vision or context of perception gives to everything its proper position and dimension. What had evidently been proved to be the superlative value of judgment is reduced to almost nothing (*fāng cún hú jiàn shǎo* [42/17/10]). The Sea is deprived of its prominent position and transcending qualities. Its own dependency and finiteness are fully revealed. Having maintained the absolute sovereignty of the Sea in the sensible world, even using it as an image of *tao*, the Sea-Spirit is reduced to a mere minor position in space. This method of affirming and negating in the dialogue creates a strong tension between the different parts of the text. A definition of a concept or thing is put forth, and apparently affirmed, only to be rejected immediately afterwards as insufficient. The proposal need not be dismissed as utterly false, but it is regarded as a half-truth; one level of insight is replaced by another, more advanced level. What the Buddhist philosophers in China discussed as 'the theory of double truth', especially in the *K'ung Tsung* or *Shūnyavāda*, was not only a product of the dialectics of Nāgārjuna imported from India, but also drew inspiration from the native tradition promoted by Chuang Tzu. The theories of Chi-Tsang (549–623) about the three levels of truth [4] show striking resemblances to the epistemological theory put forth in different sections of *Chuang Tzu* and to the method employed in the present dialogue.

The Sea-Spirit has conducted the River-Lord to an understanding of the visible world, making Nature or the universe the totality for which he has been searching. The concept of *tiān-dì*, Nature, is the new value, the new standard, in comparison with which everything else is to be judged. For a second time, the River-Lord experiences the replacement of one world-concept by another, but he is still left with the idea of an all-encircling, finite nature.

The Sea-Spirit now applies the recently established standards to certain things and ideas in order to bring out their real importance and size: the world defined by the four oceans (that is the civilized world), the geographical entity called China, the part which humanity occupies in Nature, and Chinese culture and history. By extension of the horizons defining the context of interpretation and apprehension, these objects are reduced in their relative importance, the qualities attributed to them in a positive, absolute way losing their meaning within a new world-frame. Chuang Tzu looks upon this kind of analysis as a matter of pure calculation in regard to relations and proportions between objects and values. This is implied by the use of the word *jì* ('to calculate' [42/17/10]).

It is interesting to note that the objects in question are carefully compared with objects of a corresponding species. The four oceans (*sì hǎi*) and China are measured against heaven and earth, mankind against other natural objects, and the Nine Provinces are brought into contrast with other habitable places in the world. It is also of interest to note that the Sea-Spirit claims that the place inhabited and occupied by human beings and civilization is only a tiny part of the spatial world *capable* of habitation and cultivation.

Chuang Tzu's apprehension of the traditional institutions and morals cherished by the Chinese comes out in the devastating analysis by the Sea-Spirit. This attitude towards the past and present culture is truly a piece of 'Umwertung aller Werte'. Labour done and war fought in the service of China are merely due to an overestimation (*zì dūo*) of Chinese culture, the result of insufficient understanding and insight into the world and its proportions.

The arguments in III have so far established heaven and earth, i.e. the visible universe, and the tip of a hair (*háo mò*) as, respectively, the largest and the smallest perceivable objects in our sensible world. They are reckoned as the two extremes of our standard. This preliminary conclusion is expressed by the River-Lord in a question which sums up the passage commented on in III after the Sea-Spirit has ended the argument: 'If it be thus, then may I look upon heaven and earth as great and the tip of a hair as small?' (42/17/15).

In order to judge and measure, we must have two fixed points, the superlatively large and the superlatively small. Clearly, according to the argument above, knowledge of these values is to be discovered in our sensible world. What is indubitably the greatest in extension is the universe, and as noted in II, it becomes simultaneously the most important thing. The smallest thing that our eyes can perceive, on the other hand, is the tip of a hair, a point with the absolute minimum of extension. These two extremes of the scale are used when we measure and compare everything else. We may predicate 'great' (*dà*) of Nature (*tiān-dì*) in an absolute, positive sense because everything else is not large in comparison to it. We may attribute the quality 'small' (*xiǎo*) to the tip of a hair in the same absolute manner because everything else is not small, but large, in comparison to it. In other words, everything is smaller than heaven and earth and bigger than the tip of a hair. We can pinpoint every object in our perceived world on a scale extending between these two extreme values, thereby placing the objects in relation to each other and in comparison with the greatest and the smallest.

As mentioned above, the absolute values *dà* and *xiǎo* when conferred on heaven and earth and the tip of a hair, respectively, imply a qualitative judgment. *Dà* is not only big, but also 'important' and 'significant'. *Xiǎo* is not only 'small', but also 'unimportant' and 'without significance'.

As for everything else in this world defined by heaven and earth, on one hand, and the tip of a hair on the other, nothing can be referred to as big or small except in a relative way, while heaven and earth and the tip of a hair possess these attributes in an absolute, positive sense. All other things are judged in relation to and comparison with several similar objects, and *dà* and *xiǎo* may thus be applied only in a relative sense. This relative manner of judging and measuring is evidently deemed an inferior way of understanding things, belonging to an earlier level of thought. The inferior level is fully explained and understood by the superior insight whose main feature is the comprehension of heaven and earth and the tip of a hair as the standards.

Between these two extreme values, all other values are relative and form parts of a 'floating' world. We may always find something smaller or larger than the object in question, thus adding to its importance or subtracting from it.

Knowledge at this level is no sooner established than it is demolished in the next section.

IV. The Axioms of Relativism (42/17/15–42/17/18)

The section we now come to is marked out by the Sea-Spirit's firm denial to the question quoted above. Four axioms are laid down for the argument that follows:

1. The number of things is without limit (*wù liàng wú qióng*).
2. Time has no end (*shí wú zhǐ*).
3. Distinctions have no constancy (*fēn wú cháng*).
4. Beginning and end cannot be fixed (*zhōng shǐ wú gù*).

These axioms have each the form of a negative statement. Immediately following them is an illustration of how the man possessing the

superior insight expressed in these axioms regulates his life and attitudes. The axioms must be seen in the light of the earlier arguments, and
a number of possible interpretations of them may be suggested:

1. Things in nature, natural objects (*wù*), include everything that has
extension, form, and shape. There is no limit to the number of these
objects. Their number is infinite in the Aristotelian sense, infinite in
addition; they cannot be exhausted (*qióng*) by counting, by adding
part to part. This problem should not be confused with that of whether
the universe as a whole is finite or infinite. The subject of the axiom
is only *wù liàng*, 'the number or measure of things', and this probably
includes quantitative judgments concerning the specific things, and
the relations and proportions defining them reciprocally. Above (42/
17/11), Chuang Tzu said: 'If we are to mention or name the number
of things, we call them ten thousand (*wàn wù*).' This means only that
the number of things is indefinite, a number which we are not capable
of determining; and this accords well with our present axiom.

2. Time (*shí*) has no end or will never stop. Chuang Tzu says nothing
about the beginning of time, a possible starting-point, but only maintains the view that time is infinite in the sense of continuing *ad infinitum*.
Time has no maximum, but whether it has a minimum, i.e. time =0,
is left unexplained in this section. We may interpret the axiom as
saying, correspondingly to axiom 1 in respect of the number of things,
that time is infinite in addition of parts. Chuang Tzu is clearly not defending the cyclical concept of time propounded in many schools of
Chinese philosophy. Rather, he seems to conceive of time as an infinite
line. His idea of time includes the view of it as something which brings
about changes in Nature and influences the actions of man and things.
In several contexts we must interpret *shí* as 'the circumstances or
influences caused by time'. Later (see IX and XII), when he discusses
the problem of being in harmony with time, this interpretation of *shí*
is the preferred one.

3. Distinctions or differences (*fēn*) have no constancy. *Fēn* means the
differences between things whereby we distinguish them as individual
objects. It may also denote the fate or lot of a thing or person, something
ordained by *tao* or *ming*. But unless otherwise stated, we shall take *fēn*
to denote the differences and distinctions between things. Consequently,
we can understand the common meaning of *fēn* as the 'part' or 'portion'
of something. That which is identifiable by virtue of the differences it

bears to something else is at the same time to be reckoned a part in opposition to other parts and to the whole.

Attributes, expressed in judgments of quality and quantity, may be predicated of a subject *S*, thereby defining it in relation to other things, marking it out as an individual, an object for counting and measuring (*shǔ, liáng*). The predicates act as markers of differences between things (*fēn*). However, we have established a certain relativism in defining the values and measures of natural objects. The predicates become wholly dependent upon the objects in comparison with which we judge and measure. The differences can thus be established only relatively, or in the words of Chuang Tzu, the distinctions are not constant, but are prey to the changing point of view.

4. To emphasize the distinctions of things is at the same time to draw the boundaries between them, stating where they begin and end. The classification of something as an individual object depends on the relativism of the differences. Beginning and end are thus also subjected to the same relativism; that is, they cannot be firmly settled. Thus the River-Lord had settled the beginning and end of himself, of his domain, and had determined himself as a visible object, but in his encounter with the Sea-Spirit the proportions defining the Yellow River became distorted, and his 'beginning and end' is determined anew. His position as an individual has altered; the River-Lord becomes identical with a part defined within the frame of a new context of perception.

The Sea-Spirit applies these four axioms accordingly to heaven and earth and to the tip of a hair, to show that even these entities are not exempt from the validity of the axioms and from the relativism of values. We believe they mark the beginning and end of our world, but in doing so we are ignoring, for instance, the fourth axiom.

Aside from the axioms themselves, we are offered a vivid picture of the great, wise man characterized by a profound understanding of the four theorems just quoted. The practical application of the axioms is brought out in a strict, logical way, by deducing from each axiom its effects in practical life. The wise man, when contemplating the visible world around him, refrains from passing judgment. He may accept that he perceives some things as big or small, important or unimportant, but he is aware of the fact that his seeing them in this way is totally dependent upon his context of perception. He avoids valuing them even though they look big or small (*xiǎo ér bù gǔa, dà ér bù dūo* [42/17/16]).

The following clauses (42/17/16–42/17/18) describing the theory and practice of the superior man fall neatly into four groups, each a well-shaped argument. With the exception of 4, all of them start with a restatement of an axiom, add a new premiss and draw the practical implication. We may reconstruct the arguments as follows:

1. He knows (*zhī*) that there are no limits (*wú qióng*) in the number and measures of things, (cf. first axiom). He is clearly conscious of past (*gǔ*) and present (*jīn*). Therefore (*gù*): As for the past, though it glides away, he feels no sorrow, and as for the present, though it is momentarily there, he seizes it, but without enthusiasm.

2. He knows that time has no end (cf. second axiom). He discriminates between the full and the void (*yíng* and *xū*). Therefore (*gù*): As for what he obtains (*dé*), he feels no joy; and as for what he loses (*shī*), he experiences no grief.

3. He knows that distinctions have no constancy (cf. third axiom). He is aware of or comprehends the level road, the cycle of life and nature (*tǎn tú*). Therefore (*gù*): He takes no delight in life (*shēng*), and he does not regard death (*sǐ*) as a calamity (*huò*).

4. He knows that the beginning and the end cannot be fixed (cf. fourth axiom).

The last axiom is only mentioned, the author has not drawn any conclusions from it. In fact it looks as if the rest of the argument was missing. It cannot very well form part of the succeeding argument (*jì rén zhī sǔo zhī* [42/17/18)]) which marks the beginning of the section we shall come to in V.

I have not forced the above arguments into the 'Aristotelian' form used in my reconstructions. The way in which the author himself has presented them lends itself to this lucid form.

Arguments 1, 2, and 3 serve to apply the theoretical knowledge to practical behaviour in regard to particular life situations in time and nature. As in most Chinese philosophy, theory must serve a practical aim.

Time consists of past and present. The wise man knows that what is obtained (*dé*) in the present (*jīn*) will be lost (*shī*) when the present becomes past (*gǔ*). The present is what is, here and now, the full (*yíng*), while the past, receding and disappearing, becomes absent and is therefore described as emptiness (*xū*). Time is measured in the same relative way as are things in space, judging its different parts (*jīn* and *gǔ*) in comparision with and in proportion to each other.

The concepts of far and near (*yuǎn* and *jìn*) are applicable to pheno-

mena both in space and time, as they indicate the relativism of proportions valid both for the spatial world and our perception of events in time.
The wise man contemplates on far and near, meaning that he has knowledge of the relativity involved in the measuring of objects in time and
space. The wise man looks upon death and life as mere changes, transfor-
mations in the cycle of life and nature.[5] Past and present are not constant
and well-defined concepts, but are subject to the relativism stated in the
axioms above. Consequently, the wise man shows no emotion in the face
of what happens to him now or before (*dé* and *shī, yíng* and *xù*).

V. THE PESSIMISM OF CHUANG TZU (42/17/18–42/17/20)

This passage rounds off the refutation of the thesis expressed by the
River-Lord at the end of III. Chuang Tzu himself marks the end of
the argument in this and the next passage when he sums up: 'If we
look at things in this way (*yóu cǐ guān zhī* [42/17/19]), then how do we
know that the tip of a hair is sufficiently small to determine the limits
of the smallest? Or how do we know that heaven and earth are sufficiently great to reach the outer limits of the greatest?' (42/17/20).

Human knowledge is very small in comparison with what we do not
know (42/17/18). Our life is very short in comparison with the time
when we are not living (42/17/18). We may achieve a fairly broad
insight, transcending that of the summer-insect, the well-frog, or the
cramped scholar, and reach a new level of thought from which everything, including ourselves may be looked at. The Sea-Spirit states that
despite the concrete examples in *A* and *B* of a possible improvement of
the understanding, our 'Umwelt' remains nevertheless restricted. What
we comprehend as the greatest cannot be sufficiently proved to be
actually the greatest, and our claims are even contradicted by the
axioms in IV. Chuang Tzu has entered upon a profound pessimism
concerning our power of understanding. He has denied every possibility
of maintaining our recognition of fixed values, and only the relativism
remains. Not even heaven and earth or the tip of a hair can be reckoned
as the extreme standards of measure and judgment. We must argue
ad infinitum in every case when referring to the qualitative and quantitative properties of things. Accordingly, the possibility of establishing
fixed values on the basis of the sensible world which forms our surroundings, is banished altogether. To advance any further, we must leave
the world of senses and accompany the Sea-Spirit on a rambling and
free-going excursion into the realm of pure conceptual thinking.

VI. The Absolutely Great and the Absolutely Small (42/17/20– 43/17/24)

The River-Lord asserts two theses, quoting 'those who for the time being discuss these problems' (42/17/20). One cannot say for certain whom he is referring to, but probably he has exponents of the School of Names (*Ming chia*) in mind. We have no other sources than this occurrence in Chuang Tzu for the doctrines in the precise form given here.

The theses quoted by the River-Lord are:

1. The most minute has no body (*zhì jīng wú xíng* [42/17/20]).

2. The greatest cannot be encircled or embraced (*zhì dà bù kě wéi* [43/17/21]).

The argument in this passage contains a partial affirmation and a partial refutation of these two theses. The Sea-Spirit proceeds from this theorem: 'To regard the great from the little cannot be done exhaustively. To regard the little from the great cannot add anything to our understanding' (43/17/21). We have already touched on these thoughts (in V), but certain implications of the theory in V are essential to our understanding of the Sea-Spirit's argument in VI.

(1) We cannot reach that which is positively and absolutely great, the greatest, by a mere addition of what is small, for instance by the adding of small units when measuring something. The great has no maximum, or is infinite in addition. That which we shall define as *dà* ('great') in an absolute, unrestricted sense must have this property. It cannot be a product of what is small, nor can we in thought determine it by way of what is small.

What we define as that which is *xiǎo*, absolutely small, must be of such a kind that we cannot reach it by a mere division of the great into parts. The small has no minimum, or is infinite in respect of division.

A part of something is large in relation to those parts into which it may still be divided. We can always continue dividing into parts, and the world, accordingly, has no indivisible parts. There are no simple, individual entities making up the bricks of the world. The Universe is positively infinite as regards number of parts (cf. IV above).

(2) My surrounding world and my understanding are always insufficient to gain adequate knowledge of any other being's 'Lebenswelt' (cf. V). The world-view of the well-frog is too small to comprehend the world-view of the Sea-Spirit, and conversely, that of the Sea-Spirit may be insufficient for a thorough comprehension and apprehension

of what is implied in the world-concept of the well-frog. We must realize that our restricted world is basically *ours* and we cannot thoroughly gain an adequate conception of the worlds belonging to other beings.

These opening lines may be a refutation, by Chuang Tzu, of the theoretical background of the theses quoted by the River-Lord. The author may intend to offer an explanation of why 'those who for the time being discuss these problems' hold the theory. They only feel that the smallest is without body and extension because, being situated in a restricted world-view, their thoughts cannot manage to reach it. Their feeling of the greatest as being that which cannot be determined, or embraced, is only due to the fact that the world they occupy is small in comparison, while what they try to embrace and understand is the greatest. It is the world-concept that has determined the theses put forward by the debaters referred to by the River-Lord.

(3) The great and the small are incommensurable. One cannot measure or define the great by means of the small, or the small by means of the great. It is important to remember that the only possible meaning of *dà* and *xiǎo* in the present interpretation is 'the absolutely great' and 'the absolutely small'.

In my view the theorem of the Sea-Spirit cannot be dismissed as merely a criticism of the dialecticians, though it may perfectly well serve that purpose too. We shall do best to deem it a premiss for the succeeding argument.

The two concepts of fineness (*jīng*) and coarseness (*cū*) play an important role in the present argument. They are both defined by the Sea-Spirit as belonging to that which has a body or extension (*yǒu xíng zhě* (43/17/22]). This can occupy a certain position in space and be determined and defined in relation to other objects, and may be encircled (*wéi*), where to encircle means to embrace, to draw the boundaries between the object in question and the rest of the world.

Fineness (*jīng*) is further defined as that which thought may reach (*kě yǐ yì zhì zhě, wù zhī jīng* [43/17/24]), and coarseness (*cū*) is what words may speak of (*kě yǐ yán lùn zhě, wù zhī cū* [43/17/23]). The definition of *cū* comes before that of *jīng*, and this may be taken to mean that *jīng* may be reached by thought alone, and not expressed in words. *Cū* can be expressed in words, however, and it would be very unlikely that *cū* should elude thought, even if the definitions do stress a certain contrast.

Jīng and *cū* are referred to specifically as properties of natural objects (*wù zhī cū* and *wù zhī jīng* ['the coarseness of things' and 'the fineness of things']). Other occurrences[6] in Chuang Tzu confirm that they are conceived of as a pair of qualities inherent in things.

In introducing *jīng* as the smallest (*xiǎo zhī wéi*), the Sea-Spirit contrasts it with the gigantic (*dà zhī yīn*), which is called *fú* (43/17/22). As *jīng* and *cū* occur frequently together, one might feel justified in regarding *fú* as a synonym for *cū*. But this interpretation is far from reasonable in light of the following definitions. It seems more likely that the *jīng* contrasted here with the gigantic is not the same concept as that of *jīng* and *cū*.

The Sea-Spirit offers a definition of the concepts introduced above by the River-Lord:

1. That which is without extension cannot be divided (*fēn*) by measuring units or distinguished by numbers. It is exempt from division and measure (43/17/23).

2. That which cannot be encircled is such that numbers may never reach its end. We shall never attain to its outer limits by a mere adding of parts. It is thus an infinite entity transcending every effort to determine or define it quantitatively (*shǔ*) (43/17/23).

Fineness and coarseness belong to that which has extension and can be defined, and they partake accordingly of the world which may be comprehended in thought or expressed in words. They may be counted and measured.

Everything which thought may grasp or words express presupposes the categories of *jīng* and *cū* (43/17/24). This implies that whatever does not participate in these categories — and this means whatever has no body and cannot be encircled — eludes thought and language. Such a thing must be defined by pure negation, as something which is neither *cū* nor *jīng*.

In the hypothesis put forward by 'those who for the time being discuss these problems' (42/17/20), 'what is without body' was identified with the smallest (*zhì jīng*), and 'what cannot be encircled' with the greatest (*zhì dà*). This is now established by the Sea-Spirit as a doctrine, but only after he has turned it over in his mind, defining the concepts anew and thus offering another interpretation of the same thesis. In the theory offered by the Sea-Spirit, we should more properly call 'the greatest' (*zhì dà*) *maximum absolutum* and 'the smallest' (*zhì jīng*) *minimum absolutum*.

The absolutely greatest and the absolutely smallest have finally been defined negatively, as eluding body and determination, language and thought. We are left with a negative knowledge of the absolute values which we started in search of. There remains only a relativism of the values and objects perceived in our world of senses. There exists no standard accessible to our minds, at least of great and small, of what is valuable and what valueless. Within every isolated milieu and world of one's being and understanding the values and measures have their validity, but one that is restricted and limited to this specific context. We have reached a conclusion fully in harmony and accordance with the general rule of epistemology proved above (in III and IV), namely that our limited world of insight, though it may be enlarged and brought to a certain perfection, is incapable of fathoming the absolutely greatest and smallest. We remain parts of a whole transcending our powers of understanding.

VII. The Relativism of Ethical Values (43/17/24–43/17/28)

The practical implications of the foregoing arguments are now set out and a description of the conduct and behaviour of the great wise man (*dà rén zhī xìng* [43/17/24]) offered. The relativism of values is clearly exhibited in the doctrines of moral philosophy. The wise man refrains from any judgments of right and wrong, and he totally avoids any approval or disapproval of behaviour that he observes in others. He carefully balances between the extremes, both in regard to his own behaviour and in regard to his judgments of the behaviour of others.

Value-systems such as those advocated by the Moists and the Confucianists are violently attacked. A lack of stable values in ethics is the inevitable conclusion of the foregoing ontological and epistemological arguments. The wise man refrains from fighting for gain, and neither does he practise the virtues of Meng Tzu and K'ung Fu Tzu, those of *cí* and *ràng*, 'humility' and 'indulgence' (43/17/25). These are basic moral virtues in the system of Meng Tzu, constituting the beginning of ethical behaviour, *lǐ*.[7] In *Chuang Tzu*, however, Meng Tzu is not mentioned by name at all, but the ideas of *cí* and *ràng* seem to have been present in an oral tradition upon which Chuang Tzu draws. The choice of words in this section is very deliberate, everywhere indicating the school of thought which Chuang Tzu is attacking.

The conduct of the wise man is actively neither good nor bad but eludes approbation or disapprobation in relation to a specifically chosen set of values. His supreme knowledge consists in the recognition of the impossibility of distinguishing right (*shì*) and wrong (*feī*). The distinctions whereby we judge right and wrong cannot be absolutely determined (*bù kě wéi fēn* [43/17/27]), but rest on our relative and inadequate understanding. His knowledge includes, of course, the epistemology and ontology developed above, that is, the fact that the great and the small may not be defined absolutely (43/17/27).

The arguments presented in II–VI were intended to have a general application to moral philosophy, and it is only in this section that this is explicitly brought out by the reference to right and wrong. The intimate connexion between the use of putative and descriptive verbs, emphasized in our discussion in II and III above, has indicated, however, that the notion of right (*shì*) and wrong (*fēi*) has been implicit throughout most of the dialogue hitherto.

Shì is right in the sense of what is approved of in relation to a given set of ethical values. *Fei* is wrong in the sense of what is disapproved of in relation to the same set.

The wise mind refrains from judging people's actions because he is aware of how each man and each being strives and abides in a narrow restricted world which determines emotions, ideas, intentions, and knowledge. Each being expresses in thought and action its world, and approves (*shì*) or disapproves (*fēi*) according to its set of values. Consequently, it is impossible to gain a platform of objectivity from where the notion of *shì* and *fēi* would have an unchanging, permanent value. The behaviour of each thing cannot be objectively judged. It just *is* as it is.

It is evident that the person described as 'the great man' (*dà rén* [43/17/24]), possessing 'the great knowledge' (*dà zhī* [42/17/15]), is identical with 'the man of tao' (*dào rén* [43/17/27]). He is a model of the greatest power or virtue of existence (*zhì dé*, [43/17/27]). He is without fame (*wén*) and without ego or self (*jì* [43/17/28]). By applying and possessing the knowledge expounded in II–VI, he becomes an example of the best method, namely 'the bringing together of the differences' (*yūe fēn zhī zhì yě* [43/17/28]). 'Differences' must be understood in the sense of 'apparent differences', as they have been proved to be without firmness and constancy, in other words without reality. *Yūe fēn* is taken to signify: The wise man 'brings the differences together'; that is he realizes their relativism and mutual dependence, not taking their apparent plurality for granted. On the contrary, he acts in spite of the distinctions and transcends them in a superior view of the world's unity.

VIII. Aspects of Measuring (43/17/28–43/17/34)

Having established the ontological and epistemological doctrines expounded in VI, the summit of our dialogue, and the moral philosophy in VII, the discussion is now carried on by the introduction of two new concepts, the outside of things (*wù zhī wài*) and the inside of things (*wù zhī nèi*) (43/17/28). This must correspond to the outer and inner qualities of a natural object. The outside is measured in terms of 'great' and 'small' (*dà* and *xiǎo*), while the inside is expressed in judging 'importance' (*gùi*) or 'unimportance' (*jiàn*) (43/17/28). It would perhaps be better to put it this way: What we measure as *dà* or *xiǎo* is the outside of things, and what we measure as *gùi* and *jiàn* is the inside.

The Sea-Spirit's answer to this problem posed by the River-Lord is to list six possible aspects from which a thing may be viewed.

1. Things may be looked at from the viewpoint of *tao*. This ought to be identical with the way in which things have been analysed in the foregoing dialogue, evidently establishing a superior outlook upon the world. The differences expressed in our judgments of quantity or quality do not really exist.

2. Things may possess an opinion of themselves as the River-Lord did in II and III. The subjective apprehension of oneself implies a corresponding debasement of others. Everything will naturally seek a high degree of self-esteem.

3. Things may be regarded as pure objects of common opinion (*sú*). *Sú* seems to be a kind of collective, objective opinion superimposing values from outside without any kind of self-understanding on behalf of the object valued. In dismissing the regard of oneself in judging things, one no longer has any reason for reducing others in contrast to oneself, and there remains an objective way of measuring things in their relation to each other without the contrast to oneself.

4. We may look at things and take a special interest in the differences (*chà*) immediately perceived to exist by our eyes. At a given moment, when comparing an object with another in our field of vision, this results in a judgment that attributes *dà* or *xiǎo* to the object in question. We may always compare a thing with something bigger than itself, judging it accordingly as small, and with something smaller than itself, judging it accordingly as big. This is a conclusion from the relativism established in IV. Everything in the universe, including heaven and

earth and the tip of a hair, may be small and big depending on the differences and comparisons that are taken into account (cf. 43/17/31).

5. Things may be measured from the viewpoint of *gōng* (43/17/31), variously translated as 'function'[8] or 'services'.[9] *Gōng* implies 'use' or 'function', but also 'merit'. In having a function or use and fulfilling it adequately, one acquires merit and may be deemed 'valuable' (*gùi*). Self-esteem (*zì dūo*) depends on function and merit (*gōng*). Anything which is without function is also devoid of significance and useless.

Depending on the context of comparison and judgment, each thing may be pronounced to have a function, be meritorious, or to have no function, and be without merit. East and West cannot keep their identities as different directions without the being of each other. They are mutually dependent in spite of the fact that they are opposed to one another. This is the way to determine differences in function, but everything both has and does not have a function, depending on the context.

It is tempting to draw attention to other places in the philosophy in *Chuang Tzu* which deal with the use and uselessness of things (cf., e.g., Ch. 20), the superior man's lack of merit (cf. 2/1/22), the law of reversion (*fǎn*) from one extreme position to another, and the mutual dependency of opposite powers and entities. This, however, lies beyond our present scope.

6. The final aspect according to which an object can be judged is that of one's 'preference' or 'interest' (*qù* [43/17/33]). The preferences or interests of a being are expressed in two possible attitudes or judgments pronounced by that being, that of *rán*, approval, and that of *fēi*, disapproval or condemnation. Everything may be approved of or condemned according to the one who is judging and his interests. *Rán* and *fēi* are relative to the preferences (*qù*), and these are mere expressions of a particular world-concept, restricted in space and time (cf. II and III above).

Every being affirms or denies the utility to himself of everything in his surrounding world, according to his likes and dislikes. Interests reflect the sphere of living. Anything may then be, quite accidentally, approved of or condemned. The judgment is arbitrary and emerges from only a selection or part of an individual's preferences. Things are always being looked at from different angles, being subjected to judgments from each of these perspectives. Every object in the world can thus be both approved of and condemned, depending on the eyes of the beholder.

IX. The Code of Ethics (43/17/34–43/17/35)

The translation of this next section involves certain problems, and the relation between it and the following one is not quite clear. This does not impede an understanding of the main idea, however, which I take to be that one cannot establish constant rules of behaviour by studying the consequences of past conduct and actions. One pattern of conduct may in different times (*shí*), and under different circumstances, produce different effects, and may accordingly be valued differently from one time to another, i.e. *gùi jiàn yǒu shí* (43/17/35). The past cannot be taken as a model for the present, as the Confucianists professed. There is a correct action for every point and situation in time. Patterns of behaviour must change with the course of time. Here I am anticipating the further discussion of time in XII below. The same theory is advocated by the Legalist school and certain of the neo-Taoists in the 3rd and 4th centuries A.D. It also seems to be an established doctrine of the original Taoism, expressed for instance in the notion of 'spontaneity' (*zì rán*).[10] The conclusion, in all these cases, is that we cannot search in the past for something upon which to model our ethical codes of today. The relativism of ethics (*lǐ*) is absolute. There is no norm to be discovered (*wèi kě yǐ wéi cháng yě* [43/17/35]).

X. The Inherent Qualities of Things in Nature
(43/17/35–43/17/37)

So far we have been dealing with distinctions (*fēn*) between objects in Nature. These are differences expressed in judgments of quantity and quality, function and position. According to the argument in the present section, Chuang Tzu evidently presupposes that there is another set of differences between things. These are differences inherent in the things, determining the actions and natural pattern of conduct of each object in the universe. Three categories are applied to describe how things objectively differ in regard to essence or nature: instrument or purpose (*qì*); gift, talent, or skill (*jì*), and natural endowment (*xìng*). The Sea-Spirit offers illustrations of the differences between, for instance, the horse and the wildcat in regard to the catching of mice. Things in nature are clearly objectively determined from without, that is in their given constitution, to perform and pursue a definite pattern of behaviour. The inherent character defines 'biologically' the world of existence for each species, e.g. the well-frog and the summer-insect.

The limits imposed on things by their nature in turn becomes the world of their values and understanding. The restricted 'Lebenswelt' of each thing in Nature is not the result of an arbitrary choice, but is conditioned by its essence and is to a high degree unchangeable. Everything occupies a definite position, and if we refer to other parts of *Chuang Tzu* we immediately note a connexion between this argument and his ideal of the realization by each man and thing of his or its specific happiness in his or its proper environment (cf., e.g., Ch. 1).

The three categories, *qì, jì*, and *xìng*, describing the inherent qualities of things, are not easily and clearly distinguished. Nor is it essential to our present purpose that they should be.

XI. The Narrowness of Mind Expressed in Moral Theories (43/17/37–43/17/39)

The one-sidedness expressed by any given theory of moral law is further emphasized. 'Right' and 'wrong' are always related to a definite set of values, and to say that one 'cherishes the right' (*shī shì* [43/17/37]) is equivalent to saying that one completely lacks understanding of the principles underlying the universe (*tiān dì zhī lǐ*) and the reality of things (*wàn wù zhī qíng*). The occurrence of *lǐ* ('principle') here only serves to indicate the continued argument invoked by the Sea-Spirit in II and finally brought to a close in XIV below.

The principles of the universe and the reality of things in Nature are identical with the theorems and axioms put forth above in IV and V. The universe lacks an unchanging standard of values and measures, and is, so to speak, amoral. Any set of fixed values merely expresses a one-sidedness of judgment and a narrowness of mind. We shall take neither right nor wrong, neither heaven nor earth as our model for action and understanding. We are not even allowed to take into consideration both right and wrong, both heaven and earth; rather, as in the system of Chuang Tzu, we must transcend even these pairs of distinctions and entities.

XII. The Values of Historical Actions (43/17/39–43/17/41)

We have already discussed the concept of time or the correct time for doing something (*shí*) in IV above. Time in the present context does not merely refer to a moment of time, but includes the circumstances and influences upon situations brought about in the due process of time. The universe, as conceived by Chuang Tzu, is a dynamic one, subject to eternal movement and change. When time and nature change, the circumstances in our surroundings towards which we direct our actions change simultaneously. This is beyond human control, and consequently we must adapt our behaviour in accord with time.

Those who adhere to natural changes, the situation of time, and common opinion (sú) are judged by their contemporaries and by posterity as 'disciples of righteousness' (yì dú [43/17/40]), not because they acted in accordance with some universally valid concepts of 'right' or 'good', but only because their actions corresponded to the circumstances of time. Actions are to be judged only in relation to historical settings The significant figures in history owe their fame to the fact that they were in harmony with what the times demanded. There is no question about their moral character or righteousness. The verdict of posterity in that respect is due to an illusion of the existence of moral values.

XIII. A PROPOSED COURSE OF CONDUCT (43/17/41–44/17/47)

The River-Lord is finally faced with the problem of deciding how to conduct himself and his affairs. The Sea-Spirit answers in light of the foregoing arguments (II–XII), which have terminated in a Taoist viewpoint. One cannot decide absolutely about anything, neither about what is valuable or valueless, nor about what is important or unimportant. Opposites (fǎn) are not to be determined (43/17/42).

The answer proposed is to escape from narrow-minded intentions and actions which are the product of an inferior knowledge of the world. One must avoid jū ér zhì (43/17/43), i.e. becoming obdurate in one's will, wishes, and intentions. This is contrary to tao. Accordingly, we should be permitted to infer that tao is not chained to its intentions, or in other words, tao does not have any definite aims. Tao in action is aimless, or to use the frequent statement in Chuang Tzu, is practising wú-wéi (non-action). Intentions and desires are conditioned by the world where a being exists. Its likes and dislikes, interests and preferences are expressions of its 'Lebenswelt'. Tao is something wholly transcending such an existence in a finite sphere of living.

Secondly, one must avoid one-sidedness in action: wú yī ér xíng (43/17/43), because this implies deviation from the course of tao. One must not give priority to one pattern of behaviour or one set of ethical values, for in doing so one is easily locked in an unchanging character and an inflexibility of mind, which implies an inability to change in accordance with time and nature, and also liable to produce undue self-esteem and pride. *Tao* in action is pluralism and spontaneity, it is unpredictable and without stability.

Thirdly, one should develop certain character traits modelled on *tao* : impartiality, breadth, and expansion. The 'Lebenswelt' including my thoughts, emotions, and actions, should become as limitless and undetermined as *tao*. All things should be treated equally, without preferences and partial judgments. They should be comprehended in a unity transcending the apparent, merely relative differences.

To comprehend the ten thousand things in their unity may be taken negatively to mean that one should ignore their differences, which are only real within the frames of a limited world-view. Whether the statement may be interpreted positively as saying that all things partake in an all-transcending unity, is left unexplained by Chuang Tzu. A statement in Chapter 2 (5/2/53) would defend the positive interpretation as well as the negative one.

Some properties which one can ascribe to *tao* are later outlined in contrast to the properties of the natural objects. Life and death, beginning and end, are common to all finite things, but as shown above (IV–V), they are without constancy. One should not base one's life on these apparent qualities, subjected to the principles expounded above in the main part. Needless to say, *tao* is wholly exempt from any of these qualities.

The Sea-Spirit ends with a picture of the dynamic universe, comparing it with a galloping horse. Time and movement cannot be brought to a stop. The void and the full, beginning and end, are prey to an eternal process in which everything passes from one state to another. This is called the principle of the ten thousand things (*wàn wù zhī lǐ* [44/17/46]). The only answer to the problem posed by the River-Lord as to how one should act in this universe is to let everything, including oneself, pursue the road which spontaneity (*zì rán*) offers. This is called *zì huà* (44/17/47), and denotes the natural course which is the evolution of nature based on the activity of *tao* and characterized by the structures and laws common to all Nature. The dynamism of Nature is to be taken as a model, implying that all beings, in so far as they are parts of Nature and participate in its laws and constitution, should be left alone and not interfered with. They will then take their natural course. This argument effects the transition to the last section of the dialogue, in XIV below, which discusses finally the difference between 'what is of heaven' (*tiān*) and 'what is of man' (*rén*) (cf. 44/17/50–44/17/54). Despite the fact that these problems are basic to a complete understanding of Chuang Tzu's philosophy, an interpretation of them lies beyond the scope of the present essay.

As regards the mechanism of *tao* and the universe, there are several chapters in the rest of the book which deal more exhaustively with this (Chs. 11, 12, 13, and 14).

XIV. THE GREAT PRINCIPLE (44/17/47–44/17/53)

The dialogue ends with a final reference to *tao*, the principles of the world and certain consequences of having knowledge of them. To know *tao* is to understand the principles (*lǐ*), and this may be applied to practice; that is, one may become enlightened *vis à vis* the forces of circumstances (*míng yǔ quán* [44/17/48]). This knowledge must be taken to be what the Sea-Spirit has discussed and professed above, through the arguments in II–XIII, i.e. the whole dialogue. The principles in regard to theory of knowledge and ontology are expressed in III–VII and the application of this world-concept to practical behaviour has been set out in IX–XIII. The River-Lord should thus be prepared to meet 'the forces of circumstances' (*quán*), that is whatever time (*shí*) and its influence on the events in life and Nature, and whatever the evolution of the universe might bring in his way. The consequences are portrayed, as usual in Chuang Tzu, in a vivid, sometimes exaggerated way. Such conduct, based on superior insight in *tao* and *lǐ*, ('principle'), is called the conduct of supreme virtue (*zhì dé* [44/17/48]), i.e. the best possible way of existence and of preserving one's being. The dialogue, passing through several initiatory levels of insight, ends in this appraisal of a superior way of existence in total harmony with what Chuang Tzu elsewhere maintains in his work.

NOTES

1. Quoted from James Legge, 'The Texts of Taoism' in *The Sacred Books of China*, Oxford at the Clarendon Press, 1891. Part 2, p. 142.
2. Quoted from the translation of Burton Watson, *The Complete Works of Chuang Tzu*, Columbia University Press, New York 1968, p. 175.
3. Cf. the fragments (arranged according to the numbering of Diels) 8, 17, 51, 53A, 54, 60, 62, and 94.
4. Cf. *Erh-ti Chang*, Sect. 1. *Taishō shinshū daizōkyō* 45. 90–91.
5. Cf. the death of Chuang Tzu's wife described in Ch. 18, 46/18/15–46/18/19.
6. Cf. *Chuang Tzu* 90/33/8 and 90/33/41.
7. Cf. *Meng Tzu* 2A:6.
8. Quoted from Watson, op.cit., p. 179.
9. Quoted from Legge, op.cit., Pt. 1, p. 380.
10. As for the concept of '*zì rán*', cf. *Chuang Tzu* Chs. 7, 9, and 11, and in *Lao Tzu*, Ch. 25.

CHUNG YING CHENG

VIII. *Chinese philosophy: a characterization*

This article offers a synthetic characterization of Chinese philosophy based on an analytical reconstruction of its main traditions and thinking. Three main traditions in Chinese philosophy, Confucianism, Taoism and Chinese Buddhism, are depicted and discussed, together with some comments on Chinese Marxism in the contemporary scene. Four characteristics of Chinese philosophy are presented: intrinsic humanism, concrete rationalism, organic naturalism, and a pragmatism of self-cultivation. It is clear from the discussion that these four characteristics are interrelated and mutually supporting and thus should be better understood in the context of one another. Many open problems of philosophy, such as transcendence, evil, logic, and theoretical knowledge, are raised by an inquiry into Chinese philosophy. If Chinese philosophy serves to make us critically aware of these problems and to provide alternative ways of thinking, we are more than justified in presenting Chinese philosophy as a philosophy of universal concern and universal significance.

I. Fallacies in Early Studies in Chinese Philosophy

Early studies in Chinese philosophy in the European languages have led to many confusions and misunderstandings concerning the true nature of Chinese philosophy. Four such confusions and misunderstandings are common in many writings on Chinese philosophy. There is first of all the belief that Chinese philosophy is irrational and mystical and merely to be grasped by some form of intuition. On the basis of this belief it is naturally assumed that Chinese philosophy is so radically different from Western modes of thinking that it is impossible to convey Chinese philosophy in Western terms. This assumption and its presupposed belief are fallacious and misleading, for in fact there are conspicuous traditions of naturalism and rationalism in Chinese philosophy and some other universal elements which should make comparisons and contrasts between Chinese philosophy and Western philosophy not only intelligible but profitable.

In direct contrast with the fallacy of attribution of mysticism is the fallacious belief that there is nothing new and original in Chinese thinking and that everything which is contained in Chinese thought has been dealt with in the Western tradition. This latter view is characteristic of the critics of Chinese culture in early nineteenth-century Europe, just as the former view is characteristic of the admirers of Chinese culture and philosophy in twentieth-century America. Certainly this second view is not true, for a thorough understanding of Chinese philosophy will reveal many fundamental concepts of Chinese philosophy which are not to be found in the Western tradition. Even though there are of course many similarities between Chinese philosophy and some philosophical thought in the West, it must be pointed out that similarities can be profoundly significant and inspiring in philosophical inquiries. In fact a dialogue between Chinese and Western philosophies can be conducted and developed only when similarities and differences between them are not limited to surface observations. To develop a dialogue between Chinese and Western philosophy, one has to understand first of all the languages of both traditions and to be able to translate one language into another in a constructive fashion. To do this, it is evident that one has to have creative insights so that one can see philosophical problems and solutions presented in a different tradition and thus can conceptualize them in one's own native system.

The good consequences resulting from a dialogue between Chinese philosophy and Western philosophy can be many. Among others the most relevant would be a better understanding of one's own position. If it is one of the functions of philosophy to uncover the presuppositions of an accepted view and to explore new ways of thinking and argumentation, the dialogue in question will certainly provide new light for such discovery and exploration. No improvement on self-understanding is possible without such discovery and exploration.

Related to the second fallacy mentioned above is the general erroneous tendency toward crude generalization in many Marxist-oriented studies on Chinese philosophy. Crude generalizations on the nature of Chinese philosophy are reflected in the facile classification of all Chinese philosophers into idealists and materialists, objectivists and subjectivists, proletarianists and aristocratists. On the basis of these classifications pretentious value judgments are then drawn which cannot but throw a veil on the true nature of the school under examination. This approach toward the study and evaluation of Chinese philosophy is unacceptable and undesirable, as it is based on dogmatic premises which are not open to criticism. Furthermore, the classifications in use are too general and vague to capture the individual merits and demerits of specific schools or thinkers. They naturally lead to a distorted picture of Chinese philosophy rather than to a clarification of it. A lesson which one can learn from this fallacy is that one has to be critical of one's own conceptual tools of study and evaluation before one embarks on a study and evaluation of Chinese philosophy. There can be no adequate understanding of a subject, be it Chinese or any other philosophy, if there is no adequate conceptual tool for uncovering and formulating an adequate understanding. Generalizations are in general necessary for the purpose of understanding, but we should remember nevertheless that generalizations must be reached as conclusions based on a detailed study, analysis, and reconstruction, and must also be considered as instigations to further critical studies. It is with this view of generalization in mind that I shall present a general picture of Chinese philosophy as a whole.

A final fallacious view prevalent in the study of Chinese philosophy is that Chinese philosophy can be explained in terms of socio-political or socio-economic, or even socio-psychological, conditions and features of the thinker and his times. The Marxist has of course developed a systematic method for relating philosophy to socio-economic conditions of a time period. The undesirability of dealing with Chinese philosophy on this basis has been indicated in the discussion of the third fallacy in the study of Chinese philosophy. What I am now thinking of are the non-Marxist intellectual historians who commit themselves to explaining Chinese philosophy in terms of historical events without developing any systematic methodology or theoretical justification. The result of this approach to the study of Chinese philosophy is that many significant philosophical ideas are reduced to specific historical referents and are therefore divested of universal meaning and truth-claim. This is the fallacy of historical reduction. As with any form of reduction, it is bound to impoverish the rich content of philosophical thought in China and will mislead people to disregard the independent philosophical character of Chinese philosophers.

Before we engage ourselves in a general discussion of the over-all characteristics of Chinese philosophy, it is important to do two things: first, we should explicitly state our method of study and evaluation; secondly, we should actually apply our method to bear upon our historical review of major and main trends and traditions in Chinese philosophy. The methodology which we are to adopt to characterize Chinese philosophy is one of analysis and reconstruction which we may call briefly the method of analytical reconstruction. This method consists first in analyzing various basic views in Chinese philosophy in an attempt to display and reveal the intricate implications and relationships of concepts involved in these views. It will, furthermore, be directed toward making explicit presuppositions and consequences of these views. Finally, it will lead to a systematic and critical explication of the concepts and views under analysis. It seems deplorable that in the past no such method has been applied to the study of Chinese philosophy and little attempt has even been made to state views and concepts in Chinese philosophy in clear and systematic philosophical language. A consequence of this is that Chinese philosophical ideas couched in the classical language gradually lose their direct appeal to the philosophical mind of modern man. This is due to a conceptual block and to lack of linguistic criticism. In the following our discussion of Chinese philosophy will be based on the methodology of analytic reconstruction, and will be conducted in such a way that the relevance of Chinese philosophy to modern philosophers and modern man will become manifest, and a comparison of Chinese philosophy with Western philosophy possible.

II. ARCHETYPAL IDEAS IN THE PRE-CONFUCIAN PERIOD

Historically speaking, Chinese philosophy begins with a tradition which is not characterized by any systematic mythology or dogmatic personalistic religion, but instead by a sentiment of consanguinity of man and nature, a sense of historicality and continuity of life in time, and finally a faith in the reality and potential perfectibility of man and this world. In the Shang and Chou times, long before Confucius was born, there were already developed archetypal ideas concerning ultimate reality and its determining authority, the potentiality of man for achieving goodness, the external limitation of man's existence and the need for establishing a relationship of unity and harmony between man and reality in well-tuned behavior patterns. There are ideas of *t'ien* (heaven), *ti* (lord on high, ancestral god of man), *hsing*, (nature of man), *ming* (mandate, destiny and necessity), *te* (power, potentiality, virtue) and *li* (rites and proprieties). The idea of *ti* and *t'ien* are specifically related to the practice of ancestral worship in ancient times: the ancestors of men are identified with ultimate reality and regarded as a perennial source of life. This view has profound philosophical significance. Later the more personalistic notion of *ti* is replaced by the less personalistic notion of *t'ien*, as the later represents a more general notion open to acceptance by a broader group of people. In a sense we may regard *t'ien* as a generalized notion of *ti* developed from the need to unify the ancestral worships of different groups of people. Thus *ti* may be regarded as ancestor of a specific people, *t'ien* as ancestor of all peoples. In this fashion *t'ien* becomes less personalistic than *ti*, because it is divested of the specifically personalistic characteristics of *ti*, even though *t'ien* still retains the special and moral powers of *ti*.

Apart from all this, *t'ien* is primarily a spatial notion, while *ti* is primarily a temporal notion. The development from the idea of *ti* to that of *t'ien* indicates an awareness of the physical proximity to man of the ultimate reality and supreme authority. This proximity is further indicated in the fact that *t'ien* has a close and deep concern with the well-being of people. The existence of government and ruler is made possible through the desire of heaven to raise people in happiness. Because of this concern of *t'ien* a ruler is responsible for making his people well-nourished and well-ordered. Also because of it, the will of heaven is identified with the will of people, so that the dissatisfaction and unrest of people can be interpreted as a sign of heaven's withdrawing of a ruler's appointment as ruler due to his loss of virtue or goodness. The virtue and goodness in question are nothing but powers in carrying out the intentions of heaven and in fulfilling the potentiality of one's life. This *te*, which in a sense is inherent in man, and which one can cultivate so as to fulfil oneself in accordance with the will (or mandate) of heaven — this potentiality of man and his ability to cultivate this potentiality — is called the nature (*hsing*) of man. It is clear from the fact that man is closely related to heaven — the source of his life and his model for greatness — that he must have his nature cultivated to realize *te*. Furthermore, since the order of man is based on the order of nature, the principle which should preserve the order of man is a practical concern of man. It is from this concern that *li*, governing relationships among men and between men and spirits, are developed and valued as most fundamental and essential for the development of man, as well as for maintaining the well-being of society.

To conclude, the archetypal ideas of the pre-Confucian period have profound philosophical significance. They are interrelated and founded on a sentiment of the original consanguinity between man and nature, and on a sentiment of man's existence as a potential entity capable of development. Thus the existence of virtue in man is his ability conscientiously to pursue and attain, or realize, unity of man and reality. In the following we shall see how, on this general basis, the main trends and traditions of Chinese philosophy develop and diversify.

III. THE TRADITION OF CONFUCIANISM

The Confucian age begins with Confucius's explicit recognition that the external *t'ien* (heaven) has an essential link with the internal *te* (virtue, power) of man and that man should extend himself in a graded love toward other men and thus achieve the universal humanity inherent in us. We may say, therefore, that Confucianism as represented by Confucius is an awakening of man in regard to his relationships to heaven, to other men and to himself. The relationality of man is to be realized in the practice and perfection of virtues such as *jên* (love and benevolence), *yi* (or *i*) (righteousness), *li* (propriety) and *chih* (wisdom in distinguishing good from bad). *Jên* is the universality of man. *Yi* is the necessity and actual application of *jên* to a diversity of situations and relationships. *Li* is the proper way of expressing oneself in fulfilling one's *jên* by means of *yi*. If *li* is the exterior behavior pattern of a man toward another man in a situation, *yi* is the principle which confers propriety on the behavior pattern in question, and *jên* is the natural desire for fulfilling *li* in the spirit of *yi*. Thus *jên* is most fundamental for making a man a man. For it is on the basis of *jên* that a man will seek to fulfil others in order to fulfil himself, as well as to fulfil himself in order to fulfil others. It is on this basis that a man can relate to other men and become himself.

A man who sets his mind in pursuing *jên* is called a superior man (*chün-tzu*), a man who has come to awareness of *jên* and his ability and necessity to fulfil himself by *jên*. When he succeeds in achieving perfection of *jên*, so that he may act in total freedom and yet according to strict principles of *yi* and *li*, he is not only a *chün-tzu*, but a sage (*shen-jên*). Thus *jên* can also represent the ideal perfection of man in Confucian thinking. It is to be identified with both the totality of all virtues (*te*) and the essence of all virtues.

When *t'ien* is regarded as related to the internal *te* of man, *t'ien* is a source of moral courage and moral wisdom in a superior man. But, on the other hand, *t'ien* in Confucius, and later in Mencius, is regarded not merely as an internal source of one's potentiality, but also as an external limitation and necessity which put life to trial and limit life. In understanding this phase of *t'ien* a superior man will have to accept many determined facts of life, such as death, misfortune, etc. These determinations are possible because man has his object-nature — that is, he is an object. But Confucius and Mencius recognize that besides this object-nature of man according to which man is determined by external causes, man has a dynamic subject-nature — that is, man is a subject capable of cultivating himself in the path of virtue and therefore of determining himself in the direction of achieving full autonomy and independence of his nature. This is how man may realize his spiritual freedom despite the external determination and limitation imposed upon him as an object. The importance of Confucius is his insistence that man can become a full subject, and that his life is meaningful because he has a subject-nature and thus the power to pursue perfection in the actual conduct of himself in a network of relationships.

Confucianism after Confucius has been greatly developed in the classical period in Mencius, Hsun Tzu, and in the works of *The Great Learning* and *The Doctrine of the Mean*. Mencius explicity forms the doctrine of goodness of human nature as a foundation for man's capacity of self-cultivation toward perfection. He appeals to natural sentiments of man, such as compassion, shame, modesty, or reverence, and like and dislike, as bases and beginnings of virtues such as *jên, yi, li* and *chih*. Thus it is asserted in Mencius that virtues have a natural foundation in man and that the nature of man is nothing other than the ability to pursue virtues. The goodness of human nature is therefore nothing but a fulfilment of the inherent nature-virtue in man, whereas badness is but the abandonment and deviation of one's natural sentiments and nature under circumstances which dominate man. But man cannot really lose his inherent goodness and his innate ability to know and see what he needs for the preservation of his goodness. Thus Mencius is fond of talking about 'collecting self in return to good'. His doctrine of government by the love of people and by becoming a good example in the person of a ruler is based on this doctrine of the goodness of human nature.

Though Hsun Tzu, as a Confucianist later than Mencius, argues that human nature is bad and that man's goodness is only man-made, not natural, he nevertheless remains a staunch Confucianist in his faith in man's ability and potential and his initial willingness to better himself. For Hsun Tzu, human nature is bad because it is seen to consist basically in desires which know no proper limitation and which mean only self-profit. But this is not the whole of Hsun Tzu's view of man's nature, for he recognized the power of the human mind or reason to be inherent in that nature too. By experience man must come to use his mind and reason for the benefit of himself and others. Thus Hsun Tzu argues for the importance of education and training in terms of *li*, which are regarded as principles for ordering and organizing human behavior and efforts in society and the State. *Li* in this sense is the creation of reason, and is the fundamental saving virtue of man.

Confucianism in later ages has received various formulations, but basically the minimal and necessary principles of self-cultivation of virtue, unity of man and heaven, and relevance of social order and political harmony for individual self-realization, are never abandoned and are universally affirmed from the Han to the Sung Ming period. Even though Sung-Ming Confucianism (called neo-Confucianism) has been deeply involved with metaphysical speculations over problems of *li* (principle of being and reason) and *chi* (vapor, substance, and material), *li* and *chi* have also been used to explain the essentially good nature of man, the potential unity between the nature of man and the nature of heaven and all things in reality, and not least of all why man by cultivating himself can actualize what is inherent in him.

IV. The Tradition of Taoism

Another important tradition in Chinese philosophy is, of course, Taoism. It may be suggested that Taoism represents the stage of development of the concept of *t'ien* to that of *tao* in the classical period. It is true that the term 'tao' has been used in Confucian writings, but it is Taoists such as Lao Tzu and Chuang Tzu who formulate an exclusive philosophy of *tao*. Now the concept of *tao* is altogether different from the concepts of *t'ien* and *ti* in being a completely non-personalistic concept of ultimate reality. It is more generalized in scope than 'ti' and 't'ien', because it comprehends everything in the world. There is, however, one respect in which *tao* shares something in common with the earlier concepts of *ti* and *t'ien*. *Tao* is internally related to man just as *ti* and *t'ien* are internally related to man in Confucianism. In a sense *tao* is regarded as the primordial being of man. In saying this we must bear in mind that *tao*, unlike *ti* or *t'ien*, is not regarded as being in a position to dispense a special favor to man or as deeply concerned with man's well-being, for *tao* is impartial to everything as it generates, comprehends, transforms and preserves all things. It is with regard to this impartiality of *tao* that all things can be regarded as being ontologically equal. In Lao Tzu this concept of ontological equality is implicit in the very notion of *tao*, while on the basis of this same concept, Chuang Tzu goes a step further in developing a new sense of the ontological equality of all things.

Things are ontologically equal, according to Chuang Tzu, because they are formed by a process of self- and mutual transformation. There is no substance to individual things and to their individuality, for all individual things are only relatively determined in the totality of the self- and mutual transformation of things. Thus things are ontologically equal also in the sense of being both self-activating and mutually determining.

There are several important characteristics of the philosophy of *tao* to mention. First, *tao* is a totality which is basically indefinable and unnameable. A proper interpretation of this indefinability and unnameability of *tao* is that *tao* cannot be limited by any object or be finitely characterized. This means that no object and no character can stand for *tao* without creating a partial and misleading conception of *tao*.

Because *tao* cannot be characterized by any finite character, it can be contrasted with things which are finitely characterizable. If things which are finitely characterizable are called 'being', then *tao* would be the opposite of being, and is in fact called by Lao Tzu the non-being, or the void (*wu*). Thus *tao* for Lao Tzu is not a reality merely negatively conceived, but is instead something which can only be conceived as the indeterminate, as the source and origin of all things. Although 'void' is the concept conveyed by Lao Tzu to capture the virtue of *tao*, it is better to use the terms 'indeterminate' or 'ultimateless' to suggest the possibility of actually generating things and men in *tao*. Indeed, Lao Tzu has specifically maintained that it is *tao* which gives rise to all finite things that are related to us in any way, and that it is the void or the indeterminate which one has to understand and to take into consideration in the understanding of *tao*.

Another point about Taoism is that *tao* is not conceived as a static or unchanging substance, but as a process of movement and change. This means that all things comprehended in *tao* are in a process of change and movement. Now there are two questions to be answered in this connection: By what operation does *tao* give rise to all things in being? How is *tao* as a process of change and movement to be described? The answer to the first question is that *tao* gives rise to everything by way of differentiation and self-realization. There is an apparent paradox in the process of generation by *tao*, which should be resolved from a dialectical point of view.

Tao, as we have seen, is void and yet produces everything. This is so because *tao* is the principle by which the negative can become the positive, the potential can become the actual, the void can become the substantive, and the one can become the many. It is by the very negativity and potentiality of *tao* that everything positive and actual is created and preserved. But at the same time, when the potential becomes the actual, the negative becomes the positive, the void becomes the substantive, and the one becomes the many, the converse process takes place as well. *Tao* in this sense is inexhaustible, and its workings define change in terms of dialectical oppositions and complementation. This notion of *tao* is insisted upon by Taoists as representing the most fundamental wisdom of life, which, the Taoists hold, is basically experienceable in a careful reflection on life and reality.

Because *tao* is change, and change is always change from something to something else, *tao* itself is a unity of two opposites. The two opposites of *tao* are respectively called *yin* and *yang*, the feminine force (or principle) and the masculine force (or principle). In Lao Tzu it is clear that the *yin–yang* forces represent two aspects of a unity, be it an individual or the totality of *tao*. *Yin* can be identified with the negative, the potential, the subjective, and the preservative, while *yang* can be identified with the positive, the actual, the objective, and the creative. In a sense, *yin* represents *tao* as an inexhaustible source from which every form of energy or activity is derived, whereas *yang* represents *tao* as a form of activity which is ever creative, but which has a beginning and an ending and therefore remains exhaustible. When the *yang* force exhausts itself, it will fade into the *yin*; but when *yin* dominates, there is then great promise of *yang* activity. In the process of change which is constituted by the interchange of the two forces in the twofold movement of *tao* — actualization of *yin* by *yang* and the movement of potentialization of *yang* by *yin* — Lao Tzu has specifically emphasized the notion of return (*fu*): return is return to *tao* the indeterminate and the inexhaustible. It is an emphasis on *tao* as a *yin* force. But this is no denial of the *yang*, for one thing cannot return to *yin* except by way of exhausting *yang* activity in the thing itself. Thus, as in explaining the cosmological principle of the generation of all things by *tao*, Lao Tzu also made explicit the cosmological principle of the destination of all things.

Lao Tzu has applied his cosmological principles of generation and destination to man, as the world of man is not separate from the world of nature. According to these principles, the well-being of man consists in his ability to follow the *tao*, and this means his ability to preserve potentiality for action but not actually acting out his potentiality. This is so because man is a part of *tao* and part of the production of *tao*: when he exerts himself to act and exhausts himself, he will be simply tossed away as a product of the *tao*, which can be explained as frustration and exhaustion resulting from too much effort. Thus a better way to deal with life is not to exhaust oneself and to become an object. Instead one should try to potentialize the actual and remain one with the source which is *tao*. To do this one must become aware of *tao* and cultivate the *tao* in the sense of imitating the action of non-action of *tao*, so that man will become infinitely creative and free himself from domination by destructive forces. It is in this state that one's life will flow naturally and spontaneously, and everything will be preserved in a similarly natural and spontaneous way. This doctrine has been aptly described as 'doing everything by doing nothing'. Doing nothing means doing nothing specific, while doing everything means doing everything flowing from *tao* on its own. Lao Tzu has used many images and analogies to convey the importance of preserving the potential of life and remaining effortless and natural in the conduct of life. It is not difficult to see Lao Tzu's point if we reflect on the nature and strength of such things as water, a valley, an uncarved block of wood, a child, a mother, and the female.

In regard to the movement of *tao*, and in regard to the attainment of the well-being of life, Chuang Tzu differs fundamentally from Lao Tzu. In the first place, Chuang Tzu does not stress the idea of a return to *tao* as the source and origin of everything. For him *tao* is a universal presence and the total activity of all things. It is revealed, in particular, in the relativity and relationality of all things. Chuang Tzu has put a special stress on these ideas. The relativity and relationality of things are twofold: things are relative and relational to each other, and furthermore relative and relational to the totality of things which is *tao*. They are relative and relational to each other in the sense that each thing is a 'this' and a 'that', and thus are relatively and relationally determined and defined. Things are different from one another, but are interdependent for their individuality. Thus nothing is an absolute or center of the world, because everything is an absolute and a center of the world. Things are relative and relational to *tao* in the sense that they, each of them, are part of *tao* and each of them come about by way of self- and mutual transformation. On the basis of *tao* there is no limitation to the process of self- and mutual transformation, and *tao* is itself a whole which exemplifies self- and mutual transformation. Because of this, no individuation and differentiation of things is absolute and yet there is no simple undifferentiated homogeneity.

From the point of view of *tao*, an individual is both *tao* and not *tao*. It is *tao* because it is an exemplification of the self-transformation of *tao*; it is not *tao* because it is not the totality. This principle of self- and mutual transformation, as we have indicated earlier, establishes the fundamental equality of things. It applies, furthermore, to the life of man. On recognizing the relativity and relationality of things, man could detach himself from any specific perspective of things and thus open his mind to all the possible perspectives and possibilities which are manifested in things. This attitude will lead him to a natural and spontaneous life, even facing hardships and disasters. Chuang Tzu does not regard this attitude as one of recession and passivity, but rather as a natural positive result of understanding *tao*. Positively to understand *tao* is to become *tao* and to adopt the perspective of *tao*, and thus to realize the centrality of everything. In this manner one will become creative, in the sense that one is open to all possibilities of becoming, and free, in the sense that one will not be attached to any single fixed position. We might suggest that Taoism in Chuang Tzu has made freedom and creativity the goal of man's life, besides naturalness and spontaneity.

V. The Tradition of Chinese Buddhism

A third important tradition in Chinese philosophy is Chinese Buddhism. We must distinguish Chinese Buddhism from Buddhism in China. The latter is an Indian importation, but the former is the product of the native intelligence of Chinese in later stages of the development of Buddhism in China. An interesting fact, often overlooked in the discussion of Chinese Buddhism, is that there are two schools of Chinese Buddhism which have corresponding Indian predecessors, whereas there are two other schools of Chinese Buddhism which do not have corresponding Indian predecessors and which can be regarded as having developed or evolved from the two other schools, transcending them in significance and profundity. The first two schools of Chinese Buddhism are Madhymika and Yogacara, and the second two, Tien-tai and Hua-yen. We shall first discuss briefly how the two later schools overshadow the two earlier ones by advancing concepts which are typical of Chinese Buddhism, and also how these two schools can be considered to combine theoretically to lead to a novel position which has exercised a powerful influence in later ages — the Ch'an Buddhism of Hui Nan and other Ch'an masters after him.

In Madhymika the essential idea is that one has to go beyond both affirmation of this and affirmation of not-this in order to reach the state of non-attachment and transcendence characteristic of Buddhist wisdom. But this logic of the denial of four terms (this, that, this and that, neither this nor that), when applied to ontology, will entail a concept of constant and infinite detachment and negation. This process, however, is difficult to reconcile with the actual experience of order and stability in which man finds himself. Tien-tai was apparently developed from a concern with this type of problem, namely, a concern with the problem of man's relationship with this world.

In the Tien-tai literature the negative attitude of constant transcending this and that is combined with a positive attitude toward seeing the meaningfulness of affirming this and that. The proposition that this world is nothingness and thus to be denounced, is supplemented with the proposition that nothingness is this world, and thus to be accepted in this world. The upshot of this, as far as the Tien-tai Buddhist thinker is concerned, is that to denounce the world is to accept the world and that to accept the world is to denounce it, for one can denounce what is denounceable of the world and one can accept what is acceptable of the world. The world is thus seen as both denounceable and acceptable, both affirmable and negatable. It is thus held that truth is twofold and yet remains one unity. Now we must ask how this is possible. The answer is very simple: the world can be seen from a dialectical point of view, and therefore can be seen as a dynamic unity of two opposing and yet complementing polarities. One may note that classical Chinese philosophy has provided a model of this dialectical thinking in Taoism and the *Book of Changes*.

The course of the theoretical development from the Yogacara school to the Hua-yen school seems to follow a similar pattern. In the original teaching of Yogacara the whole world is regarded as a projection of the ideational activity of a trans-this-worldly mind or potential consciousness called *alaya*. The assumption of this all-powerful mind or consciousness goes together with the assumption of the ideational attachment of this mind which accounts for the existence of the world. In other words, the world is regarded as a concomitant reality resulting from the activity of mind. Thus the cycle of life and death will not cease if the ideational activity of mind continues and persists. One of the ultimate goals of Yogacara doctrine is to show ways of terminating activities of life and death by terminating activities of mind, and to show ways of withholding the reality of the world by withholding the reality of mind. Now this view is again incompatible with the human experience of the goodness of life, as well as that of the continuity of the world's existence. Perhaps it is because of a need to resolve this incompatibility that the school of Hua-yen comes to advance the doctrine that the world can be seen in a manifold of ways and that wisdom and true salvation consist in actually seeing the world in a manifold of ways.

Thus according to Tu Shun, the first master of the Hua-yen school, the world is simultaneously a unity of every principle with every parti-cular, a unity of every principle with every principle, a harmony of particulars, and finally a unity of every particular with every particu-lar. All this means that the world is infinitely rich and real at the same time, and that mind should open its eyes to this rich and real world which is not bound by the attachment of ideation. By further holding that all is in one and one is in all, it is clear that the Hua-yen school must regard mind as a principle and as a particular which is present in all other principles and all other particulars, and vice versa. This principle of ontological interdependence and interrelationship thus serves to restore reality to both mind and world by restoring the pri-mordial unity of the two. This principle has also the implication that the subjective and the objective must be interdependent in a reality of infinite harmony, so that both necessarily contribute to a knowledge of the real. The possibility of this thinking again has to be understood in the light of the dialectical point of view developed in Taoism and the *Book of Changes*.

Next we come to the development of Ch'an Buddhism in Chinese philosophy. As we have indicated, and to express it from the viewpoint of analytical reconstruction, Ch'an Buddhism can best be described as the final and finest product of the tradition of Chinese Buddhisms preceding it. This means that Ch'an has the best of the *T'ien-tai* tra-dition on understanding the problem of nothingness (*kung*, sunyata), and the best of the Hua-yen tradition on understanding the problem of mind (*hsin* or consciousness). And in a sense it is indeed the case, particularly when we put T'ien-tai and Hua-yen in the right perspective. In the above we have explained the fundamental points of these two schools. From this explanation one can readily see that the T'ien-tai school has developed an ontology of nothingness which nevertheless confers meaningfulness on the existence and reality of this world and preserves the phenomenological reality of mind, whereas the Hua-yen school has developed a phenomenology of mind or consciousness which recognizes and affirms the ontological reality of the world. Both have indicated a possibility of unifying ontology and phenomenology in regard to the reality of this world and of the mind of man. They point to the same direction, even though they begin from the different points of view of their respective background philosophies.

Now this possibility of unifying ontology with phenomenology with regard to the reality of the world and man, that is, of unifying the ontological reality of the world and the phenomenological activity of mind, is actually and explicitly realized by the teachings and practice of Ch'an Buddhism. For according to the teachings and practices of Ch'an, when one sees the true nature and the original mind of oneself, one will realize ultimate reality and becomes enlightened, in the sense of ceasing to be bound by attachment, prejudice, and illusion of any kind. This of course does not mean that one loses one's mind or denies the existence of the world. On the contrary, it is important to keep one's mind and to affirm the existence of the world in order for a Ch'an Buddhist to achieve enlightenment. For it is only by holding to one's mind and affirming the existence of the world that one will be free from the bondage of one's mind and of the world. To use the Buddhist idiom, there is nirvana (freedom) in one's actual life, and there is actual life in nirvana.

The above dialectical combination is not only realized in an act of enlightenment, it is embodied in the practical performance of one's life. Or, to put it another way, the act of enlightenment is not, and cannot be, separate from the actual living of one's life. Even language cannot be considered intelligible in its own terms apart from living contexts. In fact, for the Ch'an Buddhist, use of language represents many aspects of reality and results from the interaction of all possibilities in reality. Thus language and its uses have many functions apart from that of stating, arguing, or making a verbal point. While language can normally make a point by stating a point, it can be used to make a point by not stating a point, or by verbally denying that point which it is making. The complex ways in which Ch'an masters use language to express enlightenment or to awaken enlightenment deserve careful analysis and explication, a work still largely undone. Such an analysis and explication will not only be significant for revealing the simple and yet profound character of Ch'an thinking, but will testify to the potential nature of language and its use. In fact, for the Ch'an masters, use of language is not the only way to induce or express enlightenment. Many other ways, such as various physical bodily actions, can be the inspiration.

What is important to note in connection with this is that every action of man has an ontological meaning which is phenomenologically transparent and a phenomenological meaning which is ontologically hidden. The insight of Ch'an is to reveal the hidden and to assimilate the transparent in simple ways of creative living and self-awareness. There is really nothing mystical or irrational in it, as sometimes claimed by outsiders who have only a superficial grasp of the spirit of Ch'an Buddhism and its historical background. What is relevant here is the natural wish to preserve the world but without confining the meaning of the world to one level of categorial understanding, which is also a message conveyed in both Taoism and the *Book of Changes*.

Man, being essentially an embodiment of *tao* or Buddha-nature, has every reason to claim an ability to realize and achieve *tao* and/or Buddha-nature in his conscious active life. The ontological relationship between knowing and doing or acting should easily lead to the doctrine of instantaneous enlightenment in Ch'an Buddhism. The instantaneousness of enlightenment is a dynamic unification of the objective with the subjective, that is, of the known object with the knowing subject.

VI. MARXISM IN CONTEMPORARY CHINA

Finally we come to the position of Marxism as a representative school of thought in contemporary China. Since China entered the twentieth century there has been a constant search among Chinese intellectuals for an enduring philosophy which will accommodate and adjust the Chinese mind, life, and culture to the needs of the modern world as shaped by Western science, religion, and technology with all its merits and drawbacks. In the turmoil of political, economic, and social upheaval in China, there is little time for analysis and evaluation of the past and for planning, construction, and anticipating the future. There is, in addition, little time for synthesizing the past with the present, the West with the East. There is time only for growing discontented with the past and for rejecting it in favor of something which can become an agent of practical change and transformation. This should suffice to explain the rise of Marxism in China in the early twenties and the general failure of the Chinese intellectuals to make the transition from the past to the future a smooth one.

Clearly, Chinese Marxism is a breakaway from traditional Chinese philosophy as we have discussed it under Confucianism, Taoism, and Chinese Buddhism. Yet it shares with the traditional views its pragmatic orientation toward social and political actions. With the rise of Marxism in contemporary China, the reconciliation of Marxist principles with past philosophical traditions becomes a theoretical-ideological problem as well as a cultural-realistic problem. Though we cannot probe the problem of intellectual continuity in contemporary Chinese thinking, one thing is increasingly clear: Chinese Marxists have made sporadic yet systematic efforts to interpret or re-interpret Confucianism, Taoism, and Chinese Buddhism in terms of the Marxist ideology, and to evaluate them accordingly. In doing this, however, they have also exposed themselves to doctrines of the past which are bound to renew their influence on current thinking. In other words, in the present context, the language and mentality of earlier doctrines in Chinese philosophy will continue to function and interact with the language and mentality of Marxism. What will ensue from this type of interaction is something which is difficult to predict. Perhaps with a reassertion of what is best in the past, the significance of Chinese philosophy for the modern world will be gradually recognized. Chinese Marxism, therefore, at the present stage represents a test and trial of the true potential of Chinese philosophy to meet the needs of man.

VII. Four Characteristics of Chinese Philosophy

In the light of our discussion we can now formulate four distinctive characteristics of Chinese philosophy. Our problem is not to evaluate Chinese philosophy, but to describe it in the most relevant terms. This description and characterization of Chinese philosophy can be regarded as a conclusion based on a comprehensive reflection on the nature of Chinese philosophy. They may also be regarded as results of our reconstructive analysis of important traditions in Chinese philosophy. They are formulated here to represent only the major, not all, characteristics of Chinese philosophy. They are sufficient, however, to provide a basis for further inquiry into the nature and significance of Chinese philosophy, and to capture and manifest both the dialectic and problematic of Chinese philosophy as a whole.

1. *Chinese Philosophy as Intrinsic Humanism*

Although there can be many versions of humanism, humanisms can be conveniently divided into the extrinsic and the intrinsic. Most humanistic thinking in the West is extrinsic, whereas the humanism in Chinese philosophy is intrinsic. In Greek as well as Renaissance philosophy the existence of man and his power of reason are given a unique place in the scheme of things. But with the background of a transcendental religion (be it Orphic or Christian) and a speculative metaphysics (be it Platonic or Thomist) which distinguishes between the natural and the supernatural, man and God, the subjective and the objective, mind (or soul or spirit) and body in an absolute sense, the affirmation of the value of man tends to be made at the expense of the value of that which is contrasted with man, be it the natural or the supernatural. That is, the affirmation of the value of man entails either a denunciation or a neutralization of the value of that which is contrasted with man or the value of man.

Thus, as a consequence of Renaissance humanism, the Western mind is guided by an interest in the exaltation of man toward exploring, utilizing, and controlling nature as an inanimate object and as a means for achieving human power, thus contributing directly to the development of modern science. But when science has grown to a respectable stature, humanism is regarded as too subjective and limited in dealing with nature and thus to be dispensable in virtue of truly scientific interests. This is so because in the light of scientific achievement, not only has nature been deprived of human meaningfulness and considered value-neutral, but human beings are themselves treated as objects of scientific investigation, subject to a methodology which regards value purely as an invention of man. This is the unavoidable result of a humanism which begins with the extrinsic assumption that man and nature are different and therefore in opposition.

The modern revolt against this scientific mentality in existentialism is no less extrinsic, for it stresses the absolute subjectivity of man as a humanistic principle to the exclusion of objective and physical nature. This leads to a depth-psychology of man which is no less frustrating and humiliating.

Now the philosophical assumption that nature is intrinsic to the existence of man and man intrinsic to the existence of nature, is the foundation of Chinese humanism. Here there is no such absolute bifurcation between the objective and the subjective, mind and body, man and God. The reason for this is not, of course, that the bifurcation has failed to be made, but that it should not be made from the viewpoint of Chinese philosophy. In all the major traditions and schools of Chinese philosophy it is considered important that man and nature or reality should be seen as forming a unity and harmony, just as man himself is a unity and harmony of mind and body. There is, furthermore, no separation of the natural from the supernatural, if indeed we can regard the pre-Chin conceptions of *ti* (lord on high), *t'ien* (heaven), and *tao* (the way) as supernatural conceptions at all. Body and mind mutually determine and define each other to constitute the existence of man, who interacts with everything else in the world, to grow and develop into an ideal perfection which has both anthropological and cosmological significance. Perhaps because there is no fundamental division between mind (or soul) and body in man, the fundamental category relating to the existence of man and to the value of his existence is 'life' (*sheng*), which applies to nature as well as to the creative activity of *tao* or heaven.

2. *Chinese Philosophy as Concrete Rationalism*

Rationalism is the belief that truth can be obtained by man through use of his reason. In fact the rationalistic tradition in Western philosophy has distinguished truths of reason from truths of fact. Truths of reason are truths known independently of experience and therefore *a priori*, whereas truths of fact are founded on sense experience and therefore *a posteriori*. Now this conception of truths of reason is related to two basic suppositions in rationalistic philosophy: first, reason is innate in man and man will naturally come to understand truths of reason through rational reflection since these truths are inherent in reason; and secondly, truths of reason are considered more certain and noble than truths of fact and are therefore considered paradigms of human knowledge. Logic and mathematics and even theoretical physics are taken as examples of truths of reason in Western rationalism. Even in ethics and metaphysics truths of reason have been the focus of attention, and only relatively recently has rationalism in the above sense been subject to severe criticism and doubt.

Now it is clear that the most significant characteristic of Western rationalism is the belief that man's rational faculty of abstraction and deduction is able to establish abstract and universal principles of knowledge. As the faculty of reason is fundamentally discrete from experience, so truths of reason are fundamentally discrete from truths of fact or experience. Western rationalism may therefore be called a rationalism of abstract reason, or of reason in its abstract use.

Chinese philosophy, on the other hand, is rationalistic not in an abstract, but in a concrete sense. The Chinese philosopher recognizes man as a rational being who is endowed with a rational faculty for knowing truths. This derives from the belief that man is in unity with nature and that nature in its development culminates in man as a being full of creative potential. That man may naturally come to know reality, or the way, is just a step in the development of the creative potential of man. Reality, in the sense of heaven or the way, as man sees it, is a rational order displayed in concrete things which can be seen and understood by man in his inquiries. Since there is no original demarcation between the objective and the subjective, the subjective in man naturally corresponds to the objective in nature. This may be regarded as a metaphysical article of faith, but it has the virtue of ruling out epistemological puzzles about knowledge of the external world and other minds. Hence there are no doctrines of solipsism and scepticism in Chinese philosophy.

There are three fundamental senses in which we may define the concrete use of concrete reason in Chinese philosophy. In the first place, man has to open his eyes to reality and observe activities and patterns of things. It is on the basis of empirical observations and experience at large that the philosophy of change, in terms of interchange of *yin* and *yang*, is developed in the *Book of Changes*. Furthermore, one can see from the use of language in the Classics that the terms for ultimate reality, such as *t'ien* and *tao*, are not general and abstract terms capable of logical definition, but terms with a universal yet concrete content, to be understood by means of direct and diverse experience.

Similarly in ethics, we see that in Confucianism ideas of virtue are closely related to the experience of basic sentiments. If we compare Mencius's doctrine of immediate feelings as beginnings of virtues with Kant's doctrine of the categorical imperative, we can readily see that sentiments of virtue are concrete realizations of experience in concrete situations, whereas commands of the categorical imperative are abstract deductions of reason. Thus whereas there is no practical problem of applying Confucian virtues, applying the Kantian categorical imperative to concrete situations does present a difficult problem. But on the other hand, whereas Kantian ethics has a deductive structure and a rational justification, there is comparatively little systematic organization for the moral insights in Confucian writings. Even though Mencius speaks of man's innate knowledge of goodness (the so-called *liang-chih*), *liang-chih* is not taken to be a faculty which enables man to arrive at moral injunctions, but an ability to distinguish between good and bad in concrete situations. Thus concrete reason in Confucian philosophy does not straightforwardly correspond to Kantian practical reason, nor for that matter, does Confucian abstract reason correspond straightforwardly to Kantian pure reason, for concrete reason, as typified in Chinese philosophy, not only deals with practical problems but guarantees the ultimate connection of reason with practice. This leads to the second sense of concrete rationalism.

Chinese philosophy is generally oriented toward action and practice in society and government, and aims at the reform and perfection of man and the world. It stresses, furthermore, that theory must be applied to practice or be considered merely empty words. In the extreme case of Wang Yang-ming, theory and practice are considered two ends of the same thing. This means that theoretical understanding must entail practical doing, and in practical doing of any kind one will acquire knowledge and wisdom of oneself and the world. In the light of this characteristic of Chinese philosophy which we shall discuss more below, concrete rationalism simply means that one has to attain moral perfection through a process of self-cultivation and of concrete realization of knowledge in practice. In practice this process is not merely a rational activity of reason, it manifests reasonableness in life and in the attainment of an ideal of perfection. Indeed, contrasting the ideal of pure rationality in abstract reason with that of natural reasonableness in concrete reason is a way of accentuating the characteristic of Chinese philosophy under discussion.

Finally, there is the following sense of concrete reason: Chinese philosophy is primarily directed toward moral and political goals. Even ontological and cosmological speculations are not without moral and political significance. The *li* (principle, reason) in neo-Confucianism for example is a concretely rational ideal and idea. *Li* is not something divorced from man's basic life-experience in relation to himself, other men, and things; it is taken to be the basis for achieving social harmony and administering political order.

Perhaps it is the lack of any differentiation between abstract principles of rationality and concrete instances of reasonableness in Chinese thinking that has prevented a cultivation in the abstract of such pure sciences as logic and mathematics, and explains why Chinese thinkers do not consider philosophy itself a deductive rational activity but a synthetic moral achievement capable of influencing the actions of men.

3. *Chinese Philosophy as Organic Naturalism*

Naturalism is an important feature of Chinese philosophy, since the Chinese world-view is basically this-worldly rather than other-worldly. In fact, as noted earlier, the dichotomy between man and God, the natural and the supernatural, does not exist in Chinese philosophy. There are, consequently, no arguments between transcendentalism and immanentism in Chinese philosophy. Every form of reality is considered a process of change and development in nature. As we have seen in the case of Taoism, the potentiality for change and transformation is in the nature of things; which means that individual things do not have static substances, and are not unrelated to one another as individual entities, but mutually determine and define one another in a dynamic process of change within a context of organic relationships.

Organic naturalism in Chinese philosophy is perhaps better described in consideration of the relation between the objective and the subjective and between the physical and the mental. Chinese philosophers consider these in terms of natural correspondence, interdependence, and complementation, in which life and understanding can be achieved and preserved. In fact the relationships in question might even be thought of, from a general viewpoint, as continuities, for there is no real break between physical and mental, objective and subjective. Ontologically and cosmologically speaking, the objective and the subjective, and the physical and the mental are transparent to *tao* as the ultimate reality and therefore parts of a total dynamic process.

The organic relationships between man and society and State constitute further evidence for organic naturalism in Chinese philosophy. In Confucianism, man is a relational being who depends upon other men for the cultivation and perfection of himself. In Taoist, and even in Chinese Buddhistic doctrines, man is relational to all things, but has to interact with and participate in the activities of *tao* in order to be good and perfect. He is not simply to identify himself with *tao*. In this context of organic relationships among men and between man and things, harmony and harmonization are the key words, and harmony and harmonization are possible only if there are organic relationships of unity in variety. Chinese philosophy provides a serious elaboration of such relationships as a basis upon which 'goodness' can be conceived as essentially the ability to achieve and preserve harmony.

4. Chinese Philosophy as Pragmatism of Self-Cultivation

As has been generally indicated, Chinese philosophy has been concerned from the very beginning with the practical question of advancing the well-being of the individual and the order and harmony of society and State. The moral ideas of Confucius and other Confucian thinkers clearly manifest this mentality. Even in the Taoist philosophy of Lao Tzu there is a concern for the best form of government. The principle of doing nothing by doing everything is both a cosmological principle of the *tao*, and a political principle of a *tao*-inspired ruler. The practicality of Chinese Buddhism and Chinese Marxism in the contemporary scene need no special elaboration. For it is clear that Chinese Buddhism has aimed at the practical solution of fundamental problems in life, and that Chinese Marxism has aimed at the practical solution of social and political problems in China. What is noteworthy is that no philosophical school and no philosophical thinker in China regards philosophy as a mere speculative activity. Chinese philosophy has a special dimension which we may call 'self-realization by means of philosophical self-cultivation'.

In both Confucianism and Taoism a special branch of studies has been developed which may be called 'theory of self-cultivation' or 'theory of self-realization'. Of the Confucian writings specifically, the *Great Learning (Chung Yung)* has formulated eight steps of self-cultivation with harmonization of the world as its ultimate goal. The first two steps — investigating things and extending knowledge — are directed toward the goal of understanding the world. The next three steps — making sincere one's intentions, rectifying one's mind and cultivating or improving one's person — are directed toward the goal of perfecting oneself within, so that one can be ready for social and political responsibility in order to better others. The last three steps — regulating a family, governing a State well, and pacifying the world — are directed toward extending one's virtues among men so that one can be said to realize one's potentiality in a reality of relationships.

There are two essential features in this process of self-cultivation and self-realization. First, the process is one of extension from individual perfection to the perfection of all men; secondly, it is one of unifying one's internal attainment with one's external efficaciousness. This process has been termed the unification of 'sageliness within and kingliness without'. Now it seems clear that Confucianism has perfectly exemplified this ideal of self-cultivation with reference to the perfection of others. It is not so clear how Taoism and Chinese Buddhism can be said to be pragmatic in this regard. Chinese Buddhism offers pragmatic instructions for attaining the salvation of the whole through the self-cultivating efforts of the individual. And although Taoism remains basically individualistic, nevertheless in the case of Lao Tzu, the ideal ruler who preserves the well-being of all must be a follower of *tao*. It is also an historical fact that Taoistic principles have suggested to later political craftsmen various practical measures in dealing with problems of State and society, as exemplified in the writings of Han Fei Tzu.

It is generally held that in Chinese philosophy man is capable of reaching the ultimate and highest state of perfection, be it called sagehood, true manhood, or Buddhahood. In other words, man is capable of generating the highest form of good without needing to look beyond and transcend his own world. Thus the pragmatism of self-cultivation in Chinese philosophy provides a substitute for the worship and dependence upon a supreme god. The moral philosophy underlying this pragmatism of self-cultivation can thus be said to perform for the Chinese mind the function performed in the West by religion, but without suffering from the dogmatism of Western religion. The religious import and autonomy of morality in this pragmatism of self-cultivation is possible also on many other grounds, none of which is not covered, however, by what we have said about the intrinsic humanism, concrete rationalism, and organic naturalism of Chinese philosophy.

VIII. Conclusion

In the above we have made a synthetic characterization of Chinese philosophy based on an analytical reconstruction of its main traditions and thinking. There are three main traditions in Chinese philosophy: Confucianism, Taoism and Chinese Buddhism. All these three have interacted and shared something in common in their historical and theoretical developments. We have noted that Chinese Marxism developed as a result of the Western impact upon China in recent times. In the light of our discussion of the archetypal ideas in the pre-

Confucian period, we can see that Confucianism and Taoism have in fact shared the same origin and source, and in a sense mutually define and complement each other. This view should fit well with the dialectical metaphysics of *yin* and *yang* accepted by both Confucianism and Taoism.

We have described four characteristics of Chinese philosophy. The first and the last, intrinsic humanism and the pragmatism of self-cultivation, deal primarily with moral, social, and political aspects of Chinese thinking, whereas the second and third, concrete rationalism and organic naturalism, deal primarily with the metaphysical and epistemological aspects. But we must remember that the moral and socio-political aspects of Chinese thought are internally and dialectically intertwined, for the moral and socio-political thinking has metaphysics as its basis, whereas metaphysical and epistemological thinking, on the other hand, always has moral practice and socio-political improvement as its goal. It is clear from our discussion that these four features of Chinese philosophy are interrelated and mutually supporting, and are thus best understood in the context of one another.

We have not dealt with every branch of Chinese philosophy. Thus we did not dwell on neo-Confucianism as a special development of Classical Confucianism under Chinese Buddhistic influences. But if we looked into neo-Confucianism, we would see that, like the other main traditions of Chinese philosophy, it possesses the same four features.

Something else we have omitted is a discussion of philosophical problems resulting from acceptance of the perspective of Chinese philosophy as we have characterized it. If Chinese philosophy can be said to be broadly based on the principles of the unity of man and nature, of reality as a process of dialectical interchange between *yin* and *yang*, of non-bifurcation between objective and subjective, mind and body, and abstract and concrete, and of the perfection of totality by self-cultivation of the individual, there are bound to be questions regarding how Chinese philosophy is to face problems of the need for transcendence, the origin of evil, and the nature of logic and of theoretical knowledge in science. We will also be led to ask how Chinese philosophical principles can be reconciled with existing doctrines of transcendence, evil, logic and theoretical knowledge in the Western tradition. Our discussion has deliberately left these questions open. If Chinese philosophy serves to make us critically aware of these problems and to provide alternative ways of thinking, we are more than justified in presenting it as a philosophy of universal concern and universal significance.

166

The Authors

Joseph S. Wu was born in China in 1934, received a B.A. from Taiwan Normal University and did graduate work in Chinese philosophy at the New Asia Research Institute with Professor Tang Chun-i (a co-author of this volume). He received an M.A. from Washington University and a Ph.D. from Southern Illinois University, taught at the University of Missouri, Northern Illinois University, and Loyola University, Chicago, and is now Associate Professor of Philosophy at California State University, Sacramento. His publications include articles in the *International Philosophical Quarterly*, *Philosophy East and West*, *Notre Dame Journal of Formal Logic*, and other, including Chinese, journals.

Shu-hsien Liu was born in China in 1934, received an M.A. from National Taiwan University, and a Ph.D. from Southern Illinois University where he is now Associate Professor of Philosophy. He has been Associate Professor at Tunghai University, Taiwan, and has held research grants both there and at Southern Illinois University. He is the author of *Literary Appreciation from a Philosophical Point of View*, *Semantics and Truth*, *Philosophical Methods and Convictions in a Changing World*, and *An Introduction to the Philosophy of Culture*, as well as articles in a number of journals.

Antonio S. Cua was born in Manila, Philippines, in 1932. He received his B.A. from Far Eastern University, Manila, and an M.A. and Ph.D. from the University of California, Berkeley. He taught at Ohio University, was Professor of Philosophy and Chairman of the Department at the State University of New York, College at Oswego, and since 1969 has been Professor of Philosophy at the Catholic University of America. He is the author of *Reason and Virtue: A Study in the Ethics of Richard Price*, and of articles in *Ethics*, *American Philosophical Quarterly*, *Philosophy and Phenomenological Research*, the *Australasian Journal of Philosophy*, *Man and World*, and other journals.

Tang Chun-i was born in China in 1909, and is Professor of Philosophy at the Chinese University of Hong Kong. He has been Professor of Philosophy at National Central University, and helped to found New Asia College. He is an Adviser of the Buddhistic Cultural Association and a Member of, among other institutions, the China Academy. His major publications (in Chinese) are *Comparative Studies in Chinese and Western Philosophies*, *Reconstruction of the Moral Self*, *Spiritual Values in Chinese Culture*, *Cultural Consciousness and Moral Reason*, *Treatise on Philosophy*, and *The Development of Ideas in Chinese Philosophy*.

Paul Wienpahl was born in Wyoming, U.S.A., in 1916. He is Professor of Philosophy at the University of California, Santa Barbara. He received a Ph.D. from the University of California, Los Angeles, has had a Ford Fellowship for study at the Sorbonne, and a grant for study at Daitoku-ji in Kyoto. He is the author of *The Matter of Zen*, and of articles on a range of topics, including Spinoza, Frege, and Wittgenstein.

William L. Cheshier was born in Chicago, U.S.A., in 1948. He studied at Loyola University, Chicago, and in 1968 completed work towards a B.Sc., majoring in psychology and philosophy. He began graduate work in philosophy in 1969 under the direction of Professor Joseph S. Wu (a co-author of this volume). He has translated *Recherches sur Les 'Os du Ho-nan'* into English, and written a book, *Iceberg*, on Mao Tse-tung's quotations. He received an M.A. in philosophy in 1970, and is now studying at the University of Chicago for a Ph.D. in Chinese and American Political Philosophy. From 1969 through 1971 he taught philosophy first as an assistant, then as an instructor at Loyola University.

Lars Jul Hansen was born in Norway in 1948. He has studied philosophy, sinology, and science of religion, and has received the cand. mag. degree from the University of Oslo. He is preparing for an M.A. in Chinese Philosophy, has taught at the Institute of Philosophy, University of Oslo, and is now undertaking research at the Institute of Sinology at Leiden, Holland, with a scholarship from the Dutch Government for the study of Buddhism in China.

Chung-ying Cheng was born in China in 1935. He is Associate Professor of Philosophy at the University of Hawaii, studied at the University of Washington and at Harvard University, where he received a Ph.D., and has been Visiting Professor at Yale University and at National Taiwan University. He is author of *Peirce's and Lewis's Theories of Induction* and of *Tai Chen's Inquiry into Goodness*, and editor of *Contemporary Issues in Philosophy of Language*, *The Present Status of Mind-Body Problems*, and of the journal *Chinese Studies in Philosophy*. He has contributed to many journals, including the *Journal of Philosophy*, *Notre Dame Journal of Formal Logic*, *Foundations of Language*, and *Philosophy East and West*.

The Editors

Arne Naess was born in Norway in 1912, studied psychology and philosophy in Oslo, Paris, and Vienna, received his doctorate in philosophy from the University of Oslo and became Professor of Philosophy there in 1939. He has taught widely abroad, and has been Visiting Professor at the University of California, Berkeley, on a number of occasions. His publications include *Interpretation and Preciseness*, *Democracy, Ideology and Objectivity*, *Four Modern Philosophers*, *Scepticism*, and *The Pluralist and Possibilist Aspect of the Scientific Enterprise*, as well as many articles. He is co-editor of *Inquiry*.

Alastair Hannay was born in England in 1932, studied philosophy at the University of Edinburgh and University College, London, from which he received a Ph.D. He has taught philosophy at the University of Oslo since 1963, has been Research Associate at the University of California, Berkeley, and Academic Visitor at the London School of Economics and Political Science. He is author of *Mental Images — A Defence*, of articles in the *British Journal of Aesthetics*, *Mind*, and other journals, and is co-editor of *Inquiry*.

of view, Kant fails to make the crucial distinction between transcendental determination and transcendental application. According to Mou, Kant believes that the categories of understanding also have the function of transcendental determination. By so doing Kant erroneously takes his categories of understanding to be constitutive principles of reality and makes them shoulder a burden which they should not carry. Kant believes that, since we cannot establish certainty of knowledge in experience, such certainty must be established in terms of the categories of the understanding. It is the legislative power of the mind that gives certainty to our scientific knowledge. But today the certainty of scientific knowledge has been shown to be only an illusion. In fact, what is certain pertains only to the transcendental schemata of the cognitive mind. Such certainty is always subjective certainty on the part of the mind, never objective certainty found in the external world. Mou detects in Kant a tendency toward realism which cannot be reconciled with his idealism. Also, the empiricist strain in his thought interferes with the transcendentalist tendency. Such interference prevents Kant from developing a consistent position of his own. Therefore, Kant's philosophy is in need of total reconstruction.[22]

In his attempt to reconstruct Kant's philosophy, Mou employs a distinction made by modern logicians, that is, the distinction between so-called existential propositions and non-existential propositions. Empirical, factual statements are existential propositions which are supposed to tell something about the world, while logical, mathematical statements are non-existential propositions which have nothing to do with the real world. From Mou's point of view, so far as empirical, existential propositions are concerned, relational propositions in the final analysis can always be reduced to subject–predicate propositions. Since the logical subject in an empirical, existential proposition always stands for something real, the problem of ontology cannot be avoided.[23] But, for the time being, we shall reserve metaphysical considerations for later attention. Let us first examine the nature of non-existential logical, mathematical propositions and the philosophical problems raised by our reflection on such propositions.

According to Mou, many logicians today maintain that logical, mathematical propositions are non-existential statements which tell nothing about the world; they are analytical, tautological statements; symbolic logical systems are many; different primitive terms and postulates may be chosen to construct a logical system. While Mou does maintain that logical, mathematical statements in themselves tried to accomplish in the three recently published monumental volumes on *Mind and Human Nature*.[18]

At the beginning Mou's analysis is much like Hume's. When the physiological organism gets into contact with the physical object, an immediate apprehension results. Both the knowing subject and the known object cannot be regarded as real ontological substances, because both are composites. And the consequent apprehension is always the apprehension of particulars; it cannot extend beyond the moment, and it has meaning only for the individual.[19]

Events are transitory; only meaning structures are stable. In order for experience to be objectified so that it may have intersubjective meaning, certain schemata such as space–time must be employed. We may apply either an empirical or a transcendental analysis of space and time. The empirical analysis is not adequate because it can never establish the universality and necessity of space and time. Since pure and exact space and time cannot be found in the external world and cannot be established by experience, space–time must be a transcendental schema of the cognitive mind. This same line of argument may apply also to other schemata as well.[20]

According to Mou, there are four basic schemata of the cognitive mind. They are: space–time, ground–consequence, whole–part, and affirmation–negation. These four schemata may be divided into two groups. Space–time is the schema for immediate apprehension and is established by transcendental imagination; the other three are the schemata for discursive understanding. Space and time have the function of transcendental determination, while the other three are involved with transcendental application. Space–time is a formal schema which does not concern itself with the content of things, and hence cannot serve as the principle which distinguishes one existent from another; it determines only the formal ground for all objects or events. It is not so with the schemata of discursive understanding. These schemata are not present in immediate apprehension as space and time. They are strictly regulative principles used by the cognitive mind to determine the specific features of individual objects and to establish correlations between events.[21]

The Kantian influence on Mou's thought is unmistakable. But there are important differences between Mou and Kant. For example, Kant does not take space–time to be a schema, while Mou does. Mou's idea of a schema is developed out of Kant, but it has acquired new meanings which cannot be found in Kant's system. From Mou's point tell nothing about the world, he feels that the other assertions need careful examination, because these assertions tell us only half of the truth; if we accept them on their face value, then we will be misled to adopt a formalistic or conventionalistic view of logic and mathematics which gives an erroneous interpretation of them.

While logical, mathematical statements may be regarded as analytical, tautological statements within a given logical or mathematical system, this fact does not preclude the possibility that from another perspective they may also be regarded as synthetic propositions, since these propositions must presuppose the synthesizing function of the mind. Therefore, even though these propositions tell nothing about the world, they do tell something about the mind. The classical philosophers, including Kant, believe that the mind has a rational structure. But contemporary philosophers shy away from this kind of talk. One reason is that contemporary philosophers know very well that we can construct more than one logical system, and that we can select the primitive terms and also the postulates for a logical system. Hence a formalistic or conventionalistic view of logic and mathematics prevails. If logical systems are nothing but conventions of man, naturally it is difficult to talk about the rational structure of the mind. But Mou is quick to point out that contemporary philosophers are committing the fallacy of taking the manifestations of logic to be logic itself. While symbolic systems of logic may be many, logic must be one. Although in theory it seems that we may construct as many logical systems as we like, in fact this is impossible. Moreover, the logical systems that have been constructed today, such as the traditional Aristotelian logic, the logic of sentential calculus, and modal logic, have strikingly similar structures. This cannot be a simple coincidence, and hence is in need of a rational explanation. Mou's answer is that all these logical systems are the external manifestations of one logical reason.

It *looks* as if we may arbitrarily construct a logical system; in fact, there is little that is arbitrary. Modern logicians are elated at finding that they need not include the traditional laws of thought in the list of the axioms or postulates within a given logical system. Laws of identity, contradiction, and excluded middle are regarded as no more than theorems within the given logical system. On further reflection, however, it seems that the 'principle' of contradiction should be kept distinct from the law of contradiction in any given symbolic logical system. We are not free to construct a logical system that is inconsistent with itself. This fact proves that the principle of contradiction is supreme; it is the regulative principle that underlies any logical system. Once this idea is formulated, it belongs to a specific logic, and hence loses its transcendental status. To contradict the principle would mean to contradict reason. If these arguments are sound, then Mou claims that he has shown that logic must be one, although its manifestations may be many. Modern developments in logic may have discredited Kant's transcendental analysis of logic and mathematics, but not *any* transcendental analysis of logic and mathematics. It is Mou's belief that only through a proper transcendental analysis of logic and mathematics can the true nature of logic and mathematics be understood.[24] For instance, the same line of argument applies also to geometry. Although geometrical systems may be many, geometry must be one.[25] Thus, Mou is able to declare that logic, arithmetic, and geometry are the external manifestations of pure reason. Indeed he has made an ambitious attempt to deduce these three from pure reason. Logic is the first step by which reason externalizes itself, arithmetic the second step, and geometry the third step. However, Mou's deduction is too complicated, and also too technical, to be introduced in the present article.[26]

Now we may return to the discussion of empirical, existential propositions. When we want to make empirical assertions about the world, transcendental schemata in themselves are no longer adequate. We must put these schemata into use and we must employ categories. In Mou's view the relationship between the schemata and the categories is one of correlation, not of identity. For example, the schema of ground–consequence correlates with the category of causality. But the two should not be confused with one another. Since categories are related to empirical content, they must be hypothetical in character. Here Mou endorses Dewey's pragmatic interpretation of categories. From Mou's point of view, Kant's deduction of categories is fallacious, because Kant mistakes one manifestation of the structure of understanding for the structure itself. For Kant, categories have certainty, and they give a guarantee of the universal validity of scientific knowledge. In fact, we can find no certainty in the realm of scientific knowledge.[27]

Now, here we face the dilemma of the cognitive mind. On the one hand, we can never establish anything with certainty in terms of empirical generalization, and yet, on the other hand, reason demands certainty and will not be satisfied with anything less than certainty. In logic, we demand complete logical systems; in fact, we have very